D1339543

VICTORIA
& ABDUL

VICTORIA & ABDUL

THE TRUE STORY OF THE QUEEN'S CLOSEST CONFIDANT

SHRABANI BASU

For my daughters,
Sanchita and Tanaya

'I am so very fond of him. He is so good & gentle & understanding ...
& is a real comfort to me.'
Queen Victoria to her daughter, Louise, Duchess of Connaught
3 November 1888
Balmoral

First published 2010

The History Press
The Mill, Brimscombe Port
Stroud, Gloucestershire, GL5 2QG
www.thehistorypress.co.uk

© Shrabani Basu, 2010

The right of Shrabani Basu to be identified as the Author
of this work has been asserted in accordance with the
Copyrights, Designs and Patents Act 1988.

All rights reserved. No part of this book may be reprinted
or reproduced or utilised in any form or by any electronic,
mechanical or other means, now known or hereafter invented,
including photocopying and recording, or in any information
storage or retrieval system, without the permission in writing
from the Publishers.

British Library Cataloguing in Publication Data.
A catalogue record for this book is available from the British Library.

ISBN 978 0 7524 5364 4

Typesetting and origination by The History Press
Printed in India by Nutech Print Services

CONTENTS

AUTHOR'S NOTE

In order to retain the authenticity of the period, I have used the old British names of the various Indian cities in this book. Hence, Cawnpore for present-day Kanpur, Benares for Varanasi, Simla for Shimla, Bharatpore for Bharatpur, etc.

Queen Victoria often underlined her words for emphasis. The italicised words in her quotes indicate the words that she underlined in her letters.

The words 'Hindustani lessons' refer to Urdu lessons and not Hindi lessons. The word Hindustani was used by the British as a generic term for both Urdu and Hindi.

Queen Victoria learnt to read and write in Urdu from Abdul Karim.

ACKNOWLEDGEMENTS

Working in the historic archives of Windsor Castle was one of the most pleasurable moments of writing this book. For this I have to thank Jill Kelsey, Deputy Registrar of the Royal Archives, and Pam Clark, for all their help in sorting through the material and for coming to my aid whenever I found reading Queen Victoria's handwriting a challenge. Thanks also for the wonderful tea and cakes which provided a welcome break every day!

Thank you to Sophie Gordon, Curator of the Photographic Collection at Windsor Castle, and to Katie Holyoak of the Royal Collections at St James's Palace for all their help and patience. I am grateful to Her Majesty the Queen for her gracious permission to reproduce material from the Royal Archives.

This book could not have been written without the complete access to the several volumes of the Reid Archives provided by Sir Alexander and Lady Michaela Reid and I am truly indebted to them for all their help and generous hospitality in their beautiful house in Jedburgh. I would also like to thank them for permission to quote from the diaries and journals of Sir James Reid and for use of photographs from his scrapbook.

My thanks to Michael Hunter, Curator at Osborne House, for all his help and especially for taking me to the basement at Osborne House to show me the menus from Queen Victoria's time. I am also grateful for his permission to use images from the files.

I am grateful to the staff at the British Library for their patience and guidance.

In Agra, I would like to thank Syed Raju and Rajiv Saxena for their invaluable help in the search for Abdul Karim's grave. My thanks also go to the staff at the Regional Archives in Agra for their help in tracing Karim's files.

In Delhi, I would like to thank Krishna Menon for translating Queen Victoria's Hindustani Journals from Urdu into both Hindi and English.

Very special thanks are owed to my agent, Jonathan Conway, who flagged me off on Karim's trail, helped me structure my thoughts and whose sense of humour kept me going.

I am grateful to Simon Hamlet, commissioning editor at The History Press, for believing in the book from the start, and to my meticulous editor, Abigail Wood.

I would like to thank Aveek Sarkar, my editor-in-chief at *Ananda Bazar Patrika*, for his constant support and encouragement with all my books. Thanks also to Vishal Jadeja, Prince of Morvi, for his input on his ancestor. For inputs and help in various ways, I am grateful to historians Indrani Chatterjee, Sumit Guha, Shahid Amin and Kusoom Vadgama.

To my sisters, Nupur and Moushumi, I owe more than I can ever say, for all their help in Delhi and Agra, in locating Karim's grave and sourcing translations. Thanks to my husband, Dipankar, for his patience and support and for brewing endless cups of tea, and to my daughters, Sanchita and Tanaya, for their enthusiasm in reading my early drafts, acting as my helpdesks for all technical problems and for persuading me to enter the virtual world and finally set up a website. To all of you, I owe this book.

Shrabani Basu
London

DRAMATIS PERSONAE

THE ROYAL FAMILY

Queen Victoria – Queen of England and Empress of India
Prince Albert Edward, Prince of Wales, Bertie, later King Edward VII – son of Queen Victoria
Princess Alix, Princess of Wales, later Queen Alexandra – consort of Prince Edward
Princess Beatrice – youngest daughter of Queen Victoria
Prince Henry of Battenberg – husband of Princess Beatrice
Princess Victoria, Vicky, Empress of Germany – eldest daughter of Queen Victoria
Princess Helena of Schleswig Holstein – third daughter of Queen Victoria
Princess Alice, Grand Duchess of Hesse – second daughter of Queen Victoria
Prince Arthur, Duke of Connaught – son of Queen Victoria
Prince George, later King George V – grandson of Queen Victoria
Princess May of Teck, later Queen Mary – consort of Prince George
Prince Louis of Battenberg – husband of Queen Victoria's granddaughter

THE INDIANS

Abdul Karim – Queen Victoria's Munshi
Mohammed Buksh – Queen Victoria's attendant
Dr Wuzeeruddin – Abdul Karim's father
The Munshi's wife
The Munshi's mother-in-law
Hourmet Ali – Queen Victoria's attendant and Abdul Karim's brother-in-law

Ahmed Husain – Queen Victoria's attendant
Sheikh Chidda – Queen Victoria's attendant
Ghulam Mustapha – Queen Victoria's attendant
Khuda Buksh – Queen Victoria's attendant
Mirza Yusuf Baig – Queen Victoria's attendant
Bhai Ram Singh – architect of Durbar Hall
Sir John Tyler – Superintendent of Agra Jail
Abdul Rashid – Abdul Karim's nephew
Rafiuddin Ahmed – solicitor, journalist, friend of Abdul Karim
Duleep Singh – son of Maharajah Ranjit Singh deposed ruler of Punjab, Queen
    Victoria's ward
Nripendra Narayan – Maharajah of Cooch Behar
Sunity Devi – Maharani of Cooch Behar
Hurwan Singh – Maharajah of Kapurthala
Sayaji Rao Gaekwad – Maharajah of Baroda
Chimnabai – Maharani of Baroda

THE HOUSEHOLD

Henry Ponsonby – Private Secretary to Queen Victoria
John Reid – Personal Physician to Queen Victoria
Frederick (Fritz) Ponsonby – Assistant Private Secretary to Queen Victoria
Arthur Bigge – Assistant Private Secretary to Queen Victoria, later Private
    Secretary to Queen Victoria
Alexander (Alick) Yorke – Groom in Waiting and Master of Ceremonies for
    Royal Theatricals
Marie Mallet – Maid of Honour
Lady Jane Churchill – Lady-in-Waiting
Harriet Phipps – Woman of the Bedchamber and Private Secretary to the
    Queen
Lady Edith Lytton – Lady-in-Waiting
Ethel Cadogan – Maid of Honour
Fleetwood Edwards – Keeper of the Privy Purse
Dighton Probyn – Private Secretary to the Prince of Wales
Edward Pelham Clinton – Master of the Household

THE VICEROYS

Lord Dufferin   1884–88
Lord Lansdowne   1888–94

Lord Elgin   1894–99
Lord Curzon   1899–1905
Lord Minto   1905–10

THE SECRETARIES OF STATE, INDIA OFFICE

Lord Cross   1886–92
Lord Kimberley   1892–94
Lord Fowler   1894–95
Lord Hamilton   1895–1903
Lord Morley   1905–10, 1910–14

THE PRIME MINISTERS

Marquess of Salisbury   1885–86, 1886–92, 1895–1902
William Gladstone   1880–85, 86, 1892–94
Earl of Rosebery   1894–95

QUEEN VICTORIA'S FAMILY TREE

VICTORIA (1819-1901) m Prince Albert of Saxe Coburg Gotha (1819-1861)

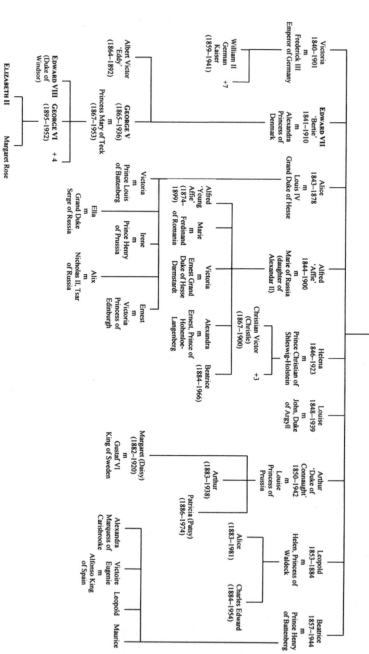

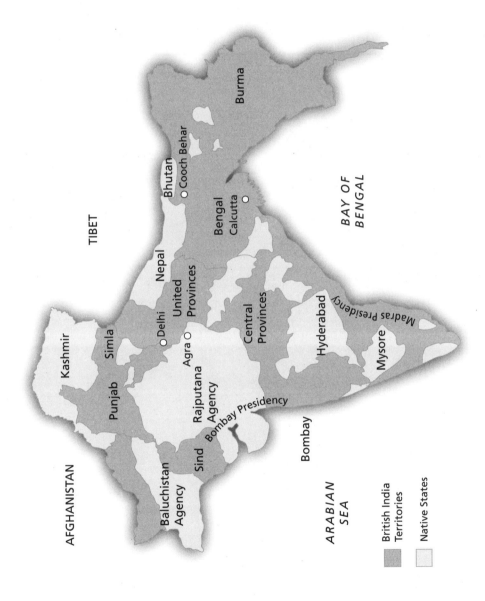

Map of India showing the British India Territories and the Native States in the nineteenth century.

Map of Britain showing the Royal palaces and neighbouring cities during Queen Victoria's reign.

INTRODUCTION

As the January mist enveloped Osborne House, a short line of mourners passed silently through the grounds towards Queen Victoria's private apartments. In the corridor outside her rooms a tall Indian man stood alone. It was Abdul Karim, the Queen's Indian Munshi or teacher. He had been waiting there since morning, his eyes occasionally looking out across the garden where he had spent so many hours with the Queen. In the distance, the ships in the Solent bobbed silently, their flags at half-mast.

The eighty-one-year-old Victoria had died peacefully in her sleep three days earlier, her family beside her. She was now dressed according to her wishes for this final journey to Windsor. The Royal family had been summoned to say their last farewells. The Queen lay in her coffin, her face covered by her white wedding veil. She looked, as one witness described, 'like a lovely marble statue, no sign of illness or age', regal in death as she had been in life. A bunch of white lilies was placed in her hand. The procession filed past – her son and heir Edward VII and his wife Queen Alexandra, the Queen's children and grandchildren, together with a collection of her most trusted servants and Household members. Each stood for a few moments before the coffin of the woman who had ascended the throne at the age of eighteen and proceeded to define an age. The King then allowed Abdul Karim to enter the Queen's bedroom. He would be the last person to see her body alone.

The Munshi entered, his head bowed, dressed in a dark Indian tunic and turban. His presence filled the room. The King, knowing his mother's wishes, allowed him a few moments alone with her. The Munshi's face was a map of emotion as he gazed at his dead Queen, her face lit by the softly glowing candles. She had given him – a humble servant – more than a decade of unquestioned love and respect. His thoughts raced through the years spent in her company: their first meeting when he had stooped to kiss her feet at Windsor in the summer of 1887; the lazy days spent together as he taught her his language and described his country; the gossip and companionship they shared; her generosity to him; her loneliness that he understood. Above all, her stubborn defence of him at all times. He touched his hand to his heart and stood silently, fighting back tears. His lips mouthed a silent prayer to *Allah* to rest her soul. After a final look and bow he left the room slowly as two workmen closed and sealed the Queen's coffin behind him.

At her funeral procession in Windsor, Abdul Karim walked with the principal mourners. The elderly Queen had given this instruction herself, despite what she knew would be intense opposition from her family and Household. She had ensured her beloved Munshi would be written into the history books.

But only days after the Queen's death, the Munshi was woken by the sound of loud banging on his door. Princess Beatrice, Queen Alexandra and some guards stood outside. The King had ordered a raid on his house, demanding he hand over all the letters Victoria had written to him. The Munshi, his wife and his nephew watched in horror as the letters in the late Queen's distinctive handwriting were torn from his desk and cast into a bonfire outside Frogmore Cottage.

As the 'Dear Abdul' letters burnt in the cold February air, the Munshi stood in silence. Without his Queen he was defenceless and alone. Postcards and letters from the Queen, dated from Windsor Castle, Balmoral, the Royal yacht *Victoria and Albert* and hotels across Europe, crackled in the flames. The Queen used to write to the Munshi every day, signing her letters variously as 'your dearest friend', 'your true friend', even 'your dearest mother'. The Munshi's distraught wife sobbed beside him, tears streaming down her veiled face. The nephew looked frightened as he was ordered to bring out every scrap of paper from the Munshi's desk with the Queen's seal on it and confine it to the mercy of the guards. The Munshi's family, once so essential to the Royal Court, stood bewildered, treated like common criminals. With Queen Victoria in her grave, the Establishment had come down hard and fast on the Munshi. King Edward VII asked him unceremoniously to pack his bags and return to India.

The fairytale – that had begun the day the young Abdul Karim had entered the Court in 1887 – was over.

Karim had been a gift from India to celebrate the Queen's Golden Jubilee. Strikingly dressed in a scarlet tunic and white turban, the handsome twenty-four-year-old youth had arrived from Agra, the home of the Taj Mahal – the world's most beautiful monument to love. Initially a servant waiting at the Queen's table, his rise through the ranks was swift. Within months he was cooking the Queen curries and, soon after, became her teacher or 'Munshi'. Whilst his colleague from India, Mohammed Buksh, remained a waiter, Karim eventually became the Queen's highly decorated Indian secretary. He was also the lonely monarch's closest confidant, filling the shoes of John Brown, her trusted Scottish gillie, who had died four years earlier.

If the Royal Household had hated Brown, they abhorred Karim, deeply suspicious of his influence over the Queen. These fears were strengthened by the increasingly violent calls for Indian independence that were filtering through to Court. But the Queen cared little for what others thought. She defended her 'Dear Munshi' relentlessly, handing him cottages in Windsor, Balmoral and Osborne and extensive lands in India. She insisted that he be treated on a par with the rest of her Household and had his portrait painted by the artists Swoboda and Angeli. She even allowed him to carry a sword and wear his medals at Court. She fussed endlessly about Karim's welfare, gave him permission to bring his wife and family to England and praised him to her family and ministers. Throughout the last ten years of her life, Victoria stood like a rock by his side.

And the more the Household complained about Karim, the more fiercely the Queen defended him, seeming to delight in her verbal spats with them over the Munshi. She went out of her way to protect Karim from any of her Household's racism. At a time when the Empire was at its height, a young Muslim now occupied a central position of influence over its sovereign. On a visit to Italy, Karim was mistaken for a young Prince with whom the Queen was in love, so majestic did he look as he rode in his private carriage through Florence.

What was it about the Munshi that attracted the Queen? Was he a soulmate for this lonely, heartbroken, elderly woman, someone who understood her and to whom she could relate? Given the current climate towards Muslims in the West, that a Muslim should have played such a key role in Queen Victoria's Court is all the more intriguing and relevant. Did the Queen represent a more enlightened and tolerant attitude, even at the peak of her Empire? Were the dawn raids on Abdul Karim's house after her death a precursor of things to come?

These and a hundred other questions entered my mind as I took the ferry across the Solent to the Isle of Wight, where I had first discovered the mysterious Abdul Karim.

He had looked out at me from his portrait painted by Rudolph Swoboda that hangs in the Indian corridor at Osborne House. I had gone to Osborne in the centenary of Queen Victoria's death in 2001 to see the restored Durbar Room whilst researching Queen Victoria's love for curry for an earlier book. What unfolded before me was her affection for the man who had introduced her to curry.

Abdul Karim was painted in cream, red and gold by the Austrian artist. The portrait showed a handsome young man in a reflective mood, holding a book in his hand. He looked more like a nawab than a servant. The artist seemed to have captured the Queen's romantic vision of the subject. I learned later that Queen Victoria had loved the painting so much she had copied it herself.

Along the Indian corridor of Osborne House were portraits of Indian craftsmen, specially commissioned by the Queen. Weavers, blacksmiths and musicians stared back from the walls, all meticulously painted so the Queen could glimpse the ordinary people of India. The striking life-size portrait of Maharajah Duleep Singh painted by Winterhalter stood out amongst the canvases. It captured the Queen's fascination for the young boy who had presented her with the Koh-i-Noor – one of the world's largest diamonds and still a part of the Crown Jewels – when the British had defeated his father, Maharajah Ranjit Singh, the last Sikh ruler of Punjab.

The Durbar Room, restored by English Heritage to mark the centenary of the Queen's death, had its own revelations. The room spoke to me of the Queen's love for India, the country she knew she could never visit, but which fascinated and intrigued her. If the Queen could not travel to India, then she would bring India to Osborne. The marble ceilings, the intricate carvings, the balconies with their Indian-style *jali* work were the Queen's Indian haven. Here she sat as Empress of that faraway land to sense its atmosphere. Fittingly, it was at her beloved Osborne, with its collection of Indian antiquities, that she had died. Was her love for Abdul an extension of her love for India and the Empire, her way of touching the Jewel in the Crown?

Five years after my visit to Osborne House, I found myself tracing Abdul Karim's past in his home town of Agra, city of the Taj. My good-natured young Sikh driver, Babloo, looked like a taller version of England cricketer Monty Panesar, although he fancied himself more as Formula 1 racer Michael Schumacher than the gentle left-arm spinner from Northamptonshire. He had driven me down from Delhi in three hours, speeding along the three-lane expressways that have been built over the last few years as proud symbols of India's march to globalisation. Soon we were bumping along the narrow roads of Agra, past internet cafes, Kodak instant photo shops and electrical outlets stacked high with frost-free refrigerators and washing machines, material evidence of India's burgeoning middle class and hunger for consumerism.

I was meeting a local journalist, Syed Raju, a wiry man in white Nike trainers, who spoke endlessly on his mobile phone and clutched two small notebooks. Political dignitaries and Bollywood film stars visiting the Taj provided his more glamorous assignments, but he had never heard of Abdul Karim and knew nothing of a place called Karim Lodge. After two days, there was still nothing. The family may have left for Pakistan, he said. Perhaps Abdul Karim died there. I could find nobody in Agra that knew anything about him.

I told him that Karim had died in Agra in 1909 and would have been buried in the city. Given his position, he would surely have had a prominent gravestone, I suggested, mentally preparing to comb the burial grounds of Agra searching for his grave and to knock at every mosque to ask for information. By evening we were in luck. Raju had found a lead. He knew another journalist who had recognised the name. He wrote historical articles in a local Agra newspaper. That night we drove to the offices of the *Dainik Jagaran*, one of the highest circulated Hindi newspapers in India, recently acquired by the Irish millionaire, Tony O'Reilly, proprietor of *The Independent*.

Skirting the bales of newsprint lying near the entrance, we went up some narrow winding stairs to the editorial offices where computers whirred in the small, dimly lit newsroom. A man with a peppered grey beard met us. He was Rajiv Saxena, the newspaper's chief sub-editor. His bearded face broke into a welcoming smile.

'You are looking for Queen Victoria's *ustad*!' he said. 'Yes, I know where he is buried. Tomorrow we will go there.'

Panchkuin Kabaristan in Agra was once a burial ground for the Mughals. Now it is a dusty expanse of mud and grass, with buffaloes grazing amongst the crumbling gravestones. A few mausoleums stand intact – graves of the lesser relatives of the Mughal emperors – their semi-precious carvings vandalised and innocuous graffiti on the walls. No one comes here anymore, said Nizam Khan, the elderly Muslim caretaker of the graveyard. He cut a lost figure in the wilderness, looking after the graves that time and history had left behind. Khan led the way purposefully through the field, picking his way past unmarked graves, bramble bushes and stray dogs basking lazily in the winter sun. The dogs soon joined our procession, wagging their tails and running ahead, as if providing an escort to the Munshi's lonely grave.

At last, Nizam Khan stopped and pointed. 'This is it,' he announced dramatically, sensing our anticipation. Resting on a high plinth and surrounded by smaller graves, was a red sandstone mausoleum. We mounted the steep stairs to the tomb. Inside were three graves. Abdul Karim's lay in the middle, his father's and wife's on either side. The marble gravestone, once studded with semi-precious stones, had been plundered long ago. There was no one left to tend the grave now or bring flowers. The remainder of Karim's extended family had left for Pakistan after the Partition in 1947. The man who had lived in Windsor Castle and been the Empress's closest confidant now lay in a bleak unkempt graveyard guarded by an elderly caretaker and a few stray dogs. His Queen had provided generously for him and ironically it was the crumbling of her Empire that had changed the world of his descendants. The land had gone, given to Hindu families who had come as refugees from Pakistan, and the high mausoleum – once fairly grand – now overlooked only derelict graves.

Nizam Khan read out the words on Abdul Karim's gravestone in Urdu, his voice rising and falling as he orated, carrying across the desolate fields:

This is the last resting place of
Hafiz Mohammed Abdul Karim, CIEVO,
He is now alone in the world

His caste was the highest in Hindustan
None can compare with him

The poet finds it difficult to praise him
There is so much to say

Even Empress Victoria was so pleased with him
She made him her Hindustani ustad

He lived in England for many years
And let the river of his kindness
flow through this land

The poet prays for him
That he finds eternal peace in this resting place

Inscribed in Urdu behind the gravestone were the words: 'One day everybody
has to enjoy the sweetness of death.'

On my return to the Royal Archives at Windsor, I sat in the castle's Round Tower
looking through the thick volumes of Queen Victoria's Hindustani Journals. For
thirteen years the elderly Queen had written a page every day. Abdul Karim
would write a line in Urdu, then in English and a third line in Urdu in roman
letters so the Queen could hear the rich cadences of the words. The Queen dili-
gently copied the lines, covering the page in her sprawling handwriting. Through
winter evenings and balmy summer days, the Journals became the strongest bond
between Victoria and Abdul. The pages entered in it were their own private space,
away from the problems of Court, a troublesome family and the ever suspicious
and demanding Household. The Queen never missed a lesson. She would com-
plain almost coquettishly if Karim was absent, writing how much she missed her
'dear Abdul' when he went on leave. We can hear Abdul's voice in his written
thoughts at the end of each volume as he assessed the Queen's progress.

As I sat daydreaming, looking out of the window at the crowds of tourists
below, a pink piece of blotting paper floated out of the Journals. It had been
lying untouched in the Journal for over a century. I held the strip of paper in my
hand and pictured Karim, dressed in all his finery, standing by the Queen, gently
bowing down to blot her signature. It was as if an entire chapter of history – that
the political establishment had tried to destroy – was lying in front of me: the
story of an unknown Indian servant and his Queen, of an Empire and the Jewel
in the Crown, and above all, of love and human relationships.

1

⊶⧫⊷

AGRA

The call of the muezzin to prayer floated over the city of Agra in the dawn, waking up the residents. The summer heat had made even the nights unbearable and Abdul Karim was almost relieved to leave his bed. His young bride was still asleep. It was the few tranquil minutes of the morning that he loved. He walked on the terrace surveying the roof-tops of the neighbouring houses. Not far away he could see the high walls of the Central Jail where he and his father worked. Soon all of Agra would be awake and buzzing, the *gullies* and bazaars full of traders, artisans, *tongah wallahs* and people getting about their work. Cows would stand on the crowded streets lazily chewing the vegetables from the vendors' carts and elephants would sway through the narrow lanes carrying their loads of logs, grain, cotton and carpets to the *mandis* and factories.

As Karim sat down on a mat to pray, the first rays of the sun fell on the Taj Mahal, bathing it in a warm glow as the gentle waters of the Yamuna flowed behind. Further upstream, strategically positioned at a bend in the river, stood the impressive Agra Fort, a towering piece of architecture built in red sandstone by the Mughal Emperor Akbar in the sixteenth century, when he was at the pinnacle of his glory. Agra was known then as Akbarabad, capital city of the Mughal Empire. Within the walls of the Fort lay the history of four generations of the Mughal Emperors: tales of war, romance, court intrigues and brutality. It was in the splendour of the *Diwan i Khas*, or the Hall of Private Audience, with its marble columns inlaid with rich gemstones – lapis lazuli, garnet, jade, jasper and carnelian – that Emperor Shah Jehan had received the embassies of William Hawkins and Sir Thomas Roe, who came seeking permission for the East India Company to trade with India. The English and Dutch subsequently established their factories in Agra. It was in the Jasmine Tower of the Fort that the ageing Shah Jehan was imprisoned by his son Aurangzeb, and here that he languished till his dying day gazing through the tiny prison window at his beloved Taj Mahal, the mausoleum he had built for his Queen, Mumtaz Mahal.

Karim's family had lived in Agra for the last four years, enjoying the city's rich Mughal heritage, which was now combined with the spit and polish of British administration. The original family home was in nearby Farrukhabad in the United Provinces. Karim's father, Haji Wuzeeruddin, had been brought up by his stepfather and worked for the British government since 1856, when he was just twenty-two. Trained as a hospital assistant, he was transferred between various cantonment towns in north and central India and it was in Lalatpur cantonment near Jhansi that Abdul Karim was born in 1863.

Karim was to grow up in an India very different from that of his father – one that was governed directly by the British Crown and not the East India Company. Six years earlier, the land of his birth had been the principal theatre-ground of the Indian Mutiny of 1857. Haji Wuzeeruddin had been an eye-witness to the event that would be described later by Indian nationalists as the First War of Indian Independence. Karim's birthplace, near Jhansi, was synonymous with the fiery Lakshmibai, the Rani of Jhansi, who had donned battle armour, mounted her faithful steed and led her troops against the forces of the East India Company during the Mutiny.

Soldiers from the cantonment of Meerut in the United Provinces had taken up arms against their commanders, liberating imprisoned soldiers and killing many English officers. Soon neighbouring towns of Agra, Cawnpore (modern-day Kanpur) and Gwalior were captured by the mutineers and the rebels began plotting the downfall of the East India Company. They looked north to Delhi, where the ageing Mughal Emperor, Bahadur Shah Zafar, still held Court in the Red Fort and chose him as their symbolic leader. The eighty-two-year-old, famous more for his *ghazals* and Urdu poetry than for his statesmanship, declared himself Emperor of India, directly challenging British authority. The rulers from various central and northern Indian states rallied under his name. The mutineers met with initial success, British forces not being prepared for the rebellion. The siege of Delhi lasted for nearly four months, but on 21 September, Delhi fell to the Company troops. Bahadur Shah Zafar was given a brief trial and exiled to Rangoon in Burma; the last Mughal Emperor and descendant of Tamerlane, leaving Delhi unceremoniously in an ox-cart, ending an era of Indian history.

The British revenge was extreme. Hundreds were hanged after elementary trials and others were executed by tying them to the mouths of cannons and blowing them up. Delhi was desecrated, many of its historic monuments raided and plundered, artefacts and manuscripts looted and destroyed, and hundreds of ordinary civilians executed. The residents of Agra were fined collectively for helping the rebels. Many Mughal buildings and houses in Agra were demolished. The blood of the mutineers stained the dusty plains of central and northern India as they were hanged from trees and public posts as a warning to anyone who challenged Company rule in the future. Karim was born on the same land six years after the guns of the mutineers were silenced.

He was only thirteen when Queen Victoria was given the title of Empress of India in 1876 by Benjamin Disraeli. The East India Company had been dissolved in 1858 and ruling power transferred directly to the British Crown. The Secretary of State for India now dealt with Indian affairs in Westminster and the Viceroy represented the Crown in India.

The Queen was delighted with her new title and sent a message to the Delhi Durbar held on 1 January 1877: 'We must trust that the present occasion may tend to unite in bonds of yet closer affection ourselves and our subjects, that from the highest to the humblest all may feel that under our rule the great principles of liberty, equity and justice are secured to them.' Karim would have heard this message as a teenager living in Meerut City.

With the British Crown now directly in charge of the administration of the provinces, radical changes were made. The railways were constructed with frenetic zeal to provide direct and quick access to the interior of the country, linking Cawnpore, Lucknow, Meerut and Agra, the major northern Indian cities that had been touched by the Mutiny. The East India Railway connected Calcutta directly to Delhi, and the Central India Railway connected cities like Bombay and Baroda to the north.

After the Mutiny, the British had regulated the running of the Indian army and Karim lived his early life in the cantonment of Lalatpur and Meerut City, watching the parading soldiers and dreaming of one day being in uniform. He was the second of six children, with an elder brother, Abdul Azeez, and four younger sisters.

Karim had no formal lessons as a child and spent his time with the other boys playing in the fields. When he was ten, he was handed over to a private tutor and he studied with him till the age of eighteen. He was taught Persian and Urdu, the Court language of the Mughals, and read books on Islam and the Prophet. But the young man had always wanted to travel, and on the completion of his studies he went on an extensive tour of the various parts of India. He set off around north India visiting the cities of Jhansi, Gwalior, Benaras, Mathura and Allahabad. On his return he joined his father, who worked in the hospital connected with the second regiment of the Central India Horse.[1]

In 1878 Britain was entangled in the Anglo-Afghan war and Wuzeeruddin's corps was ordered to go north to Kabul. Karim, eager to explore, accompanied the troops as far north-west as Jellalabad, eighty miles east of the city, enjoying the rugged countryside and the tribal terrain. It was famously to the fort of Jellalabad that the exhausted British soldier, Dr William Bryden, had come on 13 January 1842; the lone survivor of 16,000 troops who perished on the road from Kabul during the First Afghan War of 1837–42, a picture etched forever in the minds of the British administration and captured dramatically on canvas by artists to remember the war's high casualties. Nearly forty years later, Afghanistan remained on the boil and the British constantly feared that the Russians would attempt to enter India through Afghanistan. The Second Afghan War broke out in 1878, after the British and the Russians clashed over setting up a mission in Afghanistan.

No sooner had Wuzeeruddin's regiment reached Jellalabad, when they were ordered to start at once on the famous march to Kandahar under General Roberts in August 1880. Roberts had been a junior officer during the siege of Delhi in the Mutiny. Within three hours the soldiers were on the road. Wuzeeruddin accompanied them as a medical assistant, but Karim had to turn back as he had no formal position in the army. The historic march from Kabul to Kandahar with 10,000 men ended in a resounding British victory and the defeat of the Afghan lord, Sardar Mohammed Ayub Khan. A few months later the Second Afghan War was over and General Roberts returned triumphantly to England where he was knighted.

When Wuzeeruddin returned after the war, Karim travelled with him again to Kabul, where he marvelled at the sight of the Khyber Pass, the fifty-three-kilometre narrow road that cuts through the Hindu Kush mountains, used by invaders for centuries since the time of Alexander the Great. The precipitous cliffs guarded by the fierce Pashtun tribes, the austere forts standing in bleak mountain deserts and the famous bazaars of Kabul overflowing with watermelon and dry fruits, were a far cry from the gentle plains of the Yamuna that Karim had grown up in.

By their return from this trip, Karim took up employment with the Nawab of Jawara, who appointed him as the Naib Wakil to the Agency of Agar, an area on the border of Rajputana and the Central Provinces (present-day Rajasthan and Madhya Pradesh). Meanwhile, the British government issued an order permitting the exchange of military for civil appointments and Wuzeeruddin transferred to the Central Jail at Agra. After three years' service with the Nawab of Jawara, Karim resigned and joined his father at Agra, taking up a position as a vernacular clerk to the superintendent of the Central Jail. His salary was fixed at Rs 10 a month. Both father and son were now employed at the same place. Wuzeeruddin moved with his family to the Hariparbat area near the jail. The family owned about five acres of land in the surrounding area. Karim enjoyed hunting with his brother in the forests around Agra, which were full of deer, black buck and tigers. The surrounding lakes of Rajasthan were the nesting grounds of a variety of wild fowl, particularly the migrating cranes who came every winter from Siberia and stayed till spring. Agra, the city of the Taj, was now the stable family home. It was here that Karim brought his young bride, a match arranged by his father in the traditional Indian custom. His wife's brothers also worked at the jail and the closely-knit family soon became well known in the area.

On that summer morning in Agra, when Karim looked out over the city, he did not know that his life was about to change.

The first stirrings of human life had begun and the banks of the Yamuna were already crowded with camels and elephants, led by their owners to drink and carry back the day's water supply. In the markets of Loha Mandi and Sadar Bazar the traders were opening their red cloth-bound ledgers and fixing the commodity prices for the day. Spices, cotton, wheat, gram, oil, sugarcane – all the produce of the fertile region – would pass through their keen fingers as they struck their deals. Agra had been the hub of trade activity since Mughal times and so it continued under the British as the trade corridor that connected Central and West India on one side and the rugged North-West on the other.

Artisans were also at work. Carpet weavers were streaming into the looms of Otto Weyladt and Co., the largest carpet manufacturers in Agra, to weave the finest carpets for the export market. In the narrow streets and shops around the jail, the craftsmen were beginning their delicate job of stone inlay work, practised for centuries since the time of Emperor Akbar, cutting the huge slabs of marble and fashioning them into exquisite handicrafts set with precious gems.

As the clinking sound of their hammer and chisel striking the stone began to fill the air, Karim said goodbye to his father, adjusted his *pugree* and strode out of the house towards the Central Jail. A tall man, nearly six feet in height, with dark intense eyes and a neatly clipped black beard, he looked impressive. Today was an important day. He had been summoned to meet with John Tyler, the jail's superintendent.

Tyler was a busy man. A doctor by profession, he was well loved for his warmth and geniality but known for a lack of tact and a hot temper.[2] As an Anglo-Indian he was fluent in Hindustani and at ease with the natives. Tyler had just returned to Agra from London from the successful Colonial and Indian Exhibition of 1886, at the inauguration of which the second verse of the English national anthem had been uniquely sung in Sanskrit. He had been in charge of thirty-four inmates from Agra Jail who had attended the exhibition. The inmates had been schooled in carpet weaving as part of the jail rehabilitation programme, a tradition started by Emperor Akbar who brought the finest carpet weavers from Persia to India as teachers. Since the prisoners had all the time in the world, they could work at leisure to produce the exquisite Mughal carpets in silk, cotton and wool. The jail carpets were internationally famous and the tradition of training the inmates was carried on by the British administration.

The carpet weavers from Agra Jail had impressed Queen Victoria with their skills. It was Karim, Tyler's assistant clerk, who had helped him select the carpets to send to England for the exhibition and had chosen the artisans, who he had supervised before they left for England. The superintendent of the jail had also wanted to send a pair of traditional gold *kadas* or bracelets for the Queen and Karim had proven useful again. Tyler found the young man efficient and trusted his fine aesthetic sense. Karim had chosen a pair of *kadas* set in solid gold, embossed with traditional *meenakari*, or painted enamel work, with two dragon heads at the terminals. The *kadas* were wrapped in Indian silk and velvet and packed for the Queen. Tyler's gift was much appreciated. On 20 September 1886, the Queen wrote to Tyler expressing her delight and letting him know that she had worn them the previous evening.

Tyler told Karim about the success of the exhibition and thanked him for his help. The jail superintendent now had another proposition for him. During his trip to London, the Queen had discussed the possibility of employing some Indian servants during the Jubilee. She was expecting a number of Indian Princes for the celebration and felt she could do with someone to help her address the Indians presented to her.[3] Tyler felt he had just the person for her. He then asked Karim if he would like to travel to England to be the Queen's personal attendant and table hand during the Jubilee celebrations the following year.

Karim was dumbstruck. He had expected a promotion, but not of this scale. To travel the seas to the Mother Country and personally serve the Queen was a dream come true. He looked at the portrait of Queen Victoria on Tyler's office wall, sitting on the throne in all her glory and felt a sudden rush of adrenalin, before accepting the offer. It was decided there and then that he would journey to England on a year's leave of absence.

What followed was a hectic period for Karim as he was trained in English social customs and etiquette. As servant to the Queen, he would have to learn all the skills of waiting at table, the formalities of serving dinner guests and the protocol of the Royal Household. He was taught how to greet the Queen, to bow correctly and practised standing still for long periods. He was told that new servants never looked the Queen directly in the eye but at her feet. He learnt about the Queen's family – the Prince and Princess of Wales, the other Royal children and the European connections. He was told about the three Royal residences that the Queen used – Windsor Castle, Balmoral and Osborne House – and was informed that Windsor was the Queen's preferred place to stay. She rarely spent the night at Buckingham Palace, which was used for all state occasions. In the few months before his departure, Karim was given a crash course in English, enough to allow him to communicate with the Queen and Household. Every night he sat by the lamplight with an illustrated phrase book given to him by Tyler, studying the everyday words that he would have to use in England.

A well-known Agra tailor was summoned and a set of special clothes were made for Karim – long Indian-style tunics in deep red and blue – with matching *pugrees* and waistbands. These were worn with loose white trousers or *salwars*. In the little free time he had, Karim also asked his wife to teach him to cook some of his favourite recipes for when he arrived in England. In the family home in Hariparbat, excitement levels were high as young Karim prepared to cross the seas and wait on Queen Victoria. His brothers-in-law, two of whom worked in Agra Jail, came visiting and gently teased Karim as he struggled with his lessons. His mother-in-law gave him her blessings and told him to take care in the cold.

Karim was soon to meet his travelling companion and fellow Indian serv-ant, Mohammed Buksh. The portly and good-natured Buksh worked for General Thomas Dennehy, political agent in Rajputana, and managed his whole household. Dennehy was to take up his new position as the Queen's extra groom-in-waiting and would be in charge of the Indian servants when they arrived in England. Buksh had worked for several years with the Rana of Dholpore, the head of a princely state in the neighbourhood of Agra in Rajputana, and was quite used to the job of cook and waiter. Karim, who had worked as a clerk, was not familiar with the job, but was a willing learner, buoyed by the prospect of serving the Empress of India and helping in the Jubilee celebrations.

When the clothes were stitched, his English lessons complete and travelling case ready, Karim instructed his wife to pack some of his favourite *pan* and betel nuts for the long journey. He also carried a box of Indian spices. Unlike Hindu families in India, who did not approve of crossing the seas and eating food cooked by Westerners, the Muslims had no religious problems with a sea journey. Both Karim and Buksh, however, wanted to be sure that they could prepare and eat their own Indian food.

When the day arrived for Karim to leave, he said an emotional goodbye to his family and set off on his new adventure. The journey would take them by train from Agra to Bombay and then by steamer mail to England. He felt a catch in his throat as Bombay port disappeared from sight and the ship steered over the clear blue waters of the Arabian Sea.

2

∽∽∽

A JUBILEE PRESENT

Weeks before the Golden Jubilee, preparations had begun in London for what was to be the biggest party of the year. Journalists and photographers kept watch at the major ports and railway stations as royalty and nobility from around the world began their descent on London. They stepped off steamers and first-class carriages, elegantly dressed, children and nannies in tow, servants and porters in attendance with mountains of luggage. The London season was in full swing and nothing was too excessive. Showcasing Britain's Empire were the Indian Princes, who were specially invited by the Crown and who would form a major part of the celebrations. It was suggested by the government that the wealth and glamour of the heavily jewelled Maharajahs, Maharanis and Indian Princes would add to the pomp of the Jubilee and display the loyalty of the Indian rulers and the colonies.

The business of rounding up the Princes was no easy matter. Many Hindu Maharajahs were forbidden from travelling the seas – crossing the proverbial *kala pani* (dark waters) – by their religion. Others were eager to come, but were completely unsuitable. Telegrams flew between the Secretary of State at the India Office in Whitehall, the Viceroy's office in Calcutta and the offices of the political agents in the princely states. The Viceroy, Lord Dufferin, sent detailed profiles of the Princes to Lord Cross, the Secretary of State, carefully weeding through the suitable candidates, cherry-picking those who would look handsome and elegant in their native clothes, could speak English fluently and would be reasonably at home in a Western environment. Balancing the three had proven quite a challenge.

The 'best blood in India' Dufferin could get was Pertab Singh, the scion of a great Rajput house, brother of the Maharajah of Jodhpur, who agreed to 'try the experiment' of crossing the seas. But even the great Rajput had his shortcomings. 'His own appearance especially out of native clothes, is not prepossessing,' warned the Viceroy.[1] Dufferin reported that Pertab Singh unfortunately did not speak English well, his teeth were disfigured by betel chewing and 'his only notion of smart get-up is to make himself look as like an English jockey as possible'. He was, at least, very sporty and excelled in all equestrian accomplishments such as pig-sticking, riding and racing.

What Pertab Singh lacked in appearance, he made up for in rank and what the others lacked in rank, they made up for in appearance. The Maharajah of Cooch Behar, thought Dufferin, was a good choice as he quite fitted 'the British idea of what an Indian Rajah should look like'. Cooch Behar, he informed Cross, looked very gentlemanlike even in European clothes and took with him a 'dear little wife'. Lady Dufferin had done her best to persuade Cooch Behar's wife to keep to her native clothes, 'in which she looks charming', and Dufferin suggested that the Queen should also send her a message to enforce this.

Some like Holkar, the Maharajah of Indore, came with health warnings – 'He is a burly, ill-mannered, vulgar Mahratta' – but even he had his advantages. 'He will take a large following with him, whose gorgeous dresses will help to enliven the Jubilee show,' commented Dufferin.

The lists were finalised over a period of four months. Dufferin sent detailed instructions as to how the Queen should receive them, what occasions they should be invited to, the ranking and order of precedence and how the Secretary of State should entertain them. The Princes were all paying for their own travel, so would need to be given a good time in London. The English officers accompanying them would handle the sightseeing, the Queen could perhaps invite them to an Indian-style Durbar and the Secretary of State to a reception. They should all be invited to Buckingham Palace and given seats at Westminster Abbey. Protocol and formalities were a vexing question: 'Whether or not the Princes should be invited to attend a levee held by the Queen in person, where they will have to kneel and kiss her Majesty's hand, is rather a ticklish question,' noted Dufferin.

Lord Cross issued instructions from London: 'The Queen wishes them [the Princes] all to appear in Native costume. European costume would be distasteful.'[2]

These Jubilee celebrations would set the precedent for subsequent major Royal events – the Diamond Jubilee, the Coronation Durbar of King Edward VII and the Delhi Durbar of 1911. Even since the Mutiny of 1857, the British believed in nurturing the princely states that had remained loyal to the Crown. In the post-Mutiny administrative reorganisation, the eleven provinces that had been dominated by the East India Company passed directly under Crown rule, while the rest of the princely or native states were ruled by their own Maharajahs or nawabs in alliance with the British government. These had remained largely autonomous, issuing their own currency and Royal crests, although their administration was subjected to close scrutiny. The princely states were arranged in a pecking order corresponding to their land and influence and some Maharajahs were allowed gun salutes. In the premier league were the states of Hyderabad, Mysore, Baroda, Gwalior and Kashmir – all known for their loyalty to the British Crown – with twenty-one gun salutes; Cooch Behar was allowed thirteen.

The first of the Royal guests to arrive for the Jubilee were the highly recommended Maharajah and Maharani of Cooch Behar, one of the most westernised of Indian princely families. Cooch Behar was a tiny principality set in the northeastern hills of Bengal, an idyllic paradise of tea plantations and game-rich forests full of rhinoceroses and tigers. The Maharajah, Nripendra Narayan, a dashing twenty-five-year-old, was a keen huntsman who had been educated in the elite Presidency College in Calcutta and tutored by English teachers. His wife, the beautiful twenty-two-year-old Sunity Devi, was the first Indian Maharani to visit the English Court. They travelled with their three children, Sunity's two brothers, an English secretary and an entourage of servants, and received a rousing welcome. The press clamoured to see Sunity when she rode in Hyde Park, reporting every detail of her clothes, accessories and lifestyle as she socialised with Alexandra, the Princess of Wales and Princess May, later to become Queen Mary.

Nripendra Narayan wore silk embroidered Indian tunics with ornamented turbans and was never without his strings of pearls and ruby and diamond encrusted rings. Sunity Devi's gowns were fashioned by top Paris couturiers combining Eastern and Western styles and she wore saris with European-style blouses and petticoats. The Cooch Behar jewels sparkled around her neck and on her fingers. The Maharani was the daughter of the nineteenth-century Bengali reformist Keshub Chander Sen, who had established the Brahmo Samaj, a liberal branch of Hinduism that believed in women's emancipation. Sen had been one of the first Hindus to cross the seas in 1870, had preached at the Unitarian Church in Bristol and had been invited to lunch with Queen Victoria at Osborne, where he was served a specially prepared vegetarian meal. Sunity had been brought up in a liberal tradition and was the embodiment of the accomplished Victorian woman: well-educated, proficient in embroidery, music and art. She was later to become the first Indian woman to write in English when her memoir, *Autobiography of an Indian Princess*, was published in London in 1921. Her husband Nripendra had also written in English and his *Thirty Seven Years of Big Game* was published in 1909.

Sayaji Rao Gaekwad, the Maharajah of Baroda, arrived a few months later – with his wife Chimnabai. Baroda in western India, in modern-day Gujarat, was a wealthy state and the Gaekwads were a fierce and proud Maratha clan. The presence of a Maharajah of a twenty-one gun salute state added significant prestige to the Jubilee celebrations and the British had been keen to host him. The Gaekwads were as traditional as the Cooch Behars were westernised. Though Sayaji Rao was well versed in English and spoke four languages, including Urdu, Marathi and Gujarati, he preferred to retain his traditional Indian clothes and customs. He wore heavily brocaded tunics, *angarakhas*, stitched in the western Indian cities of Ahmedabad or Surat, both famed for their textile centres. He was rarely without his trademark three-string pearls. On his head was the small cap-like turban favoured by the Maratha rulers. The enigmatic Chimnabai, an accomplished veena player, was as comfortable in the kitchen as she was hunting tigers and was an active campaigner for women's emancipation. The family treasures included the exquisite Pearl Carpet, a silk and deer-skin carpet embellished with over 2 million pearls and studded with diamonds, emeralds and rubies with four solid gold weights in the corners. Sayaji Rao's elephant famously had a howdah cast in solid, jewel-encrusted gold. It needed twenty-four men to lift the howdah onto the elephant's back. At the end of the day, the elephant was given a pint of sherry.

Also boarding the steamers for England were the portly, architecture-loving Maharajah of Indore, Shivaji Rao Holkar, a state in the Central Provinces with a nineteen gun salute, and the Maharajah of Bharatpore, Jaswant Singh, a seventeen gun salute state in western India, famous for its bird sanctuary. The states with eleven gun salutes were represented by the Maharajah Bhagwatsinghji Sagramsinhji, the Thakur of Gondal, who had studied medicine at Edinburgh and was much respected by the British press; the Thakore of Limri, Jaswantsinghji Fatehsinghji, with his smartly clipped beard and turban; and the Thakore of Morvi, Lukhdirji Bahadur, who sported a neat moustache and layered turban in the Rajasthani style. The handsome young Rao of Kutch and the Nawab of Junagadh were also amongst the assembled Royalty. All the Maharajahs arrived in style with their retinue of secretaries, servants and cooks. Some brought their cows with them, others their horses. The British found them sensational.

Lord Cross and Dufferin waited anxiously as the entourage of Princes and nobility travelled across the seas to England. Pertab Singh caused a slight panic when he managed to lose his jewels on the *Tasmania* and divers had to be sent in to look for them. A relieved Lord Cross later telegraphed Dufferin: 'Foreign office have just sent word that Pertab Singh's jewels have been recovered.'[3] All was well again for the Jubilee party.

Apart from the westernised Cooch Behars, most of the Hindu kings were reluctant to eat food prepared by English cooks. Sunity had started eating meat to practise for her trip to England, initially hating it. She spent several unhappy weeks in her London flat, unable to appreciate European food, but soon cheered up as the social whirl began in earnest.

Queen Victoria requested Sunity to call on her privately before she was formally presented to the Court. She sent instructions that the Maharani must wear her native clothes on all state occasions. For the first meeting at Buckingham Palace, Nripendra chose her gown: a pale-grey satin dress with stylish but minimal jewellery. So nervous was Sunity before the meeting that she accepted a glass of port from her maid to steady her nerves, but ended up spilling it over her gown. The Queen took an instant liking to the young Indian Maharani and immediately made her feel comfortable. Sunity was delighted with the Queen and was impressed by her 'simple and kindly' conversation and the way she had put her at her ease. 'I felt eager to go back to India so that I might tell my country-women about our wonderful Empress,'[4] she wrote.

Soon Sunity was being chaperoned by Princess May, the Duchess of Teck, and being invited to dinner by the Prince of Wales. She bought her son, Rajey, a toy yacht to sail on the Serpentine and took her second son, Jit, for tea to Marlborough House with the Princess of Wales. It was the start of a long friend-ship between Sunity and Princess Alexandra. Sunity and her husband went to the opera, saw a production of *The Winter's Tale*, spent a night at Windsor Castle where they were given a luxury gilt-edged bedroom, toured Edinburgh and Brighton and visited Hatfield House, where she got lost in the maze.

This Indian summer was well under way when Abdul Karim and Mohammed Buksh arrived at Windsor Castle, three days before the start of the Jubilee celebrations. As their carriage turned into Castle Hill they felt a sense of appre-hension and excitement, looking up at the towering ramparts of their new home, so different from the familiar red sandstone forts of Agra, Delhi and Rajasthan. The Queen's standard was fluttering in the light breeze from the Round Tower. In the quadrangle of the Castle, usually guarded by the Queen's troops in their livery of red coats and furry bearskin hats, was a group of Indian soldiers with long, wild beards and fiercely curled moustaches, impressive turbans and gilt-edged swords, their bronzed faces reflecting the rugged climes in which they had served. Their presence made Windsor Castle look more like an Indian bazaar than a slice of Berkshire.

The twelve Indian soldiers were the Queen's newly arrived Escort for the Jubilee celebrations. The Queen had requested an Indian Escort earlier that year to demonstrate to the attendant ranks of European Royalty her position as Empress of India. She treasured this much-coveted title, given to her in 1876, more than any other, feeling it gave her and her family a rank now equal to the Emperors of Russia and Prussia. The Jubilee was the perfect occasion to put her Empire on display and the Indian guard made an impressive sight standing behind the Queen at all significant state functions, her black mourning clothes set against their splash of colour. But their effect was more than decorative. By choosing them as her Escort – the Queen's closest source of protection – she had placed enormous trust in her Indian subjects and elevated them before the world's eyes.

The Escort had been selected to represent Her Majesty's Indian Empire in its entirety. Officers were chosen from all corners of the Indian army and comprised eight from the Bengal Cavalry, two from the Bombay Cavalry and one each from Hyderabad, Madras and the Central Indian Horse. At her Jubilee, the Queen's Empire would sparkle before the world.

Karim and Buksh stood on the sidelines taking it all in. Soon they were to catch their first glimpse of Queen Victoria. They saw her – a commanding little figure in her mourning clothes and white veil – approaching the Indian soldiers. The

Indian Escort stood to attention as she drifted past, inspecting them with a keen eye that noticed every miniscule detail of dress and comportment. As an officer bellowed a command, they extended their ornate swords for her inspection. She then moved over to talk briefly to some Indian Princes who were visiting the Castle. Impressed by the personality that radiated from her, Karim and Buksh grew increasingly apprehensive of their impending first meeting with the Queen. At night, in the room they shared in the Castle premises, they whispered to each other in Urdu about what to expect.

The day of the Jubilee arrived, leaving the Queen in a reflective mood. 'This very eventful day has come ... I sat *alone*,'[5] she sighed, her mood a stark contrast to the atmosphere of national celebration. In the gilded bedroom of Buckingham Palace, the sixty-eight-year-old Queen missed the people she had loved and lost.

Victoria remained wrapped in widow's black. Her foreign secretary, Lord Rosebery, had encouraged her to wear a crown instead of her trademark bonnet, but in vain. He had even sent her a memo the previous year, insisting: 'The symbol that unites this vast Empire is a Crown, not a bonnet.' But the Queen would not be moved and the bonnet stayed, its solemnity even adding to her presence.

For her Jubilee, the Queen's black dress and bonnet were trimmed with the exquisite white point d'Alençon lace and diamonds. She wore a string of pearls round her neck and stepped out to meet the adoring crowds. Her mood lifted as she was driven from Buckingham Palace in a handsome landau drawn by six cream horses, her daughters Vicky and Alice beside her. Her Indian Escort rode directly in front, their turbans bobbing in the morning light, drawing cheers and waves from the crowds lining the street. It was the first time the British public had seen Indian officers on the streets. The Indian Princes, splendidly attired in their native clothes, assembled in their carriages in Hyde Park Corner and rode out in a carefully co-ordinated procession to the Abbey. Sitting in the first carriage was Kunwar Hurwan Singh, Maharajah of Kapurthala, followed by the Maharajah of Bharatpore. All together, eleven carriages transported the native Princes and Indian delegations. Sunity Devi was holding a parasol, but was urged by the crowds to show her face. She obligingly folded it and smiled at the sea of waving hands. All along the royal route, people stood on the specially erected platforms cheering, many holding up banners which the Queen found 'touching'.

The noise from the crowds faded into a hush as the Queen entered Westminster Abbey and once again she felt overwhelmed by emotion. More than ever she missed her husband, who would have stood by her side on this solemn occasion. As the elderly Queen sat on the throne with her robes beautifully draped around the historic Coronation Chair, where she had been crowned as an eighteen-year-old, she felt lonely and sad. 'I sat *alone*. Oh! *Without* my beloved husband (for whom this would have been such a fine day!) where I sat alone 49 years ago and received the homage of the Princes and Peers.'[6]

On her return to Buckingham Palace, the Queen presented Jubilee brooches to her daughters, daughters-in-law and granddaughters, and then had lunch with the Kings of Saxe Coburg, Denmark and Belgium. After lunch she watched the Blue Jackets march past and then went to the Ball Room to receive her presents; she was so exhausted by the afternoon that she was ready to faint and had to be rolled back to her room on her chair. Here she lay on the sofa and rested, opening telegrams coming from all parts of the country, too numerous to personally acknowledge anymore. A newspaper announcement of thanks, she decided, would have to suffice.

For her grand Jubilee dinner, the Queen wore a dress with the rose, thistle and shamrock embroidered in silver with large diamonds. The King of Denmark led her in and proposed the toast to her health. The Queen invited most of the Indian Princes to a reception after dinner and spent some time chatting with them, accepting their congratulations and enquiring that they were comfortable and well. The Queen had always admired the jewellery the Maharajahs wore with such ease and style. She herself always wore her biggest diamonds and pearls when she was meeting Eastern Royalty so as not to be outdone. She had once met the Shah of Persia wearing her Koh-i-Noor after hearing that he always wore exquisite jewellery. India remained to her a place of mystery, exciting her curiosity.

By late evening, the Queen was 'half dead with fatigue', though she managed to see some of the illuminations. Alone in her room that night, as she heard the crowds passing the Palace singing *God Save the Queen* and *Rule Britannia*, the Queen wrote in her Journal: 'This never-to-be forgotten day will always leave the most gratifying and heart-stirring memories behind.'[7]

A delighted Lord Cross telegraphed Dufferin in India: 'Our great day of Jubilee is over, well over. We cannot pretend to Eastern magnificence, but it was magnificent.'[8]

The next day the Queen met 30,000 poor schoolchildren at Hyde Park, who had been scrubbed for the occasion and given a meat pie, a piece of cake and an orange. They sang *God Save the Queen* 'somewhat out of tune' and were each given an earthenware pot decorated with the Queen's portrait. A little girl gave Victoria a beautiful bouquet, on the ribbon of which was embroidered: 'God bless our Queen, not Queen alone, but Mother, Queen and Friend.' The Queen was genuinely moved by it.

After that it was a train from Paddington to Slough and a drive through more cheering crowds, past balconies and windows packed with people and splendid decorations with Chinese lanterns, 'the ringing of bells and bands playing' to Castle Hill, where a statue of the Queen was unveiled, and finally to 'good old Windsor' for the night. The Indian Princes took their positions on the balcony of the White

Hart Hotel opposite the Castle watching the ceremonies from a vantage point, *The Times* reporting that 'their rich uniforms and picturesque appearance excited a great deal of interest as they gazed curiously upon the crowds below and watched the busy traffic on the hill'. In the evening they watched the illuminated Castle and the night procession by Eton boys. That night the Queen wrote in her Journal: 'These two days will ever remain indelibly impressed on my mind, with great gratitude, to that all merciful providence, who had protected me so long, and to my devoted and loyal people. But how painfully do I miss the dear ones I have lost.'[9]

The Queen had gone through a rollercoaster of emotions over the last two days. As her family and her guests had enjoyed the dancing and the partying, she had felt deeply lonely without Albert. She missed someone to talk to and gossip with about the Jubilee events. The warmth of her people had cheered her, but they had gone home to their loved ones and she had returned alone to her Castle, her maids and Household. She missed her husband and her Highland servant, John Brown; both men the Queen had loved and buried.

'A fine morning with a fresh air,' noted the Queen, as she looked out of her bedroom window at Windsor Castle the next day, but she was feeling 'very tired'.[10] It was the third day of her Golden Jubilee celebrations and the monarch knew she faced another day of buntings and presentations. The Queen sat lost in thought as she was dressed by her maids. She had chosen to wear widow's black ever since the death of Prince Albert in 1861. At last, she adjusted her cap and ascended into her carriage for the short drive to Frogmore with her daughter Beatrice. As they rode down the rolling green of the Long Walk in Windsor Park, past the rows of chestnut trees, the Queen thought of the excitement of the past two days and the fireworks of the night before. Everything now seemed so still. At Frogmore House her eldest daughter Victoria and her granddaughter Vicky were already there waiting for her; and so was a special gift from India.

Abdul Karim and Mohammed Buksh – the Queen's Jubilee presents from India – had arrived early to wait at table. The breakfast room at Frogmore, a sombre place at most times, seemed to come alive with the new arrivals. Buksh's practised elegance matched Karim's naturally regal presence. Their clothes made them look almost princely. The Queen was delighted. Dressed in striking scarlet tunics with white turbans, they approached her reverentially. The Queen noted Mohammed Buksh's appearance, 'very dark with a very smiling expression'. She described the much younger Abdul Karim as 'much lighter, tall and with a fine serious countenance'. Both servants approached her slowly, their eyes lowered to gaze at the ground as they had been instructed to do. Then, with a deep bow, Karim and Buksh bent down to kiss the Queen's feet. As he rose, young Karim's dark eyes fleetingly met the Queen's gaze. Suddenly Victoria no longer felt as tired.

3

⊶⊶

An Indian Durbar

T he arrival of the Indians had already caused a flutter in the Royal Household. Sir Henry Ponsonby, the Queen's private secretary, sat in his study writing a note about them. It wasn't going to be easy taking care of them, he thought. Their rules had to be clearly defined. The elderly Ponsonby recorded: 'Mohammed Buxsh and Abdul Kareem are taken in to the Queen's service as personal Indian servants under the order of Hugh Brown and of Hyem. They received £60 a year which I presume the Privy Purse must pay them.'[1] The Indians were to be *khidmatgars*, or table hands, and General Thomas Dennehy, who had accompanied them from India (and thankfully spoke the language), would be in charge of them. Ponsonby remembered another crucial point and pencilled a note to the Yeoman of the Cellar: 'We are anxious (and H.M. approves) to request all persons in Household not to offer spirits to the two Indians.'[2] As Muslims, their religion forbade them to drink and they could not be expected to participate in any social drinking with the other servants. Karim and Buksh would also be allowed to prepare and cook their own food as their religion demanded. Ponsonby hoped it would not get any more complicated.

Ponsonby was the senior-most member of the Royal Household, the bewildering pecking order of which Karim and Buksh would soon learn. A tall man in his sixties, with a neatly clipped beard and a slightly untidy manner of dressing, Ponsonby was well liked and trusted by the Queen. He was witty, patient, ready to listen to even the most trying and boring of people and quick at getting to the root of a problem and solving it. 'It becomes wearisome. But one must listen,'[3] he once said. He was devoted to his wife, Mary Ponsonby, a highly lettered woman with radical views who wrote articles in the *Pall Mall Gazette*. Ponsonby understood the Queen and she understood him. His duties as private secretary not only included passing on all her correspondence to her after going through it himself, and laboriously reading her handwritten replies, but also soothing the ruffled feathers of members of the Household who may be complaining about the Queen or a colleague. It was Ponsonby who was on the front line facing the

Queen when a crisis erupted in the Household and he, more than any other, knew how to deal with her demands.

Sir James Reid, the Queen's personal physician, was an Aberdeen Scot who did not believe in mincing his words and freely spoke his mind. Reid was to play an important role as the main intermediary between the Household and the Queen over the affairs of the Munshi in later years. As the Queen grew older, she relied on Reid even more and he had to deal with matters that went far beyond his call of duty.'Ask Sir James', was her usual answer to members of her Household when they came to her with problems and queries. She wrote to him daily describing her physical condition, the movement of her bowels and her digestion. He constantly despaired of the Queen's ability to eat far too voraciously for one her age, but could do little to stop her.

The women of the Household consisted of the Queen's private secretary and woman of the bedchamber, Harriet Phipps; the ladies-in-waiting, Minnie Cochrane and Lady Jane Churchill; and the maids of honour, Marie Mallet and Ethel Cadogan. The maids of honour were in charge of the mistress of the robes. It was a formidable line-up of men and women with whom the Indians would have to deal with.

The Queen was delighted with her Indian servants. Less than a week after they had arrived, she noted:'The Indians always wait now and do so, so well and quietly.'[4] Karim and Buksh had immediately taken to their duties and had cleared the first hurdle.

Her Indian guests were equally special to her. At a Jubilee garden party in Buckingham Palace, the Queen ordered that her Indian Escorts be asked to stand in a ring around the Royal Tent. This they did looking very impressive and were appreciated by Queen Marie of Belgium and other European Princes who floated past them to join the Queen for tea. The bright Indian saris and turbans worn by the Indians stood out among the sea of guests enjoying the sandwiches, cakes, jellies and bowls of strawberries and cream in the lawns of the Palace. The Queen was pleased at the ambience. The Princes did not disappoint. They wore their finest jewels, held forth on stories of Royal hunts, had the English ladies hanging on their every word and the press corps clicking wildly at them.

'English society seems disposed to put everything Indian upon a pedestal, and young ladies appear ready enough to fall in love with Indians at home,' Lord Dufferin wrote to Lord Cross. The Indians were clearly working their magic.

There was no respite from the Jubilee celebrations. The day after the garden party, Karim and Buksh were up at dawn again. Windsor Castle was preparing to host its first ever Indian Durbar. The excitement was palpable, the Queen anxious to get everything right for her foreign visitors. The Green Drawing Room in

Windsor was set up for the occasion with the great officers of state, gold stick and cross, standing behind the Queen. The Indian Escort stood opposite forming an imposing background and looking 'splendid', according to the Queen. Sir Pertab Singh, ADC to the Crown Prince and brother of the Maharajah of Jaipur, stood behind the Queen with the great officers as she waited to receive the Princes.

The first to enter was Shivaji Rao Holkar, the Maharajah of Indore, who offered his presents to the Queen. She gave him an enamel portrait of herself and invested him with the Grand Cross of the Star of India, knighting him. Holkar, who was dressed in a long Indian tunic worn over *churidars*, or tight trousers, had great difficulty in kneeling down before the Queen. The Holkars, Maratha rulers of a proud state, had been reduced in size since 1818 after their defeat against the British in the third Anglo-Maratha War. Nevertheless, the state enjoyed a nineteen gun salute.[5]

The Queen found Holkar 'beautifully dressed and handsome'.[6] He was followed by the young Rao of Cutch, who entered with his brother. The Queen thought 'he and his Brother were like a dream' and she appreciated the 'wonderful jewels' that he wore. The Maharajah presented the Queen with an address in a golden case and said a few appropriate words 'so nicely and in such good English' that the Queen was enchanted. He also presented the Queen with some beautiful silver ornaments for the table. The Queen gave him an enamel portrait of herself and invested him with the Grand Cross of the Indian Empire. Cutch was a seventeen gun salute state.

The Queen was enjoying her audience with the Princes. She noted their clothes and jewellery with fascination and was delighted with their gifts. The Princes called on her in order of rank. Next to enter the Green Drawing Room were the Queen's personal favourites, the Maharajah and Maharani of Cooch Behar, Nripendra and Sunity. Nripendra wore his princely clothes, jewellery and turban, and Sunity wore a heavy white and gold brocade gown beneath a crepe de Chine sari and carried a pair of kid gloves. She curtsied to the Queen and gave her a carved ruby pendant set with fine large diamonds. Nripendra gave her an inlaid ivory writing and work box in blue.[7] The Queen gave Sunity a miniature of herself and then kissed her on the cheek. The newspapers, excited by the presence of the young Maharani, noted that she was the only one the Queen kissed that day and that the 'Indian Princess received more attention than any of the others'.

Sunity was delighted with the publicity but confessed she had been at a loss of how to respond to the Queen. She had been told that she need not kiss the Queen when she met her, since she had already been received privately. So when the elderly Queen tried to kiss her, Sunity initially moved away. A puzzled Victoria, who nevertheless planted her kiss on Sunity's cheek, wondered later to the Princess of Wales: 'Why would not the Maharani kiss me?'

The presentation of the Indian Princes carried on smoothly without any other hiccups. The Thakores of Morvi, Limri and Gondal presented themselves

to the Queen, who knighted the Thakore of Morvi and received presents from
the last two. Then, with some help from Prince Arthur, her son and the Duke
of Connaught, the Queen placed the Imperial Cross of the Order of the Indian
Empire round the necks of the Thakores of Limri and Gondal. The Thakores were
from an eleven gun salute state. The Queen also received deputations from the
Nizam of Hyderabad, and other native Princes, who had sent her their presents;
and deputations from the Municipalities and Corporation of Calcutta and Bombay.

The Durbar ended with a dramatic flourish. Sir Pertab Singh stepped forward
and placed his sword at the Queen's feet and offered her a lovely pearl ornament
which he had taken from his turban, saying everything he possessed was at the
Queen's service.

The Queen was then asked to go to the quadrangle for another surprise. The
newly knighted Thakore of Morvi came riding up on a splendidly caparisoned
young horse that was completely covered with a heavy ornamental coat of mail,
with tassels hanging down and an amulet on one leg. The horse was of the rare
Chaitana breed and recognised instantly by the Queen. The Chaitana was a mix
breed between the Rajpipla and Kathiawar horses and bred specially for playing
polo. It was led prancing into the yard by two Indians. The Thakore alighted and
begged the Queen to accept the horse as a present from him, which she did,
thanking him for it. The Queen returned indoors, pleased with the events of the
day and the display of gratitude and loyalty she had just witnessed. Karim, who
was seeing a parade of Indian Royalty at such close quarters for the first time,
watched in wonder. Even Buksh, the seasoned servant who had served under the
Rana of Dholpore, was impressed by the grandeur of it.

The Queen and her guests were all enjoying the hot Indian summer. The Queen's
list of Jubilee engagements was long, but she took it all in her stride. At sixty-eight
she displayed great energy for her constant commutes between Windsor and
Buckingham Palace. She would be in London for the day and return by evening to
Windsor. Over the next few days she presented silver medals to the Indian Escort
and laid the foundation stone of the Imperial Institute in South Kensington, which
would house the exhibits of the Colonial and Indian Exhibition.

Watched by crowds of thousands and her loyal Indian Princes, she called for
the welding of 'India and the Mother Country into one harmonious and united
community'. The Princes – many of whom had donated to the building of the
Institute – were pleased by this. The Imperial Institute would now house all the
works of the Indian sculptors and artists that the Queen had so admired when
they had come to England for the exhibition. She had had portraits of the artisans painted by Austrian artist Rudolf Swoboda and purchased a large vase from
Bakshi Ram, the 102-year-old potter from Agra. She had admired the carpets
from Agra and had been pleased to learn that it was Karim who had helped Tyler
to bring the artisans to England. She looked forward to learning more about
India from the sombre-looking youth.

Karim and Buksh were soon to discover the hierarchies, rivalries and the prejudices of the Court. The routine in the Royal Court was more or less the same every year. It usually sat in three places – Windsor, Osborne and Balmoral. The Queen rarely stayed in Buckingham Palace, never really liking the Palace that had been bought by her grandfather, George III. She only visited it on special occasions, like Jubilee celebrations, weddings or to host receptions for the presentation of debutantes. The Queen liked travelling by train and journeys to Windsor, Balmoral and the Isle of Wight were always made in the luxury of the Royal train.

Windsor was the most popular residence and the senior officials lived in various towers in the castle so they could be with their families. Quick access to London also made it an attractive place for the government.

Osborne House on the Isle of Wight was one of the Queen's favourites. The Queen had enjoyed her days with Prince Albert in Osborne and the house had been an ideal family home for the young Royals. The third residence was Balmoral in Scotland, a place disliked intensely by her Household and the government as it was 600 miles from London. Ministers calling on the Queen had to make the long journey to the Highlands and they did not enjoy it. At Balmoral the Queen had only a small Household, just enough for the day-to-day running. The equerry-in-waiting did the job of the Master of the Household.

The Royal Court moved in the late summer to Balmoral and usually returned to Windsor by September. The Court shifted again to Osborne for the winter and Christmas was nearly always spent in Osborne. By February, the Royal entourage returned to Windsor and the Queen left on a European tour around April or May.

The Queen's routine was more or less the same in all three of her residences. Breakfast was at 10 a.m. followed by some time spent writing letters and going through her boxes. Lunch was at 2 p.m. Afternoon tea was at 4 p.m. followed by a ride in the pony chair. Dinner was at 9 p.m. When out in the pony chair, she would be accompanied by a servant and a lady-in-waiting. The rest of the Household were not to be in the grounds when she was out. Once she had left, they could go out. The Queen always dined with some members of her Household and would summon those she wanted to see each day. They were informed of this by late afternoon by a footman. If they were to have dinner with the Queen, the men were expected to wear knee breeches and stockings, which they hated. Those not having dinner with the Queen could have dinner separately and enjoy a more informal surrounding. After dinner, the Queen remained in the Drawing Room till about eleven. Here the Household and guests usually played a game of whist or cards. Once the Queen left for the night, the guests could retire to the Billiard Room where they were allowed to smoke. The Queen abhorred smoking and every effort was made to ensure that the whiff of tobacco did not reach the Royal nostrils.

The maids of honour worked for four months at a stretch with the Queen and then went on leave. Ponsonby and Reid accompanied her at most times and her new Indian servants were expected to do the same.

In the summer the Queen liked nothing more than breakfasting outdoors under the trees. Since their arrival, Karim and Buksh were always by her side. She usually enjoyed a hearty breakfast of eggs, toast and marmalade with her handsomely liveried Indians waiting on her. As she ate from her golden egg cup with her golden spoon, and Karim served her on a golden plate, everything seemed perfect. The garden and pond looked tranquil and she could hear the rustling of the breeze in the oak trees. After breakfast she would always spend some time reading and writing before starting the day's hectic events. The Jubilee mail was still pouring in. As the Queen sat in her tent, Karim would stand at a respectful distance by her side gently helping her along with her boxes, leaning forward only to blot the Queen's signature with a pink blotting paper. The Queen liked his serious countenance and found him 'extremely helpful'.

From Windsor, the Royal Household moved to Osborne in the Isle of Wight as part of the continuing Jubilee tour. The Queen loved Osborne as it was here that she had always enjoyed informal days with her children and grandchildren. She was in a particularly good humour now as she made the ferry crossing sitting on the deck of the *Alberta*, her Indian servants by her side. As her carriage passed by the cheering crowds near the pier, the Queen's face suddenly lit up with a rare smile. It was a novelty for those who saw it, as it wasn't the stern image usually associated with Queen Victoria.

In the relaxed atmosphere of Osborne, just weeks since he had kissed Queen Victoria's feet, the young Karim decided to surprise her. One day he came to the kitchen in Osborne House with the spice box that he had carried from India. He was going to cook a curry for the Queen. To the amazement of the cooks in the Royal kitchen, Karim was soon chopping, churning and grinding the *masalas*. The aroma of cloves, cinnamon, cardamom, cumin and nutmeg wafted through the room. Before long, Karim had prepared a fine Indian meal: chicken curry, *daal* and a fragrant *pilau*. More was to follow. Karim was soon stirring up exotic *birianis* and *dum pukht*, dishes from the Mughal kitchens. Kormas simmered in the cast-iron pots and ground almonds and cream laced the rich curries. For the first time in her life, Queen Victoria was introduced to the taste and smell of India. She described it as 'excellent' and ordered the curries to be made regularly.

The Queen would serve curries to the visiting Indian Princes and nobility who continued to call. On 28 July she received the Kunwar Hurwan Singh Ahluwalia and his wife in Osborne. The Queen noted that the wife was 'in her native dress' and that they were both Christians.[8] She gave them the gold Jubilee medal. The Indian Princes usually performed an elaborate ceremony before the Queen. The

Maharajah of Bharatpore and his delegation laid their swords at the Queen's feet and took out a handkerchief containing money which they dropped on the ground. Then they held their swords crossways in both hands for the Queen to touch. Served by Buksh and Karim, the Queen had tea with her visitors in the grounds of Osborne under the cedar tree.

The Indians had mastered the art of waiting at table. They would always serve the sweets and chocolates at the end of the meal and had learned quickly the personal favourites of the members of the Royal family and the Household. They would move in a 'cat-like manner, never forgetting which particular kind of chocolate or biscuit each guest preferred, so twisting the dish in order that it could be taken with apparent ease', noted Marie Mallet, maid of honour to the Queen. The Queen herself had a healthy appetite for one her age and thoroughly enjoyed her meals.

The Indian servants now occupied her full time. She fussed about their clothes, their duties and wanted to make sure they were comfortable. Tutors were engaged to teach them English and their wives were invited to join them. Always enthusiastic about India and wanting to learn more about the country she ruled from a distance of over 4,000 miles, the Queen chose Karim to be her link with the exotic land. The ageing Queen wanted to learn Hindustani and asked Karim to teach her.

The youth from Agra was undaunted at this new job. He proved a serious teacher and a hard taskmaster. Karim ordered special gold-lined journals from the Royal stationers and sat with the Queen every evening, filling these up. He began by teaching her a few everyday words. A phrase book was devised with simple words written in Hindustani in the roman script and their meanings in English. The small red and gold pocket-sized phrase book became the Queen's constant companion. Soon the lessons progressed further. Karim would write a line in Urdu, followed by a line in English and then a line of Urdu in roman script. The Queen would copy these out.

Barely a few weeks after their arrival, an excited Queen noted in her Journal: 'Am learning a few words of Hindustani to speak to my servants. It is great interest to me for both the language and the people. I have naturally never come into real contact with before.'[9] Sir Henry Ponsonby was not spared the Queen's new-found enthusiasm and was handed a phrase book of common Hindustani words by the Queen. He wrote with dry humour to his wife, 'She has given me a Hindi vocabulary to study'.[10]

Karim's presence was transporting Queen Victoria into another world. The times spent with him learning Hindustani were the elderly Queen's moments spent in India, in a different land and culture. The Queen liked the sound of Urdu, the rich language used in the Mughal Courts, a mix between Persian and the native *Brajbhasa*, and she would try to say the words after Karim. He would also tell her about India; about his own native city of Agra, home of the Taj Mahal, and the romance of seeing it on a full-moon night. He told the Queen the story of Shah Jahan and his Queen, Mumtaz Mahal, and how the news of her death during childbirth affected the Emperor deeply. The Queen listened in rapt silence, understanding the anguish of Shah Jahan at losing his Queen. She learnt how Jahan had then built the Taj Mahal, taking twenty-two years to create the tomb that would be an everlasting monument to love. The Queen thought of the mausoleum she had built at Frogmore for her own beloved husband and how she would one day join him there. She shuddered when she heard how the ageing Emperor was imprisoned in Agra Fort by his son Aurangzeb; its position on the bend in the river providing the most enchanting view of the Taj, and how the Emperor spent his dying days there gazing at his beloved monument, and mourning his Queen.

Karim's soft voice brought the tragic story to life. He described the splendour of the Taj Mahal, its marble dome rising towards the sky, framed by four elegant minarets in perfect symmetry. He described the inlay work with precious gemstones, the feeling of being in heaven when light filtered in through the latticed framework and fell on the two tombs, and the words of the Koran that were inscribed all around. The Queen was entranced, letting Karim take her into this Mughal paradise that was as sad as it was beautiful. As Karim gently described his homeland, India came alive before the Queen: she could see the bazaars, the colour, the crowds and almost feel the heat.

Meanwhile, at Osborne, the Indian season continued and the Queen remained surrounded by the Indian Princes and nawabs. The Maharajah of Cooch Behar, who was in the vicinity for a Jubilee Club Ball and was staying on board the *Alive* docked off the Isle of Wight, visited Osborne on 6 August and dined with her. The Queen was once again taken by his charm. 'He looked beautiful all in white,' she recalled, 'a necklace of lovely emeralds and pearls round his neck and a diamond aigrette in his white *pagri*.'[11] The band played beautifully that night and the Queen sat outdoors with the Maharajah and enjoyed herself immensely, describing it as 'quite like an Italian night'. The Queen's sense of romance and beauty would always stay with her.

A few days later, the Thakores of Morvi and Limri came to take their leave. Again the Queen noted that they were 'beautifully dressed in white & gold and had their jewels on'.[12] They each presented her with their photographs, handsomely framed, and she gave them a gold Jubilee medal. Karim and Buksh served lunch. Karim was by now regularly cooking Indian curries in the kitchen at Osborne House and these were served to the visiting Indian guests. Communication with the other staff was still difficult but he was learning quickly. The Queen enjoyed serving the elaborate Indian meals to the visitors. On 20 August she wrote: 'Had some excellent curry made by one of my Indian servants.'[13]

The Queen was experiencing the flavours of the East like never before. She was, after all, Empress of India, *Kaiser-e-Hind*, or *Mallika-e-Hindustan*. With her new servants waiting by her side, her family next to her and the Empire stretching over one-fifth of the globe, she felt complete. Her passage to India was only just beginning.

4

⠶⠶⠶

CURRIES AND HIGHLANDERS

One afternoon in Osborne, as the Queen was sweeping out of the Dining Room accompanied by her ladies in waiting, she stopped near Karim and gently told him: 'Speak to me in Hindustani, speak slowly, that I may understand it, as I wish to learn.'[1] Watched by the critical eyes of the Household, Karim bowed and nodded. He realised just how serious his Queen was about her Hindustani lessons and knew he would have to devote even more time to them. He also felt a sense of pride that he had been chosen to be her teacher.

The few days before the Royal party moved to Balmoral were now spent in a flurry of activity, as the Queen plunged into the planning and assumed complete charge of her new servants. She wanted Karim and Buksh to be prepared for the chill of Scotland and, her maternal instincts in full flow, she issued detailed instruction about their care to James Reid, her personal physician. The Queen drew up a list of things herself. First, they would need gloves: different types, for different occasions. She requested:

6 pairs of brown kid each
6 pairs of white cotton each
3 pairs of white wool each
3 pairs of black wool each.
Total 36 pairs

The list was copied again by a member of the Household and labelled 'Gloves requested by Hindoos', not aware that both Karim and Buksh were Muslim.

A surprised Reid was sent a long memorandum by the Queen on 20 August 1887, titled *Rules For Scotland*.[2] The heavily underlined note captured the Queen's excitement and eagerness as she prepared to take her Indians to the Highlands. She wrote:

Mahomet Buksh and Abdul Karim should wear in the *morning out of doors* at breakfast when they wait, their *new* dark blue dress and always at lunch with any 'Pageri' [pagri] (turban) and sash *they like*, only not the *Gold Ones*. The Red dress and gold and white turban and sash to be always worn *at dinner in the evening*.

There were also instructions on their duties:

If it is wet or cold the breakfast is *indoors* when they should of course always attend. I may take the tea indoors (and of course later on always) and they should attend. As I often, *before* the days get too short take the tea out with me in the carriage, they might do some extra waiting instead, either before I go out, or when I come in. Better before I go out, stopping half an hour longer and should wait *upstairs* to answer a hand-bell. They should come in and out and bring boxes, letters etc: *instead* of the *maids*. In the same way they would alternately or *both* according to the number at tea, wait at my tea *instead* of the maids.

Knowing that Karim and Buksh came from warmer climes, the Queen worried about how they would cope with the Highland weather. She felt they should let their bodies adjust slowly to the cold and instructed them not to put on their thickest underclothes at once. She felt they could wear at breakfast '*if they choose*' their own thicker clothing. Gradually, she felt 'a warm tweed dress and trousers can be got for them at Balmoral to go about in, when off duty in their own room'. The Queen insisted, however, that it 'must be made in Indian fashion and the Pageri always be worn'.

'The woollen stockings and socks and gloves, as well as thick shoes for walking can be got at Balmoral,' the Queen instructed Reid. Almost like a school matron making lists for the children coming to boarding school, the Queen covered reams of Osborne House notepaper with her instructions, underlining and emphasising certain points as was her habit to do. Reid had to write the memorandum neatly again and then hand it to Major-General Dennehy. It was clear that the Queen was not going to leave the care of her Indian servants totally in the General's hands.

Though she worried about them being warm and comfortable, she was also clear that she did not want them to lose their exotic touch and insisted that the Scottish tweeds be cut in the shape of Indian tunics and then worn over warm loose trousers which could replace their cotton *salwars*.

As the days grew colder with the approaching winter, she wanted Karim and Buksh to know that 'tea will be taken *indoors*. And when the days become short (in seven or eight weeks or two months time) they better wait after tea to answer the bell as there will be no time after luncheon.'

The Queen was also concerned that the two Indians – uprooted as they had been from their country – should not feel lonely or isolated in England. Knowing the prejudices that existed in the Household and among her servants, she sent further notes to Reid about what carriage they should be given on the train to Balmoral:

> Pray take care that my good Indian people get one of the *Upper Servants places* which Hyem [her footman] knows is their proper position and they are *not* put far from our saloons, also that they have every comfort so that they are warm *at night*. They must be near. To put them at the very end would be too bad.
>
> If there is no room Morris should go with them, otherwise he better go on 1st and someone else be specially told to look after them. I *hope* Francie [Francie Clark, the Queen's Highland attendant] has had no hand in the arrangement for he is very prejudiced and was not inclined to be kind.

The notes reflect the Queen's thinking. She did not want Karim and Buksh to suffer either on account of the weather or prejudice and wanted her Household to have no doubt about the fact that the Indian servants occupied a special place in her heart. She wanted them to feel welcome in the Palace and went out of her way to learn about their culture. She was looking forward to the break in Balmoral where she would have more time to catch up with Karim and listen to his stories.

On 25 August the last of the Royal bags was packed; the final instructions given and the entourage crossed the Solent and boarded the Royal train from Bridport in Dorset to Ballater in Scotland. The men servants were in the sleeping carriage number 870, while the Queen's personal servants (including Karim and Buksh) and dressers were closer to the Royal saloons. The Queen shared a saloon with Princess Beatrice. Ponsonby and Reid shared a double saloon numbered 131, and the train chugged its way up to the Highlands, arriving next morning in Ballater, forty miles west of Aberdeen, to the sound of a traditional bagpipe greeting. The carriage drive from Ballater to Balmoral, winding through the purple heather-covered hills of the Highlands along the course of the River Dee, was always a pleasure for the Queen. Karim and Buksh took in their first glimpse of Scotland, watching with fascination as they drove past the scenic lochs and glens. They passed the pretty bridges over the Dee, many of which had been opened by the Queen. Karim was reminded of his trip to Afghanistan a few years before. It was the last time he had seen mountains and valleys.

Six hundred miles from London, Balmoral was one of the Queen's favourite homes. Here she could not usually be disturbed by visiting dignitaries as she was at both Windsor and Osborne. The Queen had happy memories of her time with Prince Albert at Balmoral, a place she described as her 'paradise in the Highlands', and the journey here in late summer was always special. From her room she could

enjoy the views over Lochnagar and the Grampian mountains on the left and
on the right she could see the River Dee winding through the glen. She took
pleasure in riding around the grounds of the castle and enjoying her tea in the
summerhouse. The sound of the Dee in full spate as it flowed past the castle lulled
her senses and she encouraged her children and grandchildren to walk along
the banks. Her first visit to Scotland had been by sea in 1842, a rough ride by
ferry from Woolwich Docks in London to Leith near Edinburgh, followed by a
carriage drive through the Highlands to Balmoral. Her first sight of the Scottish
coast had filled her with awe: 'so dark, rocky, bold and wild, totally unlike our
coast,'[3] she had remarked. In 1848 Prince Albert had purchased the castle and
ever since then it had become her Highland home. Though the Queen loved to
escape there, it was not a favourite with her Court and government, who found it
draughty and uncomfortable. Besides, the Queen hated fires. There was no holiday atmosphere in Balmoral and the Queen was a strict disciplinarian. No one
was allowed to go out until the Queen had left. The Household often found they
had nothing to do to kill time. Ponsonby went on long walks and wrote every day
to his wife, Mary. Reid bore it all with his usual patience, spending a lot of time in
the gardens. The days were always longer in Scotland and the Queen was worried
about her Indian servants fitting into the rhythm of the Royal Household. A few
days into their stay, she sent another of her pencilled instructions to Reid. She had
obviously been anxious about what Karim and Buksh should do after meals.

'It seems to me that they need not hurry away after their meals to their rooms,
and may stay either in the corridor below or above, or with anyone if they like,
for, from living out of the house they are out of reach.' She continued that this
problem would not arise in Osborne and Windsor as she would build rooms for
them. In Osborne she was planning rooms which would communicate with the
house. At Balmoral, she decided, it was better for the servants to stay after dinner
so they were available if needed. The Queen was keen to see more of both Buksh
and Karim and had already given them instructions to do many of the jobs previously done by her maids.

On 30 August, after a meeting with General Dennehy, where she discussed
further arrangements for her servants, she noted: 'Abdul is beginning to teach
me a little Hindustani which interests me very much.' A few days later, the ever-
patient Reid received another of the Queen's notes titled 'Attendance'. This
time the Queen was worrying about their English lessons.[4] 'Abdul Karim and
Mohd Buksh will wait at the Queen's breakfast daily, whether it be in the house
or out of doors,' she wrote. 'After breakfast is over, they will go to their quarters
and from 11.30 to 1.30 p.m. be engaged with their English teacher in learning colloquial English. At 2 p.m. they will both always be in attendance at Her
Majesty's luncheon.'

The Queen instructed that after lunch they would, on alternate dates, remain
in attendance on her. Mohammed Buksh, she said, on '*his* day', would remain

with her till she went out unless he was desirous of going to his room. She had different plans for Abdul Karim, however, who was rapidly becoming her favourite. She insisted that Karim, on his day, would not remain with her beyond one hour, as he would have to join his English teacher for lessons in reading and writing. The Queen wanted Karim to quickly become fluent in English as she felt she had a lot to learn from him. As a result, Karim was to have nearly double the lessons that Buksh had.

Buksh had to take on the extra work while Karim attended his extra lessons. The Queen wrote: 'When he [Karim] goes, Mahomed will relieve him in his attendance on her majesty and during the hour while Abdul is on duty, will go to the nursery to wait about where he pleases.'

The Queen wanted Buksh and Karim to be in attendance for some time before dinner, 'commencing when her Majesty comes in [after her tea-time carriage ride] and remaining till the time to dress for dinner'.

Further complicated instructions followed. Depending on what time the Queen returned from her evening ride, Karim and Buksh were to do some additional waiting, replacing the Queen's maids. If the page was on duty at the foot of the stairs, then they could remain in attendance upstairs. Reid handed the notes to Ponsonby. Between their studies and attendance on the Queen, it was clear that Buksh and Karim had a busy schedule on all days. Karim was busier; in addition to his extra lessons he still had to teach the Queen. Both servants braced the Scottish chill and took enthusiastically to their duties, enjoying a quiet walk in the grounds when they could snatch some time.

The Balmoral routine involved outdoor pursuits. Deer-stalking was a favourite pastime and the evening ended with a torch-lit dance around the carcasses. The Queen always indulged her Scottish subjects and allowed the gillies to down large amounts of whisky and sing songs. Often they drank to the memory of Prince Albert round the cairn erected for him, the Queen watching with a mixture of sadness and joy. The senior members of her Household, like Ponsonby and Reid, had little enthusiasm for these events, but she enjoyed them. She now had Karim and Buksh for company to watch the dances. It was their introduction to the Highlander's life at Balmoral.

The Braemar gathering for the Highland games was an annual event that the Queen always attended, though her Household never cared for it. This year, the weather was like a 'matchless August morning', recorded Reid. The slight traces of fog which had enveloped the castle all night had vanished before the bright sunshine and the woodlands were richer in russet brown and gold. The gillies' ball was held on 10 September in the iron Ball Room of the castle, with the servants from the Household in attendance in the Royal Stand. The walls of the Ball Room were decorated with the heads of stags that had fallen to Royal bullets over the years. Karim learned that the prized catch was The Imperial or 14-pointer. Most Highland stags were 12-pointers. The Ball was patronised by

WATCHING THE BONFIRES ON THE HILLS ROUND BALMORAL

Sketch of the Queen with an Indian attendant taken from a magazine. The caption says: 'watching the bonfires around the hills at Balmoral'.

the Queen, who was a surprisingly good dancer. She had enjoyed reels with John Brown, her Scottish gillie and close friend, when he was alive. Wearing a tartan shawl over her widow's black, the Queen would give in to the gaiety and dance with the frequently inebriated John Brown, forgetting her grief in the spirit of the evening.

To Karim it was all a new world. He had enjoyed hunting in the jungles around Agra and Rajasthan, but stepping out early morning on a Highland hunt, with the mist still curling round the hills, was a different experience. He saw his first stag – a 12-pointer – framed against the purple hills and it filled him with awe.

'It is great joy,'[5] he wrote about the hunt. 'I like this much more than dance or other games.' Karim specially enjoyed the hunt for stag, or *barasingha*, as he called it in his native tongue, though he found it rather difficult in the winter. Trout fishing in the streams was also another of his favourite activities, as was hunting for birds, particularly in the months of November and December.

The climate in Scotland, often damp and windy, was a contrast to the splendid summer they had enjoyed in London, and unlike anything Karim had ever seen in Agra. Dressed in his Indian-style tweeds he enjoyed walking in the grounds, attending on the Queen and the gamut of lessons he had to go through. While waiting at table, he would always wear his elaborate tunic embossed with the letters VRI (*Victoria Regina et Imperatrix*). Every evening the Hindustani lessons were held without fail, the Queen beginning to fill the first of the thirteen closely packed Journals that she would eventually complete. As Karim's English improved, he started having lengthier conversations with his Queen about India and she listened, rapt with attention, marvelling at being Empress of such a land. He told her more about himself and managed to convey to her that he came from a good family, that his father was a doctor in Agra Jail and that he himself had been a clerk in the jail and had never done menial work before. The Queen was impressed and began to rely increasingly on the polite young Indian who was taking his job of man-servant so seriously.

On 11 September she wrote in a letter:

My dear Indians are going on admirably. General Dennehy was invaluable and settled everything and found out all they wished and wanted and now everything goes on as smoothly as possible.

The youngest [Karim] is evidently *almost* a gentleman who could not be treated like a common servant and is extremely well *educated* and the other stout one is quite excellent. He was seventeen years with General Dennehy whose whole house he managed.[6]

Karim was a fast learner. He was quickly improving his English so as to communicate with the Queen and was soon helping her with her papers. Victoria was delighted with him. While the smiling and portly Buksh remained waiting at

tables, Karim now started doing secretarial jobs. On 12 September she wrote to
Sir Henry Ponsonby from Balmoral:

> Sir Henry will see what he [Lord Dufferin] says about the Indian servants. It is
> just what the Queen feels and she cannot say what a comfort she finds *hers* [her
> Indian servants]. Abdul is most handy in helping when she *signs* by drying the
> signatures. He learns with extraordinary assiduity and Mahomet is wonderfully
> quick and intelligent and understands everything.[7]

The Queen continued to ask Karim about India and their conversations now
grew weightier as he moved from descriptions of colour and local customs to
deeper political issues. As Karim helped the Queen with her boxes and her
mail, he also progressed beyond just blotting her signature. She was curious to
know about Indian religions and customs and Karim explained the difference
in customs between the Hindus and Muslims. He told her about the conflicts
the differences could cause and described the riots that sometimes broke out in
Agra when the Muslims took out the religious procession of Muharram to mark
the martyrdom of Hussain, the grandson of the Prophet, and it clashed with the
Hindu procession of Sankranti (a festival celebrated with ritual bathing in the
Ganges river and the flying of kites). The Queen was distressed to hear about the
rioting and decided she would pursue the matter with the Viceroy.

To the Royal Household, the Queen's attitude to Abdul Karim began to gradually remind them of her relationship with John Brown, her Highland servant.
Balmoral was always associated with John Brown. It was here that Brown had
started his working life as a stable-boy for Sir Robert Gordon, the owner of
Balmoral. When Prince Albert bought the property and rebuilt the castle, John
Brown was employed by the Royal couple as a gillie. He immediately became a
favourite of both the Queen and the Prince Consort.

After Albert's death, when the Queen was inconsolable, it fell to John Brown to
bring her out of seclusion. At forty-two, the Queen had chosen to wear black all
her life and had withdrawn into a shell. The Court became disgruntled with her
absence at public ceremonies and lack of interest in state affairs, and John Brown
was brought in as her personal servant to try to cheer her up.

Brown was a commonplace, coarse man with a typical Highland sense of
humour. He loved his whisky and was often rude to the Prince of Wales and
the Household, who disliked the influence he had on the Queen. Brown was
known to call her 'wumman', dropping all civil etiquette, openly scolding and
arguing with her; but he was completely devoted to her and took every care to
see she was comfortable and well. He ensured she was cosily wrapped in her
tartan rug when she went for her ride and even laced her tea with whisky to
keep her warm. Shocked bystanders once heard him tell the Queen, while he
was adjusting her bonnet ribbon under her chin: 'Hoots then, wumman. Can

ye no hold yerr head up?' A handsome bearded man always dressed in a kilt, he accompanied the Queen on her rides and she felt safe with him. He would keep her amused and take no nonsense from her, and the widowed Queen enjoyed his rustic charm.

Very quickly John Brown became her soulmate and she depended on him. Often isolated in her own home, as her children were awed of her and the Household always maintained a formal distance, she leaned on Brown who treated her as a normal human being. She liked the fact that this strong young man scolded her, looked after her and was always caring for her smallest needs. Rumours about the Queen's relationship with Brown were a major source of gossip among the staff, especially when she retired to the secluded Widow's Cottage at Glassalt Shiel for a few nights with Brown. Victoria, however, never let the rumours bother her. If anything, they amused her. She would not hear any ill of Brown and was blind to his faults. So close were the Queen and her Highland servant that she was often referred to as 'Mrs Brown' and there were whispers in Court circles that she had secretly married him.

The presence of a servant whom she could trust sustained the Queen, who was often lonely (as people in power often are). Without Albert by her side, she relied for many years on Brown. The Scottish gillie shared with her many political views, including a dislike for Gladstone. He wanted the government turned out in 1872 and in 1878, when the Queen asked him whether he wanted a war, the gillie replied: 'Damn it, no – I beg your pardon – but I think it would be awful; dreadful deal of fighting and at the end no one would be better and a' would be worse for it.'

However, John Brown died at Windsor in 1883, leaving the Queen devastated once again. After the death of her beloved Albert, this was the most painful to her. She wrote to Ponsonby in a letter after his death:

> The Queen is trying hard to occupy herself but she is utterly crushed and her life has again sustained one of those shocks like in 61 [the year of Albert's death] when every link has been shaken and torn and at every moment the loss of the strong arm and wise advice, warm heart and cheery original way of saying things and the sympathy in any large and small circumstances – is most cruelly missed.

The Queen was so distressed after Brown's death that she became very weak and could not stand or walk. She laid a special memorial stone in his name at the mausoleum in Frogmore and inscribed it with the words:

> In loving and grateful remembrance of John Brown, her faithful and devoted personal attendant and friend of Queen Victoria, whom he constantly accompanied here.

These words are inscribed by Her whom he served devotedly for 34 years.
Matthew 25th Chapter, Verse 21

'His Lord said unto him well done good and faithful servant: thou has been faithful over a few things. I will make thee ruler over many things, enter thou into the joy of the Lord.'

She also built a special granite fountain in his memory just outside the Tea House in Frogmore, where she enjoyed sitting on summer days, and a bench was put up in his honour in the grounds of Osborne where they had often walked together. In Balmoral she erected a statue of him.

Even Ponsonby, who had no love lost for Brown and often clashed with him, was forced to admit: 'He was the only person who could fight and make the Queen do what she did not wish. He did not always succeed nor was his advice always the best. But I believe he was honest, and with all his want of education, in roughness, his prejudices and other faults he was undoubtedly a most excellent servant to her.' Four years after the death of John Brown, the Empress now had another servant she was beginning to rely on. Surely and steadily, and to the horror of the Royal Household, the young Karim was filling Brown's shoes.

Beneath the regal trappings, the Queen was very much a people's person. She enjoyed nothing more than getting to know her subjects, especially the country folk and the under-privileged. At Balmoral, she regularly went to the village shops and chatted with the locals, often buying knick-knacks. She disapproved of the snobbery of the upper classes and reached out to the ordinary people whenever she could. Her mothering of her Indian servants and protecting them from the prejudices of the Household was natural to her.

In the quiet setting of the Highlands, the Queen became closer to Karim. He described the hunting in India and the journeys he had made to Kabul and the North-West with his father. He informed her that his father had accompanied General Roberts on the famous march to Kandahar in 1880. The Queen was impressed by his candour and felt relaxed in his company, much to the discomfiture of the Household. They did not approve of the closeness that seemed to be developing between the Queen and the young Indian servant.

In a sense, they were also reminded of the Queen's closeness to her previous ward, Duleep Singh. When the Queen was thirty-five years old, she had taken this young Indian Prince into her custody. He had been only eleven when the British defeated his father, Maharajah Ranjit Singh, the last Sikh ruler of Punjab, and seized the prized Koh-i-Noor as war booty. The young Prince was torn from his mother's side and exiled to Britain where he arrived in 1854 at the age of fifteen. He had become a Christian. Whether out of guilt or a genuine motherly instinct, the Queen became his guardian. Duleep Singh formally presented her with the Koh-i-Noor. Victoria felt the young Prince looked sad and vulnerable and became a mother figure to him, allowing him to wear his native clothes.

Fascinated by Duleep Singh's good looks, she had him painted in all his princely finery at the age of fifteen by Francis Xavier Winterhalter. Over three decades later, the Queen was taking the young Abdul Karim under her wing. She was soon to have portraits of Karim painted by Von Angeli and Rudolph Swoboda.

Despite being devoted to the Queen as a young boy, Duleep Singh had grown up and rebelled against her, wanting to be recognised as the sovereign ruler of Punjab and demanding the return of the Koh-i-Noor. While at Balmoral, the Queen received further bad news from Duleep Singh, and she recorded:

> The unfortunate Maharajah Duleep Singh has published a most violent crazy letter, speaking of being 'the lawful sovereign of the Sikhs' and 'England's implacable foe'. I heard this evening that his poor abandoned wife, the Maharanee Bamba, had died quite suddenly yesterday. I feel terrible for the poor children who are quite fatherless and motherless.[8]

To Karim, the actions of Duleep Singh were deplorable and he sympathised with the Queen in her moment of sorrow. To the Household, Duleep Singh's conduct was another reason for the Queen not to be indulgent with Abdul Karim and grant him special favours.

Karim was not aware of the Household's early wariness of him. He remained close to the Queen and asked her many questions of his own. She told him about her family, her grandchildren and the relations in Europe. The Queen reminisced about Albert and the happy times they had spent in Balmoral. Karim saw the statues of John Brown that the Queen had erected in Balmoral and learnt about the Highland servant who had been so close to her. He told her about his extended family, his father, wife, brother and sisters. In the slight chill of the September days, Karim and the Queen got to know each other better. In less than two months he had mastered reading Queen Victoria's handwriting, which at most times defeated even the patient Ponsonby. The Queen started writing to him directly instead of giving instructions through her Household.

In a letter to Reid she said: 'You might I think *see* Abdul alone to give him this letter which I think he will be able to read. Good kind Mahomet I will read those few words to myself.' Clearly Buksh had not benefited from his lessons as much as Karim.

The Queen, always interested in Indian affairs, now pressed her Viceroy for more news. She also wondered if she could have some Indian troops around her permanently and wrote to Lord Cross, the Secretary of State for India, who in turn asked the Viceroy: 'Would it not clash with the Mutiny Act?'[9] She began discussing India with her ministers and the Indian Princes who called on her. One of her frequent visitors was the Maharajah of Cooch Behar, who visited her again in Balmoral, brightening up the bleak castle with his sparkling jewellery and embroidered tunics. The Queen found the Maharajah 'very amiable',[10] as he described to her the thrill of a tiger hunt. The Thakore of Morvi, who had presented the Queen with his special horse at Windsor, left from London in mid-November after having fulfilled his desire to see a London fog. 'He had one yesterday, to his heart's content. It was horrible,'[11] a cynical Cross informed the Viceroy. Most of the Indian Royalty had left before the onset of winter and they had all expressed their satisfaction at the Jubilee celebrations, much to the relief of the British administration.

Victoria, however, was troubled by news from other quarters. Duleep Singh had plunged into an even more rebellious mode. He had already published inflammatory documents inciting the Sikh community and telegraphed the Queen demanding a trial so that he could prove in a court of justice that his proclamation of himself as the ruler of the Sikhs was not disloyal. He had returned to Paris after an unsuccessful attempt to go to India and sent a telegram to Ponsonby stating: 'I return to Paris, being unable to obtain justice, resigned stipend, thus ending annexation treaty and getting rid of all the dealings with the most tyrannical government in the world, Indian Administration.' By October, Duleep Singh had sent wild letters saying he was going to the East and would attach himself to Russia; he was apparently trying to set up a Russian party in north-west India.[12]

'Bertie [the Prince of Wales] showed me a really monstrous letter from the Maharajah Duleep Singh to Sir Dighton Probyn [private secretary to the Prince of Wales], who in spite of all the Maharajah's violent rebellious letters and publications had written in Bertie's name to condole with him on the death of his wife. He surely must be off his head,'[13] despaired the Queen, still reluctant to condemn her former ward completely. She slept badly, troubled by his attitude.

As the leaves turned golden in the autumn, the Royal entourage returned to Windsor. The journey from Ballater to Windsor was made on 25 November, the Queen comfortable in the Royal Saloon and Karim and Buksh close by. The summer had been a learning curve for the Queen. She had discovered more about India in the few months with Karim than she had ever done before. He too had learnt about her, her family, her habits and her preferences. She lay back and thought about how she would enjoy her interactions with Indian Royalty even more from now on. Maybe she would even speak to them in Hindustani.

The Maharajah, Sayaji Rao Gaekwad, of Baroda and his wife, Chimnabai, were expected at Windsor and the staff were in a flurry to get things right. The Gaekwads of Baroda were a powerful Royal house and the Secretary of State had informed the Queen that the highly educated Maharajah needed some pampering. The Maharani was famed for her skills in classical music and was also known to be a good hunter – she had felled tigers in the jungles around Gujarat and been photographed standing with her kill, dramatically dressed in a sari with a rifle in her hand. The Maharajah was known to be a proud Mahratta and a well-known patron of the arts. On 2 December the Queen received Chimnabai and her sister in the Audience Room. All the men were kept out of the way and the 'Indian attendants in particular'. The Queen was fascinated by the Maharani, whose demeanour was very different from the shy and retiring Sunity Devi of Cooch Behar. Chimnabai bent low and shook her hand.

'She is a pretty little thing,' recalled the Queen, noting what she wore in great detail: 'a close fitting jacket & trousers, no petticoat, of pale blue satin over the whole a long crimson and gold gauze veil, which passed over the head and covered her completely excepting her face, which she uncovered as she came into the room. She had splendid jewels on.'[14] The Maharani was wearing the sari draped in a traditional Mahratta way, passing between the legs, giving the impression she was wearing loose trousers. 'She looks very gentle, but is said to be very wilful and to wish to see everything without being seen … both princesses had a red spot [*bindi*] painted in the centre of their foreheads,' the Queen added, clearly impressed by her visit from a second Indian Maharani.

Chimnabai spoke a few words of English and told the Queen she regretted not having seen the Crown Prince, Bertie. Her sister did not speak any English. The Queen ventured upon a sentence in Hindustani which Karim and Buksh had taught her.

'I also presented Beatrice in Hindustani,' said the Queen, evidently quite pleased with herself for having made the effort. The Queen received Sayaji separately, noting that he was 'small, dark and not distinguished or good looking, but he seems very intelligent. He speaks English perfectly well.' The Maharajah was dressed in white and wore a low red turban or cap and a necklace of large emeralds.

That evening, the Queen held a reception in the White Drawing Room where she awarded Sayaji with the Star of India. Everyone was in uniform all around and the Queen herself wore a ribbon and the Star of the Order. She also presented the Maharajah with one of the enamel portraits of herself that she had given the other Indian Princes over the summer. She had enjoyed meeting the Gaekwads, even if they had come to see her a bit late in the Jubilee year.

A few days later, Karim and Buksh watched in wonder as the giant Christmas tree went up in Osborne House and the colourfully wrapped presents were laid below. Christmas was always spent at Osborne with the traditional decorations and festivities. Karim had seen the English families going to church in Agra on Christmas Day dressed in their Sunday best. To celebrate *Bada Din*, as they called Christmas in India, with the Queen in her own house was something special. The idea of decorating Christmas trees and putting presents out with them was a German custom and believed to have been introduced in England by Queen

Charlotte, the wife of King George III. However, the tradition was popularised further and brought to its present form by Queen Victoria and Prince Albert, who laid out a table beside the tree laden with chocolates, cakes and Christmas delights. The Queen did not forget to give a present to Karim and Buksh on their first Christmas; both received a signed photograph of her. There was even a chance for Karim to go pheasant shooting after Christmas and he enjoyed the outing, noting that it was 'quite absorbing and interesting'.[15]

The Queen's favourite Indian Prince, the Maharajah of Cooch Behar, dropped in during the Christmas season to say goodbye before returning to India. Karim and Buksh had gotten quite accustomed to serving him and now knew his favourites. The Maharani had already turned back for India as she could not stand the cold.

The Queen went to bed on New Year's Eve in a reflective mood. That night she wrote in her Journal:

> The Jubilee time was so richly blessed, not one mishap or disturbance, not one bad day … Never, never can I forget this brilliant year, so full of the marvellous kindness, loyalty and devotion of so many millions, which really I could hardly have expected …[16]

It had been a year of celebration and splendour and the Queen had been moved by the devotion of her servants. Her discovery of India, her Indian servants and her freshly acquired knowledge of Hindustani had all given her a new-found happiness. Looking out of her window in Osborne, over the grounds she had walked with Albert and John Brown, she thought of the years past and what lay ahead. She was learning a new language and discovering a new culture. The Queen gave a satisfied sigh. The possibilities were endless.

5

BECOMING THE MUNSHI

Karim felt a thrill of excitement as he took his first curtain call. Sitting in the front row, leading the clapping, was the Queen. He was on stage, wearing costume and make-up and performing before a select audience in Osborne House during the New Year celebrations. The tableau was the *Queen of Sheba* starring Princess Beatrice in the title role and Ponsonby as Solomon. Both Karim and Buksh were playing Indian servants.

Theatricals were an essential part of the festive season at Osborne. The Queen loved the shows. She would often drop in for the dress rehearsals, supervise the costumes and the backdrops and even look at the scripts. Alick Yorke, the Queen's equerry, was the director of these productions. Known for his easy wit and penchant for telling rude jokes, Yorke famously was the subject of one of the Queen's classic reprimands. Once, during a dinner party at the Palace, he had whispered a rather risqué joke to a German guest seated next to him. When the Queen heard the laughter from the top of the table, she asked Yorke to repeat the joke. Though there were several ladies present at the table, Yorke repeated it for the Royal ear. Yorke's joke immediately invited the famous Victorian one-liner: 'We are not amused.' The good-humoured equerry, however, took all this in his stride and concentrated on staging the Christmas plays before the Queen and her guests. The tableaux were very much a family affair; treading the boards were the Queen's children and members of the Royal Household. Ponsonby dreaded dressing up for the performances, but the Queen's enthusiasm for these evenings left him with no choice. Karim and Buksh also found themselves swallowed up in the costume extravaganza.

After the sound of a silver-toned bell, the dark red curtains parted disclosing the various groups. *Queen of Sheba* was the first tableau to open the 1888 season, with the Indians making their theatrical debut. They took their place in full costume standing behind Ponsonby's King Solomon. Next was *Carmen* with Minnie Cochrane, lady-in-waiting to Princess Beatrice, playing the lead role. Prince Henry of Battenberg, Princess Beatrice's husband, took on the role of

Toreador, and Major Arthur Bigge played Don Jose. The third tableau – *Queen Elizabeth and Raleigh* – was performed by Princess Beatrice and her husband. All the tableaux were staged with elaborate backdrops and costumes and the Queen applauded heartily, congratulating each person individually. Karim and the other Indian servants were soon to take an active part in these tableaux, with Karim later getting a lead role in some. Visiting dignitaries and local families would often be present and Karim found it exciting to be on stage with the Royals. He had lost some of his initial reserve and shyness and could often be seen laughing and talking with the Queen's maids.

In the family atmosphere of Osborne, the Queen treasured her moments with Karim. Her ever-increasing demands on his time, to attend to her boxes and correspondence and give her Hindustani lessons, left Buksh struggling to manage their regular tasks alone. Keen to relieve Karim from some of his menial duties, the Queen decided she needed reinforcements and ordered for more Indian servants to be brought to the Royal palaces. In February she wrote to her eldest daughter Victoria (Vicky), Princess Royal, and Empress of Germany:

> I take a little lesson every evening in Hindustani and sometimes I miss writing by post in consequence. It is a great interest and amusement to me. Young Abdul (who is in fact *no* servant) teaches me and is a vy. strict Master, and a *perfect* Gentleman. He has learnt English wonderfully—and can now copy beautifully and with hardly any faults. He will I hope remain and be vy. useful in writing and looking after my books and things and a third is coming to wait at meals. Mahomed, the stout one, is going on 4 months leave to our great regret and the new one will arrive before he goes.

The Queen had decided that when Buksh returned, 'Karim would no longer wait *at meals* wh. is what he feels a good deal'. She felt that Abdul deserved to be elevated in rank from the other servants.

In March 1888 she recorded the arrival of another servant: 'Have a new servant, called Ahmed Husain, a fine soldier-like looking man, very tall and thin.' Other Indian servants who were soon added to the Queen's services were Hourmet Ali, Abdul Hussain, Sheikh Ghulam Mustapha and Sheikh Chidda. The portly and cheerful Buksh immediately welcomed the newcomers and taught them the ropes. Karim was always more reserved, though he too was happy to have more Indian company and catch up with the news from back home. Nearly all the servants were from Agra.

The Indian servants could now be seen everywhere and formed a small coterie, enjoying cosy after-dinner chats by themselves. They became a familiar sight on the streets of Windsor as they wandered around on their days off, looking in at the shop windows and strolling along the river. Their colourful clothes and turbans always set them apart and inevitably aroused curiosity among the locals.

Karim remained the Queen's favourite. He had a proud bearing and the Queen's reliance on him increased every day. She had already started discussing the contents of some of her letters with Karim. He listened politely, sometimes offering his comments. The religious riots during Muharram continued to trouble him and he discussed it again with the Queen, pressing her gently to do something about it. She never tired of praising Karim to her children and her Household, and wrote to Reid:

> I wish to observe with respect to Abdul that he has changed very much and though his manner may be grave and dignified he is very friendly and cheerful with the Queen's maids and laughs and even jokes now – and invited them to come and see all his fine things, offering them fruit cake to eat ... he is very handy and intelligent and obliging and is useful for his great knowledge of his own language and of course I am now quite accustomed and at home with him.[1]

The Queen's favourite Indian Prince, the Maharajah of Cooch Behar, came visiting in March and she invested him with the Knight Grand Cross of the Indian Empire. She also met Duleep Singh's children, Princesses Bamba, Catherine and Sophy and Prince Edward Duleep Singh, who called on her. Despite the indiscretions of their father, the Queen showed the utmost affection for the children. The Queen hosted the first Drawing Room of the year at Buckingham Palace and proudly wore the Koh-i-Noor as a brooch, revelling in her new-found knowledge of India.

Soon it was time for the annual trip to Europe. The Queen had decided that Karim and the other Indian servants would accompany her. She travelled *in cognito* as the Duchess of Balmoral when she went on her European trips. However, since her annual departure was always reported in *The Times* newspaper, there was little secrecy about it. The entourage that left for Florence was particularly colourful as it included a band of newly arrived Indian servants dressed in their traditional clothes and turbans, who attracted large crowds at each station. The Household always marvelled at how the Indians managed to travel so light, carrying their things on board in a small cloth bundle, while they themselves struggled with several boxes. The Queen herself travelled with her entire paraphernalia, including the memos, souvenirs, medals, photographs, diaries, ink-pots and pens that usually cluttered her desk at Windsor, Balmoral and Osborne. In later years, her donkey went too as she often took a ride on the donkey cart. Boxes of food were carried from Windsor packed in special containers, looked after by the Indian servants and the Queen's maids. It felt very much like a picnic.

The crossing took place from Portsmouth to Cherbourg on 22 March, the *Victoria and Albert* escorted by torpedo boats. The Queen spent the night on board at Cherbourg, not forgetting to have her Hindustani lessons with Abdul in the evening. These would continue no matter where the Queen was. Abdul had made a phrase book of everyday Urdu words for her and written them out in the Roman script. The red pocket-size book with gold edging contained words and phrases that the Queen would use with her Indian servants and visiting Royalty.

The words set out from A to Z included under A:

Anyone	*koick*
Animal	*janwar*
Again	*phir*
Advice	*sallah*
Anger	*khafa*

The phrases included a selection of everyday terms plus some intriguing sentences reflecting the Queen's life in Court:

You may go home if you like	*Tum ghar jao agar chhate ho*
You will miss the Munshi very much	*Tum Munshi ko bahut yad karoge*
The tea is always bad at Osborne	*Chah Osborne men hamesha kharab hai*
The poor boy has a very bad pain in his hand	*Garib laundi ke hat men bahut sakhat darad hai*
The egg is not boiled enough	*Anda thik ubla nahi hai*
Hold me tight	*Ham ko mazbut Thamo*[2]

For the Indians it was their first trip to Europe. From Cherbourg, the Royal train took them to Florence, passing through the French countryside into Italy. The carriages were designed for maximum comfort. The day car consisted of a drawing room and a small compartment which was once used by John Brown and later by Karim. The sleeping car had a dressing room, bedroom and a compartment for light luggage where the maids slept on sofas. The Queen shared the bedroom with Beatrice; she occupied the large bed, while her daughter slept on the smaller one. The dressing room had a Japanese motif with the washstand covered in dark red Moroccan leather and toiletries made of white metal. The drawing room was luxurious, the walls covered with silk drapes in pale yellow brocade with the shamrock, rose and thistle. A dark Indian carpet lined the floor and the curtains were blue and white. The furniture was comfortably regal, consisting of a sofa, two armchairs and Louis XVI style footstools covered in blue silk with yellow fringes and tassels. Four lights suspended from the padded ceiling completed the look of 'antiquated splendour'.[3]

The Queen stayed at the Villa Palmieri in Florence, which was specially decorated and painted for her visit. The Indians took in the splendour of the Italian city admiring the churches and galleries. They accompanied the Queen everywhere and looked so exotic that locals mistook them for Indian Princes. The Queen spent a month in Florence, meeting European Royalty, going for rides in her carriage and practising her Hindustani with Karim. She spent several hours being wheeled round the Uffizi Gallery by the Indians and stopped sadly by the Casa Gherini where Prince Albert had stayed in 1838. She was invited to lunch by the King and Queen of Italy along with the Emperor of Brazil, his wife and the Queen of Serbia. The lunch took a comic turn when it was realised there were more Queens than Kings, so the King and the Emperor had to take two Queens on each arm into the dining hall. In later years, the Queen would always walk on the arm of one of her Indian attendants.

Not everyone approved of them. The Indian servants caused a flutter of discontent when the Queen gave them a prominent position at a function at the Bigallo. The Queen had gone to view the *Scoppio del Carro*, the ceremony of carrying the holy fire, by means of a mechanical dove on a wire, from the altar of the Duomo to a cart in the Square drawn by white oxen. She had placed her Indian servants on the loggia adjoining the Queen of Serbia, a move that did not go down well with the Italians who considered it to be a great slight to the Serbian Queen. The Italian media noted that the Queen of Serbia and the Dukes of Edinburgh and Leuchtenberg had been in the same loggia barely five minutes before the Indian servants took up their position there. The Queen, always protective of her Indian servants, had probably assigned them the seating position herself, quite unaware of the hostility it would cause. Nevertheless, it was Karim's first exposure to the ways of European monarchies and crowds, something he would see a great deal of in the coming years. The Queen by now found him quite indispensable.

From Florence, the Royal convoy moved to Berlin where the Queen met her eldest daughter Vicky and her son-in-law, the German Emperor, Frederick (Fritz), who was very ill with throat cancer. She also had a meeting with Bismarck who reportedly said afterwards: 'That was a woman; one could do business with her.'

The Royal party arrived back at Windsor on 27 April and the Queen headed for Balmoral the next month. *The Daily Telegraph*, dated 23 May 1888, reported: 'The second carriage from the Queen's carried the Indian attendants of Her Majesty, who were picturesquely attired in their native garb.' The Indian attendants now took up a prominent position in the Royal train, occupying a double saloon number 71, next to the double saloon number 131 occupied by senior members of the Household like Alick Yorke, Thomas Biddulph, Arthur Bigge, James Reid and Maurice Muther, the Queen's German secretary.

A few months after her visit to Berlin, the Queen received the dreaded telegram that Fritz had died and her daughter Vicky had been widowed. The Queen knew the pain her daughter would have suffered at the loss of her husband and the lonely life she would lead in Germany. As she 'cried her eyes out' for her daughter and son-in-law, Karim stood by her, comforting her and offering his support in this moment of grief. When the Queen wrote several emotional letters to her daughter, Karim helped her, gently blotting the paper and providing a friendly ear. She confided in him that she was very upset about the behaviour of her grandson Wilhelm II, the new Kaiser of Germany, and felt that he did not treat her daughter with any respect. Karim listened sympathetically to the distraught Queen, consoling her as she sat alone in Balmoral. His very presence and understanding manner helped her feel better and she now decided to promote her 'dear Abdul' and give him a special rank. It was the moment that Karim would cross the threshold. No longer would he be a humble servant waiting on the Queen. He was to become her *Munshi*, or clerk and teacher.

Having made up her mind, she immediately conveyed her wishes to Henry Ponsonby; he replied to her on 31 July saying that he had had a conversation with General Dennehy, who was very pleased at Abdul's promotion. Ponsonby revealed in his letter that Dennehy did, however, have a few reservations on the matter. He was worried about what the other Indian servants would feel about the promotion and had alerted Ponsonby on this. Dennehy had suggested that Abdul Karim have no command over the others as this would create jealousies. Ponsonby told Dennehy that there was no intention of this, but that as Abdul alone was able to understand the accounts, he would be responsible for them. Dennehy agreed to this arrangement and thought it was a good one.[4]

The affairs of Abdul Karim were already beginning to cause some discontent in the Household, with Dennehy anxious that Karim should not antagonise the others. The Queen was determined to go ahead with her plans. Karim was completely relaxed in her presence now. He would talk freely to her about his views on various political issues, sympathise with the Queen in her grief at her daughter's plight in Germany and criticise the arrogance and rudeness of Kaiser Wilhelm II. He had managed to convince the Queen that he was a cut above the other Indian servants.

On 11 August 1888, the Queen noted in her Journal: 'Am making arrangements to appoint Abdul a *munshi*, as I think it was a mistake to bring him over as a servant to wait at table, a thing he had never done, having been a clerk or *munshi* in his own country and being of rather a different class to the others.'[5] Karim had told her that he was unhappy with his position as a table-hand and that he wanted

to return to India since it was a demeaning job. The Queen immediately decided
to raise his rank and make him stay.

> He [Abdul] was anxious to return to India, not feeling happy under the existing
> circumstances. On the other hand, I particularly wish to retain his services, as he
> helps me in studying Hindustani, which interests me very much, and he is very
> intelligent and useful.

Abdul Karim was now given the grand title of Munshi Hafiz Abdul Karim. He
became the Queen's official Indian clerk and said goodbye to waiting at tables,
a job now left to his colleague Buksh and the other Indian servants. All photographs of Karim waiting at table were destroyed and the Queen commissioned
his portrait to be painted by Joachim von Angeli. While the other Indian servants
watched in wonder and slight envy, Karim grew in importance. He was always by
the Queen's side, talking to her in his gentle voice, caring for her needs and providing a sympathetic ear when she needed it. The Hindustani lessons continued,
the Queen making remarkable progress.

When Louise, the Duchess of Connaught, brought her children to Balmoral,
the Queen immediately wrote to her that Sir John McNeill would look after
them along with 'my good, excellent Abdul Karim'. 'I am so very fond of him,'
she added. 'He is so good & gentle & understanding all I want & is a real comfort
to me.' She also praised Karim for being 'such a good influence with the others ...
he & *all* of them set such a good example and so respectable'.[6]

Her letters were filled with praise for Karim and his philosophical attitude to
life. To her friend, Sir Theodore Martin, the Scottish poet and author, she wrote
how he and the other Indian attendants dealt with tragedy and put everything
down to fate.

> One can but say as one of her Indian attendants, (who are all Mohammedan)
> & who is now her personal Indian clerk & Munshi, who is an excellent, clever
> truly p[i]ous & very refined gentle man, who says, 'God ordered it'. Not a
> murmur is heard for *God's Orders* is what they implicitly obey! Such faith as
> theirs & such conscientiousness set us a gt. example.[7]

The Queen now began leaving instructions for the other Indian servants with
Karim, who was placed in charge of them and given the job of managing their
uniforms and accounts. She handed Karim a strict dress code for the Indians
at Balmoral:

> Will you please explain to Muhammud & Ahmad Husain, the Indian servants,
> the dress they should wear at various times when on duty, the same not to be
> changed except by Her Majesty's command.

Breakfast,	Blue uniform with white waistband,
Luncheon	white trousers,
And Tea	and almond coloured boots

The head-dress to be optional at these three meals; but the lungi must not be worn except at dinnertime with the Full Dress red uniform.

When the weather is warm a white or other coloured summer coat may be worn, but the waistband &c to be used at the three meals must not be changed.

Black boots must be worn at meals out of doors – almond coloured boots are for *indoor* use only and should not be used for walking or riding out.[8]

The instructions were given to Mohammed Buksh and Ahmed Husain by Karim the same day. A note attached to the Queen's letter signed in Urdu said 'Yek huq Muhammud Buksh aur Ahmad Husain ko suna do' (Give these instructions to Mohammed Buksh and Ahmed Husain).[9] She was now constructing full sentences in Urdu on her own.

As language barriers between them dissolved rapidly, the Queen grew closer to Karim. He had developed a good working knowledge of English and the Queen was steadily improving her Hindustani. She now wanted to recreate the spirit of India even in the family tableaux and the themes were often oriental. In October 1888 the Queen's daughter and granddaughters staged a tableau vivant called *India*. Princess Beatrice played India dressed in an elaborate silk gown. Attending her in native Indian dresses were her nieces, Princess Louise of Wales (dressed as a Muslim) and Princess Alix of Hesse (dressed as a Hindu). Abdul Karim had a role in the tableau as did the other Indian servants, Khairat Ali, Mohammed Buksh and Ahmed Husain.

Abdul Karim also played the starring role of Eleazer in the tableau *Rebecca* performed at Osborne the same month. Buksh and Ahmed Husain had supporting roles. Preening in his turban and robes, Karim proudly plunged into the mini-theatricals, his face capturing the expressions of the devoted servant Eleazer as he waited near the well for Rebecca to choose a bride for his master. Minnie Cochrane, playing the title role, would have been less enthusiastic starring opposite Karim. The ladies of the Household were none too fond of the Indian and clearly resented the fact that the Queen was so dependent on him. Despite their reticence, the Queen had to be indulged as she delighted in watching the tableaux and was the loudest to applaud as the Indians took their bow. The theatricals, already a vital part of life at Osborne, became richer now with the Indians included in them. Karim and Buksh were cast in nearly all the plays.

The Royal Household now began to notice the Queen's preference for Abdul Karim. They realised that, like John Brown before him, the Queen would not hear any criticism of her Munshi. But while the latter had been coarse and blunt, Karim was the complete opposite. He was always polite to the Queen, making her feel special and taking every care to be indispensable in her eyes.

The Queen now gave Karim the room previously occupied by John Brown, the symbolic act being immediately noticed by the Household. 'I am rather surprised that Abdul occupies John Brown's room,' Sir William Jenner, the Royal physician, wrote to Reid. 'I don't believe in the ghosts of those long dead or I should expect one in that room.'

Inevitably, the rest of the Household began to resent Karim and some of the Indian servants also grew jealous of him. But if Ponsonby or Reid pointed out a discrepancy in Karim, the Queen would not tolerate it.

In November 1888 Abdul Karim prepared to go to India on leave. The Queen, already so dependent on him, entered in her Journal on 2 November: 'Had my last Hindustani lesson, as good Abdul goes home to India tomorrow on leave, which I regret, as it will be very difficult to study alone, and he is very handy and useful in many ways.'[10]

Karim had landed on British shores to be a *khidmatgar* and waiter. A year later, he was returning to India on annual leave as a Munshi, the Queen's teacher and official Indian clerk. He was still only twenty-five.

The days immediately after Karim's departure for India were filled with news reports of the Jack the Ripper murders in Whitechapel in East London. The Queen busied herself with responding to the gruesome killings and indulged in her own spot of detective work. She shot off a letter to the Prime Minister, Lord Salisbury. 'This new most ghastly murder shows the absolute necessity for some very decided action. All these courts must be lit and our detectives improved. They are not what they should be …'

The Home Secretary, Henry Matthews, got a rather more detailed note as the elderly Queen made her own suggestions on solving the crimes:

– Have the cattle boats and passenger boats been examined?
– Has any investigation been made as to the number of single men occupying rooms to themselves?
– The murderer's clothes must be saturated with blood and must be kept somewhere.
– Is there sufficient surveillance at night?
These are some of the questions that occur to the Queen on reading the accounts of this horrible crime.[11]

The Queen wrote to Karim regularly while he was away and enquired about his family. Karim let her know that his father, Wuzeeruddin, was due to retire soon and the family could face some financial hardships. He said his father was hoping the British government would give him a pension. Karim also informed her that Dr John Tyler, superintendent of the Agra Jail, wanted a promotion.

The Queen needed little prompting. She immediately wrote to the Viceroy, Lord Lansdowne, asking for a promotion for Tyler and a pension for Dr Mohammed Wuzeeruddin, the father of her 'dear Munshi'. The Viceroy had barely taken up his new position from the outgoing Lord Dufferin and was still settling in when he was asked to make enquiries about Wuzeeruddin. He replied that he thought it advisable 'not to take steps' on the matter immediately upon his arrival, but suggested that he would do so when he visited Agra and ascertained the facts about both Tyler and Wuzeeruddin.

His answer did not satisfy the Queen, who was always impatient when she was on a mission. The Viceroy would soon learn that Queen Victoria could be very persistent when she needed something. Within days he received another telegram from her encouraging him to look at the matter urgently for Karim was returning to England on 25 February. The Queen wanted Karim to know that she had listened to his request and was trying to do something for his father while he was in India. She informed Lansdowne that while the Tyler matter could wait, he must attend to Wuzeeruddin's request immediately.

On 22 February the Viceroy received another urgent telegram from the Queen at Windsor Castle:

> It is much better to do nothing about Sir John Tyler till the Viceroy can see him himself. As regards Dr Wuzeeruddin, he wants nothing, the Queen believes, but a pension to live comfortably after *30* years' service both as Military and Civil Doctor or rather Hospital Assistant.[12]

Karim returned to Windsor in the spring of 1889 and the Queen was delighted to have him back, telling him how much she had missed him. The lessons were resumed and Karim watched over the boxes once again. The Royal entourage soon left for their European holiday, the Queen visiting Biarritz in France.

The Viceroy – given the job of enquiring after Tyler and Wuzeeruddin – decided to consult Sir Auckland Colvin, Governor of the North-West Provinces. After a lengthy conversation with Colvin, the insights he received into Tyler did not please him. He wrote to the Queen telling her what he had heard, that the jail superintendent was 'somewhat tactless'. In recent times, Tyler had apparently not been 'altogether reasonable in his tone'. He had even pressurised Colvin to dispossess the present Inspector General of Prisons in order to make room for him and when informed that it was not possible, threatened to resign.[13]

As for Wuzeeruddin, the Viceroy informed the Queen that the Munshi's father had recently met Sir Auckland Colvin who had told him that he 'desired nothing but to express his supreme sense of absolute contentment'. Lord Lansdowne said he would make it his business to inquire about Wuzeeruddin's claim to a pension.

The letters did not please the Queen, who was getting annoyed with the delay at granting a promotion to Tyler and the negative remarks she had heard about him. One morning, with Abdul standing patiently by her side, she wrote a long angry letter to the Viceroy defending John Tyler and saying he had been unfairly passed over for promotions as 'jealousies and ill-disposed persons interfered and Lord Dufferin was induced not to let him have it'.

Lansdowne was soon to realise that the Queen was not a person to give up easily. Despite her advancing years, she would write lengthy letters and send telegrams even when she was travelling. These arrived regularly on his desk, her spidery handwriting covering the black-lined notepaper, which she had used ever since the death of Prince Albert.

The Queen was determined to get Tyler promoted. She had been pleased with the man who had helped arrange the Colonial Exhibition and sent her Abdul Karim. She did not hesitate to express her dissatisfaction with the previous Viceroy and to indulge in some gossip with Lansdowne.

> The Queen must say she thinks it was wrong of Lord Dufferin not to fulfil his promise towards her, but she feels that the person who influenced Lord Dufferin most against him (and she says so in *strictest confidence*) is Lady Dufferin, as she does not favour the Female Medical Schools, or at least the manner in which they are organised, and is very bitter against Sir John Tyler. The Viceroy should hear what his (Sir John Tyler's) reasons are for *himself*.[14]

The Queen had heard nothing about a pension for Wuzeeruddin and she now sent another urgent telegram to the Viceroy who was on tour in Umballa: 'Wrote about Dr Tyler and Wuzeeruddin on 22nd. Latter wishes pension after more than 30 year's service.'[15]

In May she wrote again to the Viceroy. She had clearly had an update from Karim about what had transpired between his father and Colvin at the railway station. She now explained to the Viceroy that Wuzeeruddin had no time to speak to Colvin except a few minutes at the station and he would not have asked for anything, as he has a much easier place than before, 'but he is getting old, and wd. gladly retire on a pension, to which he is fully entitled for his long and good services, and the Queen wd be glad if he cd. have a little more than the actual ordinary pension on account of his son's confidential position about the Empress and his (Abdul Karim's) very exemplary conduct'.[16]

The Queen was eager to help Karim in what she thought was a very reasonable request for his father's pension. She realised how much she had missed him over the four months that he was away and how happy she was to have him back at her side. Having returned from the Continent, Karim seemed to be picking up some French as well. She wrote to Ponsonby:

> As for Abdul Karim, the Queen can never praise him enough. He is zealous, attentive and quiet and gentle, has such intelligence and good sense, and (as all the Indians are) *entirely* intent on his *duty* and always ready to obey the slightest *word* or hint given. He will soon be able to *copy* a good deal for the Queen – even in French – and is an excellent accountant. He is a *thorough* gentleman in feelings and manners.

The Indian servants were not too pleased at this lavish praise for Karim. One of them, Ahmed Husain, began to show signs of depression and the Queen sent Reid to find out the reason. Reid informed her that Husain had told him he was upset because of Karim's high-handed and dictatorial behaviour. Never one to tolerate any criticism of Karim, the Queen accused Reid of listening to complaints from other servants and wrote another of her lengthy letters to the doctor clarifying Karim's stature in the Household.

> The Queen wishes to repeat in strong terms her desire that Dr Reid should never allow Ahmed Husain to complain and speak against the Munshi Hafiz Abdul Karim who *is* the *first*, and from the position his family have always held, and his superior education holds a position *now*, and this he was *from the first* entitled to, which is equal to that of Clerk in her Privy Purse and with this addition that Karim is *Personal Indian Clerk to the Queen*.

Karim, she said, looked after the accounts of all the Indians, ordered them clothes, and was '*the* person' who besides these duties also took care of the Queen's boxes, letters and papers. The Queen also made clear her wish that the others should look to him for advice and help in every way.

> Abdul has shown them every reason of pride in his promotion and has always wished to do what the others like and has objected to nothing. But he disapproves with right of any extravagance and likes the Queen's *written* orders to be strictly *adhered to*. He knows Ahmed Hussain thoroughly and his wish to be the 1st or at least equal in every thing, which will *not* do. The Queen is greatly shocked at Ahmed's conduct behind Abdul's back and Dr Reid must on no account listen to or encourage his complaints which are extremely wrong. This is very wrong that he should behave as he does as she likes him personally.[17]

With the Queen backing him at every stage, the Munshi was growing in self-importance. An incident at Sandringham House made the Royal Household realise just how demanding Abdul Karim was becoming. On 26 April 1889 the entire Royal entourage, including the Queen and the Prince and Princess of Wales, arrived at Sandringham for a gala performance. The Ball Room had been converted into a theatre for the staging of *The Bells* by Émile Erckmann and Alexandre Chatrian. It was a melodrama translated from the original French *Le Juif Polonais* (*The Polish Jew*). Starring the magic pair, Henry Irving and Ellen Terry, along with a cast of sixty and a live orchestra, the play had already had a successful run at the Lyceum Theatre in London. The Queen arrived at 10 p.m. to find there were nearly 300 people in the room including neighbours, tenants and servants. She sat in the front row between Bertie and Alix. The stage had been arranged on a lavish scale with many scene changes. The Queen described the piece as 'very thrilling' and thoroughly enjoyed the performance, thinking Henry Irving had acted 'wonderfully'. Ellen Terry played Portia at the end of the evening, winning a huge round of applause for her 'quality of mercy' speech.

But there was one member of the audience who was not pleased. It was the Munshi. He found that he had been seated with the servants. Taking it as a deep personal insult, the Munshi stalked out and spent the rest of the evening sulking in his room. The next morning he told the Queen about it. Immediately she came to his defence and declared that Abdul Karim should always be seated with the Royal Household. The Munshi had climbed his first step on the social ladder.

The following year, at the Braemar Games, the Munshi was seen fraternising with the gentry. When an amazed Duke of Connaught saw the Munshi's turban bobbing among the top hats in the pavilion, he sent for Henry Ponsonby and asked him how the Munshi had come to be seated with the gentlemen. An equally exasperated Ponsonby replied that Abdul stood where he was 'by the Queen's order' and that if it was wrong, as he did not 'understand Indian etiquette and HRH did, would it not be better for him to mention it to the Queen'. Ponsonby wrote to his wife that 'This entirely shut him [the Duke of Connaught] up'.

That summer, another episode at Balmoral connected with the Munshi convinced the Household that they risked saying anything adverse to the Queen about him at their own peril. She would not tolerate any negative remarks about her favourite Munshi.

One afternoon in June, the Queen had driven to the Summer Cottage wearing a brooch that had been presented to her by the Grand Duke of Hesse. As she was getting into her carriage on her way back, she missed the brooch. It had been pinned to her shawl by her dresser, Mrs Tuck, when she was leaving for the Cottage. The Queen thought Mrs Tuck had forgotten to pin the brooch and was very angry with her, but the dresser assured her that she had done so. A search was made at the Cottage and all the gravel outside turned over, but the brooch was not found.

Rankin, the footman on duty that day, privately thought the brooch had been stolen by Hourmet Ali, one of the Queen's servants, who was Abdul Karim's brother-in-law, as he had seen the former hanging around the Cottage after serving the Queen's tea. Since nobody could suggest this to the Queen, the brooch was given up as lost and the dresser was frequently scolded about it.

A month after the incident, on the way back from the Earl of Fife's wedding at Osborne, another Indian servant, Mahomet, told the dressers Mrs Tuck and Mrs MacDonald, on board the *Alberta*, that Hourmet Ali had sold the brooch to Wagland, the jeweller in Windsor for 6s. He said he did not know where Hourmet had got the brooch, but he did not think it belonged to him.

The next day, Mrs Tuck wrote to Wagland asking for the brooch that he had bought from an Indian servant to be sent back. The brooch was immediately returned by Wagland with a note confirming that it had indeed been sold to them by an Indian servant who had claimed it as his own property. In fact, Wagland informed them that the Indian had come to the shop several times and he had finally bought it off him to 'save himself further annoyance'.[18]

Mrs Tuck took the brooch and the note to the Queen who was first surprised and then annoyed with both Mrs Tuck and Wagland for insinuating that Hourmet Ali had stolen the brooch. 'That is what you English call justice,' she shouted at Mrs Tuck, who informed Reid that the Queen 'was dreadfully angry'.

The Queen discussed the matter with Abdul Karim and then told Mrs Tuck that she was not to mention 'a word of it' to Rankin, Miss Dittweiler, the housekeeper at Balmoral, or a single soul; Hourmet was a model of honesty and uprightness and would 'never dream of stealing anything'. Abdul had said Hourmet Ali had picked it up and that it was an Indian custom 'to keep anything one found and say nothing about it' and that he was only acting up to the customs of his country, the Queen told Mrs Tuck.

Abdul had apparently said that Hourmet had picked up the brooch at the policeman's box, but Reid noted that on the day it was lost, the Queen had not been in that direction at all.

'So the theft, though proved absolutely, was ignored and even made a virtue of for the sake no doubt of Abdul about whom the Queen seems off her head,' wrote Reid in his diary.[19] The incident of the brooch and the Queen's blind love for Abdul Karim had upset the Household.

A slightly miffed Reid wrote to Jenner in July 1889 from Osborne:

I am in my new room, which is very nice and comfortable. I hear the Queen has given Abdul not only my old room but also the large central sitting room off it, which she declined to give me last year, and then only under conditions and restrictions. I am not grumbling at all, but merely mention the fact to show you the relative estimation in which Abdul and I are held!![20]

The Munshi was increasingly drawing the Queen into Indian politics. As he provided her with information about the insecurities of the Muslim minorities, the Queen wrote lengthy letters to the Viceroy about the issues that Karim raised. She felt her discussions with Karim helped her get a feel of the pulse of Indian affairs, as she was getting the native's view of the British administration and its effects. The Viceroy was surprised to receive a letter from the Queen regarding the British proposal to set up Provincial Councils, expressing her doubt as to whether India was ripe for such an enormous change. Her reason for hesitation on the election of Provincial Councils was on account of Karim's view that Muslims may not be well represented on these Councils as they were a minority in India.

The burning issue of riots during the Muslim procession of Muharram continued to be a constant in her letters. As Karim updated her about the riots, the Queen scratched off another of her innumerable letters to the Viceroy informing him that she had been concerned of late about the 'bitterness and heartburning' between the 'Mahomedans and the Hindoos' over the issue of Muharram. The bitterness had led to fighting between the two parties and clashes had occurred even at Agra, where till now this had never happened. She requested the Viceroy to take 'some extra measure to prevent this painful quarrelling' so that the Muslims could carry out their ceremonies 'quietly and without molestation'.[21]

Clearly influenced by Karim, the Queen wrote:

> It [Muharram] only comes once a year, whereas the Mahomedans complain that the Hindoos, who have many religious festivals, *try* to have one of their *own* at this very time, hence the quarrelling. Could not the Viceroy arrange that the Hindoos held *no* feast during the 13 days of Muharram? This wd. avoid all fighting and enable the Mahomedans to carry on with their religious festival in peace. If this is impossible, perhaps the Viceroy wd give strict orders and prevent the Mahomedans and the Hindus from interfering with one another, so that perfect justice is shown to both. But the former course would be far the best.[22]

Lord Lansdowne was clearly getting a little annoyed by the volley of letters from the Queen. Her suggestion of banning the Hindu processions did not go down well with him at all. He replied to her that he was aware of the hostilities during Muharram and the outbreak at Agra in 1888 to which she specifically referred. Changing the dates for Hindu festivals, he said firmly, was not a viable option.

> It is, the Viceroy fears, impossible to arrange that the Hindus should hold no feasts at all during the period of the Moharram. The dates of many of the Hindu festivals are fixed with reference to the progress of the lunar month to these; dissatisfaction would be occasioned if such festivals, which can only, according to the tenets of the Hindus, be properly celebrated upon these special dates, were to be postponed by the order of the government.[23]

On the troublesome business of Tyler's promotion, he informed the Queen that she must realise that higher appointments in India were governed by 'well-established rules of procedure' and that the manner in which they are filled up was 'closely supervised'.

Barely a few months in office, Lansdowne was already beginning to understand how persistent the Queen could be and, to his relief, Muharram passed off peacefully and without incident that year. In September he was able to appoint John Tyler to officiate as Acting Inspector General of Prisons in the absence of Colonel Sir Stanley Clarke. The Viceroy confided that since Colonel Clarke was not likely to return to take up his position, the job would go to Tyler.

On 20 September the Queen replied briefly to him from Balmoral: 'Very glad at Tyler's appointment.'

The Tyler episode over, the Queen returned with satisfaction to her routine duties, enjoying the Highland break at Balmoral with Abdul. The Household watched in shock and horror as she breezily left with Karim for Glassalt Shiel, a remote place three hours ride from Balmoral accessed only by a narrow road running along the lake. The house was the only one for miles around, nestling in the shadow of the towering Lochnagar Hills and surrounded by dense forest. Known as the Widow's Cottage, it was the first house built by Victoria after the death of Albert. She had celebrated the housewarming with John Brown in 1868, dancing some animated reels and drinking a toast with 'whisky-toddy' on the occasion. It was to this isolated getaway – tucked away among the pine trees on the banks of Loch Muick – that she used to retire with John Brown, fuelling Court gossip. After Brown's death she had sworn she would not return there.

As she took Karim to Glassalt Shiel, Reid wrote to Jenner: 'The Queen is off today to Glassalt Shiel to stay there till tomorrow. She has not done this since 1882, having given it up when Brown died, and said she would never sleep there again. However, she has changed her mind and has taken Abdul with her.'[24] There were no doubts in the Household anymore. Abdul Karim had replaced John Brown, and no one was pleased.

6

A GRANT OF LAND

The Munshi was ill. He was suffering from a painful carbuncle on his neck and the Queen was beside herself with worry. Reid was summoned to examine him, but Victoria continued to fret. She visited Abdul several times in his room, stroked his hand and comforted him. Reid was ordered to give him all his attention. She wrote to Reid:

> The Queen is much troubled about her excellent Abdul, who is so invaluable to her, and who has hitherto been so strong and well. She trusts Dr Reid is not anxious about him? He has always been so strong and well that she feels troubled at the swelling. She is always very anxious about them *all*, lest the climate should not agree as they are so useful to me and I was happy to think that they are well and did *not* suffer. Abdul is excellent, so superior in every sense of the word that she feels *particularly* troubled about anything being the matter with him.

Reid attended on Karim, poulticed him regularly and gave him opiates. But the Munshi was taking longer to recover than normal and the Queen grew more anxious by the day. By the beginning of March, when he remained confined to bed, she started visiting him twice a day and even carrying her boxes to him so they could work together as he convalesced.

Reid noted in his diary on 1 March 1890: 'Queen visiting Abdul twice daily, in his room taking Hindustani lessons, signing her boxes, examining his neck, smoothing his pillows, etc.'[1]

The twinge of jealousy and sarcasm in Reid's voice is evident. The Queen fussed about all her servants and staff if they fell ill, but the personal care being taken of Karim had raised many eyebrows. Once again visions of John Brown and the Queen haunted the Royal family and Household. The gossip below stairs was that the Queen's behaviour was out of line and the excess attention being given to a servant was not dignified for the monarch. But the Queen never cared about gossip. To her, Abdul was a dear friend, a close confidant and moral support. He was alone in this country and must not feel neglected. She may be the Empress of India and he a mere subject, but he was ill and she would tend to him.

Another letter was despatched to Reid as the Queen wondered if a second opinion on Karim was needed. When Reid decided that the best procedure would be to perform a minor operation, the Queen delicately suggested that perhaps he should take Sir J. Fayrer's opinion as to the cutting of Abdul's neck, 'on account of the difference of Indian constitutions'. Lest the good doctor feel that she did not have faith in him, she hastily added: 'I *don't* wish it, I only ask what you wd. like yourself. Of course, he could be telegraphed for, but if you are not alarmed or anxious of course it is unnecessary. I am a little over-anxious for I feel a sort of responsibility about the dear good young man, and about them all indeed, away from all their own.'

On 8 March Dr Ellison came from Windsor and helped Reid with the operation, following which Karim made a quick recovery and all was well at Osborne House again. As the tulips and daffodils carpeted the grounds in spring, it was time for the European sojourn. The Queen and her entourage, including a fully recovered Karim and the other Indians, left for Aix-les-Bains in France.

Ahmed Husain developed a high temperature as soon as they arrived and the Queen had another ill Indian on her hands. However, Husain's constant grumblings about Karim vexed her and she wrote a note to Reid:

> Though I have been speaking to you on this subject, I wish to say a few words with reference to what you told me on several occasions of Ahmed Husain's complaints and insinuations, I think that you should *at once* have told the Munshi Abdul Karim of them and to have ascertained what reasons there were, or were not for the complaints. I of course, told the Munshi of the complaints and especially with respect to the cook. He is *naturally* most deeply hurt at them and I must say I have *also been* and I must confess that I am *much* annoyed at your *always seeming* to believe Ahmed's complaints and not to ask explanation from the *responsible* person, whose greatly superior education, very high character, and confidential position about me, *warrant* implicit credence being given to what he says.

The Queen was clearly annoyed not only with Ahmed Husain, but also with Reid for seemingly being sympathetic to Husain. She told him the Munshi had been very hurt by Husain's behaviour as he had always been very kind to him and done everything he had wished for. She instructed Reid to inform the Munshi immediately when complaints were made. 'It would be better even now to ask the Munshi about the cooking,' she said, as Husain seemed to be having a problem with the meals that were being prepared. What hurt the Queen was the fact that Reid was reiterating Ahmed Husain's complaints to her, as she felt it was a slight to Karim. 'I am much pained and hurt at your speaking against *him* and thinking ill of such a person *whom I know* so thoroughly and who is in every way such a high-minded and excellent young man,' she told him.

In keeping peace between the Indian servants, the Household and Karim, Reid found himself being drawn into areas which were well outside his remit as a doctor. Increasingly, however, this would become the norm, as he became the mediator between the Queen and the rest of the Household over the affairs of the Munshi. The Queen may have written angry letters to him, but she had a high opinion of her Scottish doctor and relied on him more than anyone else in her Household.

When Reid explained to the Queen that it was necessary for him to ask Husain what was distressing him, since he was treating him medically, the Queen relented. She, however, made sure she told Reid again that he was on no account to think ill of the Munshi. 'I hope that you will not again think that the Munshi is to blame, when *I tell* you *I know* it is a fact *not* to be so,' commanded the elderly Queen.

Karim was a clear favourite over the others. The Queen wanted his portrait painted by Von Angeli. She explained to her eldest daughter Vicky that the artist was very keen to paint Abdul Karim as he had never painted an Indian before. 'He … was so struck with his handsome face and colouring that he is going to paint him on a gold ground!' she wrote in delight. 'I daresay it will be very fine …'[2] The Queen watched the portrait being painted and a few days later wrote that he had done a 'fine head of Abdul Karim, whom he [Von Angeli] admired so much'.

By summer that year, the Queen had another mission on her mind. She had sensed the hostility towards the Munshi from her Household and family. Knowing that they were capable of racism, she decided that she would provide for Karim so that he was comfortable after her death. She foresaw that they would not be very kind to him after she was gone.

With this in mind, the Queen started writing the first of what was to become a volley of letters to the Viceroy, Lord Lansdowne, and to the Secretary of State for India, Lord Cross, to get a generous grant of land for the Munshi in India.

As was her style, the Queen sent a telegram, then a detailed letter, always referring to herself in the third person. She wrote to the Viceroy saying she had a request which was 'much at heart, viz, a grant of land to her really exemplary and excellent young Munshi, Hafiz Abdul Karim, who is quite a confidential servant, – (she does not mean in a literal sense, for he is *not* a servant) – and most useful to her with papers, letters, books etc'.[3]

The Queen pointed out that it was the '*first time in the world*' that any native had ever held such a position and that she was anxious to mark this permanently. She felt strongly that she needed to do this as her wish to help his father, Dr Wuzeeruddin, had failed on account of his age. Promotions for other members of Karim's family had also not been granted, despite her request, and she reminded the Viceroy that people with lesser merit had been given promotions in the past by officials who were 'interested in them'.

The Queen wrote to the new Viceroy: 'The Queen hopes … that this *will be done* as a mark of approbation of the Queen Empress. The Queen always rewards and promotes those who have served, or do serve her well in England, and has generally found those whom she asked to assist her in this ready to do so.' She also asked him to call on Dr Wuzeeruddin when he visited Agra and tell him how satisfied she was with his son.

The tone of the Queen's letter left no doubt as to her displeasure in not having been able to do anything for Wuzeeruddin or other members of Karim's family, and the fact that she expected the Viceroy to co-operate fully. As was her habit, the letter was severely underlined. She would also refer to herself as the 'Queen Empress' whenever she wanted to make it clear that her command had to be followed. The letter, written on Windsor notepaper on 11 July 1890, would have been blotted approvingly by Karim. The Queen also mentioned her wish to the Secretary of State, Lord Cross, who conveyed the request to Lord Lansdowne in Calcutta.

The Viceroy was uneasy with the request as there was no precedence for a land grant of this sort for an Indian attendant. He made enquiries with the Governor of the North-West Provinces, Auckland Colvin, who informed him that local government had no power to make land grants. Gifts of land were only made very occasionally for recognition of a very long and meritorious military service. Karim did not qualify on military grounds, besides he had served for only a year. The Viceroy wrote cautiously to the Queen explaining his reservations that 'under ordinary circumstances a man of Abdul Karim's age would be regarded as too young for such a reward'. The Viceroy pointed out that the Munshi's father had been transferred from one appointment to another and that an appointment had also been given to his brother, Hafiz Abdul Aziz, in recognition of the Queen's approval of Abdul Karim's services. He would, however, if the Queen wished, take the necessary steps for the land grant. The Viceroy suggested a grant of land that would yield an annual revenue of Rs 300 to the government and probably double that to the grantee. It was the equivalent amount given to an old soldier for exceptional service. 'The Viceroy thinks that such a grant would be sufficient in Abdul's case, having regarded to what would be considered proper and reasonable in his caution,'[4] he wrote.

The distance between India and Britain, and the difficulty of communication in those days, meant that letters would take fifteen to twenty days to arrive by ship and train. The Queen travelled between Windsor, Osborne and Balmoral and the Viceroy was often on tour in various regions of India, when not at his head office in Calcutta or the summer capital of the British Raj in Simla. Telegrams were inevitably quicker, but not suitable for lengthy despatches. The business of government, nevertheless, carried on via letters and telegrams over the thousands of miles: a triangular round of letters between the India Office in Whitehall, the Viceroy's office in India and the Queen's various palaces. The Queen wrote practically every day, especially when driven by a particular issue. The Viceroy replied less frequently, busy as he was with the troublesome business of governing the Indian Empire.

The Viceroy, careful not to upset the Queen, said he would make a point of seeing Dr Wuzeeruddin at Agra, and 'conveying to him the expression of your Majesty's satisfaction with his son'.

The Queen had been spending a peaceful summer in Osborne and was not happy with the Viceroy's letter. Once again she sensed the attempt to slight Karim's achievements. She decided it would be best to give the Viceroy precise instructions about how much land she wanted for Karim, as she did not think his idea of Rs 300 was generous enough.

A telegram dated 1 August instructed the Viceroy: 'Wish you to proceed with grant of land for Munshi. Think that ought not to be less than five to six hundred rupees. Position peculiar and without precedent. Father was only transferred, not promoted. Brother's place not much promotion either. My last letter explains ...'[5]

A few weeks later yet another telegram reached the Viceroy, this one was from Balmoral. 'Glad, if possible, land little more than six hundred as that so little yearly.'[6] And just in case the telegram hadn't reached or been instructive enough, she wrote again the next day: 'She [the Queen] sent him another telegram yesterday expressing a hope if it *were possible* to give land to the Munshi Abdul Karim worth a little more than Rs 600 as that sum brings in so little yearly.'[7]

The Queen was on a roll. She was determined to give Karim what she thought he richly deserved and had little patience for the bureaucracy or the prejudice she seemed to be encountering from her Viceroy in India.

Realising that the Queen was determined to achieve her objective, Lord Lansdowne gave instructions to the officials to hunt for a plot of land for the Munshi and informed the Queen of this. He had requested that the land, if possible, 'be not far from Agra'.[8] Over a month later, no land had been identified and the Queen was getting impatient. The letters and telegrams were flying from Balmoral on the matter. The Queen was also pressurising the Secretary of State, Lord Cross.

The Viceroy updated the elderly Queen, delicately giving her some good news first. The good news was that John Tyler had been confirmed in his position and his appointment was to be recorded in the *North Western Provinces Gazette* dated 27 September. Lansdowne informed the Queen that it had given him 'much pleasure' to carry out Her Majesty's wish in connection with this matter. With regard to Abdul Karim, however, the Viceroy did not have any positive updates.

The case of Abdul Karim is being attended to, but there is in these days v. gt. difficulty in obtaining land suitable for such a purpose. Your Majesty may rely on the Viceroy doing his best. These grants appear insignificant in amount, when judged by European standards, but in India they are *immensely prized* and given only in the most exceptional circumstances.[9]

The delay vexed the Queen further. The Munshi was to leave for India soon on holiday and she wanted the matter wrapped up urgently. On 1 October she sent a telegram to the Viceroy from Balmoral: 'Is there chance hearing about land before 30th, when Munshi leaves for India?' The elderly Queen's request was proving to be a headache for the Viceroy.

The bureaucratic process of procuring vacant land was quite involved. The matter had to go from him to the Revenue Board, from the Revenue Board to the Commission, from the Commission to the Collector and from him again to the local officials, who had to enquire into and report on the land available. The Viceroy was also not sure that any land was available in the Agra area as government lands, other than waste lands, were infrequent in these provinces. He promised the Queen, nevertheless, that he would 'expedite the matter'.[10]

Apart from getting her Munshi a land grant, the Queen was also keen that his position in her Court was recognised in official circles. She made her request to Lord Cross, who had been visiting her at Balmoral, and asked him whether the India Office could recognise Karim's appointment as her Munshi and Indian clerk. When Cross explained to her that this was not an official appointment but a personal one in her Majesty's Household, she wrote to him asking whether it would be possible to have it gazetted in India. She was eager for the Munshi's position to be recorded in India as she had some concerns that Sir Auckland Colvin may not be very co-operative about the grant of land for him and therefore felt the need to make his seniority clear in Colvin's eyes. Though the Queen was sitting thousands of miles away from India, her instinct told her that the British authorities would not be willing to give Karim a senior status unless she absolutely insisted on it. She was particularly wary of Colvin's attitude knowing how he had tried to block Tyler's promotion in the past.

Cross passed the request through Lansdowne saying he had informed the Queen that a gazette was an official thing and he did not see how a private appointment could be treated as official. He told the Viceroy that he could 'make it [Karim's position] known anyhow you think best, if you think fit to do so'.[11]

The Queen was particularly sensitive to any attempt by her Household or a government official in India or Westminster to lower Karim's position. Once, when she had learnt that the Keeper of her Privy Purse, Sir Fleetwood Edwards, had not addressed Karim as the Munshi, she was so annoyed that she wrote to Ponsonby about it. Ponsonby replied that he was surprised that Sir Fleetwood did not know that Abdul was to be called the Munshi. He said he had given the order to this effect through the house and to Major Bigge and it had been recorded in the Red Book. Ponsonby explained that perhaps Sir Fleetwood was away at the time and escaped hearing it. He said he would write to Sir Fleetwood about Abdul's 'proper place at the performance'.

Victoria also made sure that Karim was cast in the tableaux vivant that were staged in the palaces. The roles in these tableaux were usually performed

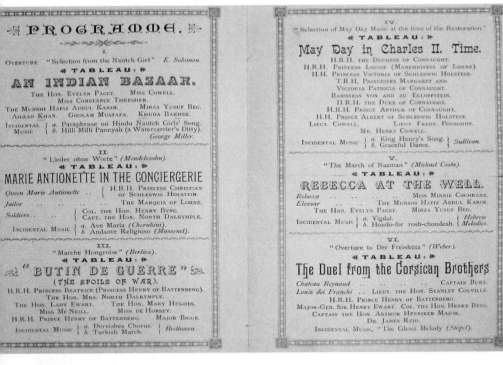

Picture of a tableau programme.

by senior members of the Household and the Royal family. That October, Karim played a major role in the tableau *Oriental Bazaar*, which was done at Balmoral in the presence of Lord Cross and many other invited guests. The Munshi helped organise the characters for the Bazaar scene and co-ordinated the costumes and sets. He chose the incidental music for the piece – an Indian folk song called *Hilli Milli Pannyah* – translated in the programme as 'A Watercarrier's Ditty' and prided himself on his work. The Queen was delighted with the colourful tableau, which she praised as being 'a really lovely and realistic scene, with such beautifully painted scenery'.[12] Karim and the Indians were also part of another tableau called *Arab Encampment* and the Queen could not have enough praise for Karim's efforts in putting these together. Lord Cross watched in amusement.

At the same time as the Queen was writing to Lansdowne, the Viceroy and Cross were having their own private exchanges on the matter. On the delicate issue of the Queen's request for gazetting Karim's appointment, the Viceroy assured the Secretary of State:

I do not think we could Gazette him [Karim] to an appointment entirely unconnected with the Indian Service ... but I will take steps to have it made known that AK has been duly appointed by Her Majesty, and the knowledge that he has been appointed will be sufficient to define his position satisfactorily and to prevent any misconception as to the nature of his employment.[13]

He also confirmed that he would 'take care that there is no misconception as to Abdul Karim's status'.[14]

All the negative responses from both her Viceroy and the Secretary of State to her ideas of procuring a generous land grant for Karim would not throw the Queen off course and she continuously pursued her objective over the next weeks. In October she wrote to the Viceroy that she had the highest regard for Karim and was keen to reward him. She informed him that the news of Tyler's appointment was a relief, especially since she had been getting the sense of 'being unable to get done what she has asked for, for nearly 3 years'.

But on the subject of 'the grant of land for her excellent Munshi, Abdul Karim', she was 'a little disappointed that the grant had not yet been accomplished', as she would have liked the matter to be settled before he left for India on leave on the 30th. However, the Munshi had told her he was 'quite content to wait' till it could be arranged. She informed the Viceroy that Karim would be the bearer of a letter from the Queen Empress to the Viceroy, whom he hoped to pay his respects to at Agra. 'The Queen is very glad that he is going out in the same ship as Lady Lansdowne, and she trusts that the gales which we have had many of lately will have subsided by that time,' she wrote.

The Queen was taking no chances. By handing the Munshi a letter to carry, she had ensured that the Viceroy would definitely have to meet Karim. She had even suggested that he may meet Lady Lansdowne on the ship. Victoria wanted to make sure that Karim's journey to India did not go in vain. She herself would miss him terribly when he was away. The young Indian had become a part of her life now. She was at once mother and friend to him and felt he understood her more than many others in her Court.

The night before Abdul Karim left Balmoral for his trip to India, the Queen wrote to the Viceroy again:

The Queen gives these few lines to be delivered to the Viceroy by her excellent and much esteemed Munshi and Indian clerk, Hafiz Abdul Karim, whom she recommends to the Viceroy's *special notice*. His absence for four months will be severely felt by her, as he is very useful and helpful in so many ways. The Queen Empress trusts that the gift of land may soon be effected, for it is four months since it was first spoken of.

The Munshi's father, Dr Wuzeeruddin, is the Queen believes about to retire after 32 or 33 years good service, as she hopes he will have a good pension. The Queen will be glad if his son-in-law also a doctor, Ilam Ullah, who has 25 years' service and is a doctor in Agra jail could succeed to Dr Wuzeeruddin's place, if feasible.[15]

The letter was sealed and given to Karim to carry back to India. Before he left Balmoral, the Queen also bestowed upon him the decoration of the Eastern Star, the first of many medals and honours that she would give him.

A few days later, the Viceroy seemed to have made a breakthrough and sent an urgent telegram to Balmoral on 30 October. 'Arrangements for land grant are making satisfactory progress. Land will be in suburbs of Agra.'[16] Delighted at having received some sort of assurance before Abdul Karim's departure, the Queen replied the same day: 'Much pleased by telegram. Munshi just leaving. Hopes to see you at Agra.'[17]

There is no record of how Lady Lansdowne reacted to the Munshi, who was travelling back to India on holiday on the same ship. Karim, still a youth of twenty-six, would have been polite and gentle and informed her that he was carrying a letter for the Viceroy from the Queen. The ship arrived at the port of Bombay on 18 November and the Munshi alighted carrying a sword and a gun, both with permission from the Queen.[18] The Viceroy had ensured his smooth passage so he was not troubled by any authorities.

The Queen missed her Indian companion and wrote to her daughter Vicky in Germany:

> My good Abdul Karim's departure is vy. inconvenient as he looked after all my boxes – letters etc. besides my lessons and I miss him terribly! 4 months is a long time; I have such interesting and instructive conversations with him about India – the people, customs and his religion, *das geht mir alles sehr ab …*[19]

The Viceroy had, meanwhile, confirmed from the provisional government that the grant of land for Karim would be above Rs 600 as the Queen had desired. The land had been identified in the suburbs of Agra and the Viceroy sent a telegram to the Queen to say he looked forward to meeting both Abdul Karim and John Tyler in Agra. In a separate letter to Lord Cross, the Viceroy confided:

> Did she [the Queen] tell you that I had obtained a grant of land for her Munshi, Abdul Karim, in the suburbs of Agra to the value of Rs 600.00 a year. The arrangement would be a most unusual one if the case was that of an ordinary employee of the state, but there is perhaps nothing very unnatural in the Empress of India desiring to reward a favourite servant in this manner. At any rate Her Majesty had set her heart upon obtaining this concession for him.[20]

The Munshi had informed the Queen about his safe arrival in India and she waited eagerly for news about the meeting between him and the Viceroy. Like a nervous mother sending her son out on his first day to school and hoping he would make a favourable impression, the Queen waited to hear from Lansdowne. On 21 November she wrote to him:

> By this time the Viceroy will doubtless have seen her good Munshi, who went in the same ship with Maud [Lady Lansdowne], and they had such a quick and good passage. The Queen Empress hopes and trusts that this time the fatigue and heat have not tried her, as they did the first time.[21]

The Queen was in a flurry of excitement at the prospect of the meeting. 'Thanks for kind reception for Munshi Abdul. Trust allow him and father to attend levee tomorrow,' she telegrammed. But she was informed by return telegram that it would be inappropriate for the Viceroy to include Karim and Dr Wuzeeruddin in the levee, as it would upset protocol and other senior officers would be left out. She replied immediately the same day: 'My mistake about levee. Quite understand. Most grateful for kind distinction for Munshi.'[22]

The next day she sent another excited telegram: 'Was not aware when I telegraphed about Munshi and father that it was Durbar. Understand that father cd not attend that though he might attend platform. Much gratified at your giving Munshi place with your staff.'

The Munshi had updated her by telegram about his reception by the Viceroy. He had been to the Viceroy's Durbar and stood in a special enclosure with the Viceroy's staff. Important Indian zamindars and landed gentry from Agra and the vicinity had watched him take his place. Though his father, Dr Wuzeeruddin, had not been invited, the Munshi had been welcomed as a member of the Queen's personal Household. His standing in Agra society had been firmly established.

The Queen was delighted. Another telegram to the Viceroy followed the same day: 'Accept warm thanks from me and Munshi for great kindness to him today.'[23] A few days later she thanked him again, both for the land and the courtesy shown to Karim. It was clear that the Queen longed to be in India. She craved to see the Taj Mahal in Agra and her beloved Abdul standing proudly at the Viceroy's Durbar. She had read the Viceroy's description of Bombay with eagerness and her heart ached that it was not possible for her to ever go there. 'The Queen is jealous of all that he [the Viceroy] has seen, for she would give anything to visit India! But she fears her age puts a bar to it, though really the journey is wonderfully quick now, and it is said will still be shortened in time.'

Being able to present her Munshi to the Viceroy had given the Queen immense satisfaction. The Viceroy, however, had had a few headaches trying to balance his Queen's demands with the strict formality and protocol of the British Raj.

The Viceroy had arrived at Agra station on 21 November to a red carpet welcome. The military band played on the platform as he alighted with his wife and regular entourage. Standing in the ring to greet him was the Governor of the North-West Provinces, Auckland Colvin, and other officials, including John Tyler. But the Munshi was not allowed to welcome the Viceroy. Though John Tyler had applied in advance on his behalf for permission for him to meet the Viceroy at the station, Colvin had rejected it on the ground that only persons of 'high official positions or native personages of rank' were allowed on the platform.

Lansdowne, learning of this, was quick to make amends and asked Tyler to invite Karim to meet him personally that afternoon. Karim, dressed in his turban and impressive clothes and proudly wearing the medal of the Eastern Star, was produced for an audience with the Viceroy. He handed him the letter sent by the Queen and later that day had an interview with Lady Lansdowne. The Viceroy was impressed with the young man and thought he looked 'very smart'. That evening the Viceroy was holding a levee, and with the Queen's request in mind, he issued an order that the Munshi could attend it with members of the Viceroy's staff. However, protocol required that Karim make an application to the Deputy Commissioner for permission to attend the levee and he had not done so. By the time the Viceroy realised this, it was too late for his staff to contact Karim and he missed the levee.

The Viceroy wanted to make sure that the Munshi did not miss the Durbar, as he had already missed two previous functions. He sent a message to the Munshi through Tyler to invite him to attend the Durbar with the Viceroy's staff. Since Karim's position as Munshi did not give him the right to be included amongst the regular 'Durbaris', the Viceroy thought that this was the proper course to adopt. All officials below a certain rank were excluded from these and the admission of any person of lower standing would be resented by the rest. However, as Karim held an appointment in the Queen's Household, 'it seemed only natural and proper that he should, upon such an occasion, attend upon your Majesty's representative with the members of his staff', the Viceroy later explained to the Queen.

Karim's father, Dr Wuzeeruddin, however, had to be excluded from the Durbar. Local officials at Agra informed the Viceroy that Dr Wuzeeruddin's position did not entitle him to be included among the Durbaris since no official drawing less than Rs 3,000 a year was admitted and nearly all the *tehsildars*, or local magistrates, were excluded under this ruling.

Though the Viceroy had been happy to meet the Munshi and had been impressed by him, he was less pleased with John Tyler. After a lengthy conversation with the superintendent of the jail, he felt that Tyler seemed to be dissatisfied with the manner in which he had been treated and also underrated the value of the Queen's gift to Karim. The Viceroy felt that Tyler was inclined to think there was a conspiracy against him, though he himself had never detected any animus against him from Auckland Colvin. He felt it was 'very unfortunate' that Tyler little appreciated all that had been done for him and that he spoke about the grant of land to the Munshi, in his presence, with indifference.

Feeling strongly about this, the Viceroy felt it was his

> duty to tell your Majesty that a grant such as that which has been made to
> Abdul Karim, is most rarely bestowed in this country, and then only to officers
> of very long and meritorious service. As an illustration he may mention that
> quite recently one of the men who at the peril of his life, and under a wither-
> ing fire helped to blow up the Kashmiri Gate of Delhi in the Mutiny, received,
> on his retirement from the service, a grant of land yielding only Rs 250 for life.
> Abdul Karim, at the age of 26, has received a *perpetual* grant of land representing
> an income of more than double that amount in recognition of his services as a
> member of your Majesty's Household.
> The Viceroy does not for a moment, question that services rendered to the
> Queen Empress should receive special and signal recognition, but he must pro-
> test against such rewards when they have been given at your Majesty's express
> desire, being underrated, or spoken of as if they were not of serious importance.

He felt that judging from the language used by Tyler, it was clear that the gentleman did not sufficiently recognise the consideration with which he and Abdul
Karim had both been treated.

The Viceroy enclosed a seating plan for the Durbar and said he had given the
Munshi a special place between the Viceroy's staff and the 'distinguished visitors'.

Before the Viceroy left Agra, he made it a point to receive both Karim and his
father privately. Lady Lansdowne, too, gave an interview to the Munshi's wife and
mother-in-law, who were brought to the camp with much secrecy and 'many
precautions for the strict observance of the purdah rules'. Lansdowne informed
the Queen that 'Abdul Karim looked extremely well and was very smart'.[24]

The Queen read the letter several times, absorbing each detail of the events in
Agra. She filled with pride at the Viceroy's praise for Karim, but was equally upset
about what she had learnt about John Tyler, the man she had worked so hard to
promote. She was also nervous that Tyler's behaviour and his remarks could reflect
badly on the Munshi and wanted the Viceroy to have no misconceptions about him.

On 27 November the Viceroy informed Lord Cross how he had delicately
secured the position of the Munshi at the Durbar.

> I have had a great deal of correspondence with HM [Her Majesty] by letter and
> telegram about the position to be accorded to her Munshi, who is now here on
> leave. His status in HM's household did not entitle him to be included amongst
> the regular Durbaris, but I got over the difficulty by giving him a place next to
> my own staff and close behind my seat. This arrangement, I am glad to learn, has
> given HM satisfaction. I bestow an excessive amount of recognition upon the
> Munshi, who as you know, has got a grant of land to the value of Rs 600 per
> annum permanently, a very liberal mark of Her Majesty's favour.[25]

His final despatch to Cross from Agra was equally tongue-in-cheek.

I have arranged to see the Queen's Munshi and his father privately before I leave, and Lady Lansdowne is, I fancy at this moment, engaged in interviewing the Munshi's wife and her mamma, who are to be smuggled into the camp with the utmost secrecy. I think you will agree with me in considering that the family should be well satisfied with the recognition which they have received.[26]

Lord Cross replied:

I felt quite sure that you would do nothing to cause the Munshi, Abdul Karim, to lose his head. I always told the Queen that I was sure that you would do what was right, and no more, and that I could not myself say what was right and proper, and what was not, but that I left it all to you, and that the Queen might rest quite satisfied.[27]

It was the first time the Viceroy of India had been asked to meet an Indian clerk, who had once been no more than a humble servant. It was clear to him, however, that the Queen held the Munshi in high regard and the Viceroy did not want to upset her, even though he clearly found her demands trying.

The Queen replied to him by telegram on 16 December: 'Received kind letter of 26th and am most grateful for kindness to Munshi.' The Viceroy's letter, however, needed to be responded to in full. The Queen sat at her desk in Windsor Castle, missing as she always did on these occasions, the reassuring presence of Karim by her side, and replied to Lord Lansdowne. After thanking him once again for his kindness to Karim, she added:

But she wishes to express to him how much she regrets the extraordinary behaviour of Sir J Tyler, who had nothing to do with the Munshi at all on this occasion. He was a personal friend of Dr Wuzeeruddin, and when the Queen Empress asked Sir John Tyler, after the Colonial Exhibition in 1886, to procure her 2 Indian attendants, Abdul Karim and another excellent man, but of very inferior class were sent over and only engaged for a year. It was the Queen's own selection. On account of the intelligence, education and very high character of the Munshi that the Queen engaged him as her Munshi and clerk early in 1888, and persuaded him to remain permanently with her, which he hesitated to do on account of the separation from his parents and family to whom he is devotedly attached. He has written and telegraphed to beg the Queen to thank the Viceroy for his and Maud's great kindness to him and his family.

The Queen Empress is entirely satisfied and pleased with what the Viceroy has done, but she trusts that the unfortunate language of Sir John Tyler has not given the Viceroy a bad opinion of the poor Munshi, as he really is a most

excellent, high principled and gentlemanlike young man, worthy of the kindness and distinctions which have been bestowed on him. Sir John Tyler did
express his gratitude to the Queen for all that had been done for himself, but
he is a very irascible man, with a violent temper and a total want of tact, and his
own enemy, but v. kind-hearted and hospitable, a very good official, and a first-
rate physician. He has, from his knowing so many people all over India, been
very useful in procuring servants for the Queen, all of whom have turned out
extremely well.

Though Sir A Colvin may not have said anything to the Viceroy against
Sir John Tyler and his friends, the Queen must tell him frankly that he is very
much disliked for his overbearing manners, and that he is ill-disposed towards
Sir John Tyler and those who he imagines are Sir John's friends. The Queen
thinks it was very wrong of him, and not respectful towards herself, though he
might have been right *au pied de la lettre*, in not allowing Munshi Abdul Karim
to be at the station to present the letter the Queen Empress had entrusted him
with, and she is sure that Sir John Tyler's asking for it was the excuse for the
refusal. That protection has been rather a misfortune to the family, though it
was v. kindly meant.[28]

The Queen's reading of the situation was clearly from the letters and telegrams she
had received from Karim after the eventful meeting with the Viceroy. Karim would
have filled her in on all the gossip, the reason for his refused entry at the station and
the kindness shown to him afterwards by the Viceroy and his wife. Co-ordinating
Karim's presentation to the Viceroy long-distance had quite exhausted the Queen
and she retired to Osborne for the family Christmas, hoping that Karim had made
his mark on the Viceroy and would soon be rewarded with land.

The Munshi was to return from India in February. The Queen hoped he would
be able to complete all the paperwork and leave with the land registry documents. She telegraphed the Viceroy on 17 January saying she hoped the land grant
would be settled before the Munshi sailed out on 21 February. As was her style,
a further telegram followed within a few days on 26 January: 'Trust deed will be
executed before 18 February when he leaves Agra.'[29]

The Viceroy replied the same day: 'Collector Agra has been instructed to put
Munshi in possession and deed will shortly be executed.'

Lord Lansdowne also responded in full to the Queen's explanation of why Sir
Auckland Colvin disliked Tyler and why the Munshi was being wrongly judged
by his association with Tyler: 'It would no doubt have been better for Abdul
Karim and his family if they had not been quite so ostentatiously "protected"
by Sir John,' wrote Lansdowne. 'Your Majesty has summed up that gentleman's
strong and weak points in language which exactly meets the case.'

Though the business of the land grant for Karim had nearly been tied up,
the Queen was still feeling uneasy about a few things. These had bothered her

through the Christmas break and the start of the year at Osborne, and they were concerning the Viceroy's letter about Tyler. She decided to put pen to paper once again and wrote to the Viceroy to tell him that she could not help feeling a good deal annoyed, as she had wished that her 'good young Munshi' would make the most favourable impression on the Viceroy, something he deserved for 'his character, education and excellence', but she was afraid that the Tyler episode may have actually done him harm in the Viceroy's eyes. She reiterated that the Munshi himself was deeply grateful to both Lord and Lady Lansdowne and that he was shy and nervous and had no one to befriend him at Agra, but Sir John Tyler, on the occasion of his presentation. He was, however, quite aware of 'the want of circumspection on his poor friend's part'.[30]

The Queen thanked the Viceroy for expediting the execution of the grant of land and said it should be settled before Karim's departure from Agra. Another letter followed on 6 February. The Queen was calmer now and delighted that Karim had received his grant. She was also looking forward to his return even more than ever before. Soon she received the final telegram on the subject which had consumed her for over eight months: 'Deed of transfer duly executed and handed to Abdul Karim.'[31] The Queen replied immediately: 'I am very much pleased!'[32]

Making every effort to satisfy the Queen, Lansdowne ensured that the deed was delivered to Karim before he left for England. The affair of the Munshi's land had finally been settled. Karim would return to English shores a man of property. Nonetheless, a cautious Lord Cross wrote to Lord Lansdowne: 'I only hope that his [the Munshi's] head will not be turned when he gets back, but I feel quite sure that on this head you will have been careful.'[33]

—⊗⊗⊗—

7

INDIAN AFFAIRS

His property papers sealed and signed, the Munshi returned to Windsor in early March and the delighted Queen resumed her Hindustani lessons immediately. However, Ahmed Husain was not having such a good time. His constant complaints against the Munshi had annoyed the Queen and she delicately suggested to him that he should return to India as he was not keeping in good health in Britain. Husain agreed, but wanted a few favours. He had learnt that the Munshi was allowed to carry arms in India and he demanded the same privilege. The Queen wearily requested Ponsonby to secure a permit for Husain to bear arms in India, as a special favour from her. Ponsonby wrote to Lord Lansdowne, explaining the situation:

> Ahmed (commonly called in our Household as the Sergeant Major) cannot get on with Abdul, whom he is jealous of. One must go, so Ahmed, whose health is bad, goes. We want to let him down easily, and are trying to get him employment at Hyderabad. Hearing that Abdul can bear arms, Ahmed asks, and the Queen hopes he can get it.[1]

With the troublesome issue of Husain resolved, it was time once again to sail to Europe for the spring break. The Queen would go to Grasse this year, an attractive floral town in the foothills of the Alps, fifteen kilometres from the coast. She was returning to the Riviera after an absence of four years and took over the whole of the Grand Hotel for her entourage of forty people, which included her retinue of Indian servants. *The Standard* newspaper reported cynically about the preparations: 'It will require dexterous management to find accommodation for the whole of the royal party in the Grand Hotel, although it is a very large building, as special arrangements have to be made for the pampered Indian domestics who Her Majesty insists on carrying about with her.'[2] Seventy-six boxes and horses and carriages were sent on ahead to await the arrival of the Queen.[3] The donkey and donkey cart went too, the Queen finding the latter convenient for travelling around the grounds. The crossing to Cherbourg was smooth and the Queen enjoyed her Hindustani lessons with Karim on board the *Victoria and Albert.*

The Indian attendants were now placed in the fourth carriage from the Queen on the Royal train, next only to the carriage carrying the Household, much to the jealousy of the other staff. On the way from Cherbourg to Grasse, the Queen's journey was held up following an incident. *The Standard* newspaper carried the report from its Paris correspondent:

> Some forty miles from Cherbourg the alarm bell was rung, and the train was of course, immediately pulled up, and the officers rushed to find out what had happened. It was discovered that one of the Hindoo servants in the suite had been amusing himself by handling the alarm signals, which is conspicuously put up in every carriage, and accidentally set it in operation. The authorities were greatly relieved at finding it was only a false alarm and the train sped on its way.

The reporter used 'Hindoos' as a generic name for Indians, as the attendants were, of course, all Muslims. No doubt Karim – in charge of all the Indian attendants – would have had a stern word with the errant servant who had stopped the Queen's train.

The Queen had chosen Grasse on the recommendation of her daughter Princess Louise, who had told her about the beautiful gardens set out by Alice de Rothschild in the Villa Victoria near the hotel. The Queen's day would begin after breakfast with the Hindustani lessons and the usual chat and gossip with Abdul Karim. This would be followed by her looking through her letters and boxes (which were brought to her every two weeks from London) and then a round of the gardens in the donkey chair.

While she was at Grasse the Queen had a visit from the errant Maharajah Duleep Singh, her previous ward. Some months ago, he had written to her begging forgiveness for all the wrongful acts he had committed against the British government over the last few years. The Maharajah had written to Lord Cross: 'I write to express my great respect for my past conduct towards Her Majesty, the Queen Empress of India. I humbly ask Her Majesty to pardon me, and I trust entirely to the clemency of the Queen. Should her Majesty grant me pardon, I promise obedience to her wishes for the future.'

Duleep Singh had been living in Paris ever since he was arrested at Aden and prevented from returning to India in 1886. He had tried to link up with the Russians and the Irish in his attempt to regain the throne of Punjab and the prized Koh-i-Noor, declaring that he would shed his last drop of blood in liberating his beloved subjects. 'I know Sri Sutt Gooroo will help me. I shall free them from the English yoke,' wrote Singh.[4] It had all come to nought however. The Russians had lost interest and stopped funding him. His protector, Katkoff, had died and the Prince had suffered a massive stroke that had left him half paralysed. The Prince then asked his son, Prince Victor, to write to the Queen on his behalf:

> It seems to me now that it is the will of God that I should suffer injustice at the hands of your people. I can find no one to curse Great Britain, and in spite of all her faults and her injustices, God blesses and makes her Great, and when I look at her, I feel that, in fighting against your country, I have been fighting against God. I would return to England if I were assured of your free pardon.[5]

The Queen pardoned him in August 1890, after Lord Salisbury, the Prime Minister, agreed to it. Cross wrote to Duleep Singh telling him that provided he remained obedient to the Queen and agreed to regulate his movements with the instructions that would be issued to him, 'Her Majesty, by the advice of her Ministers, has been graciously pleased to accord to you the pardon that you have sought'.[6] The meeting in the Grand Hotel in Grasse, a few months after she had pardoned him, went off reasonably well, though it left the Queen rather drained emotionally. She recorded in her Journal:

> He is nearly paralysed down his left side. He was in European clothes with nothing on his head and, when I gave him my hand he kissed it and said 'Pray excuse my kneeling'. His 2nd son Frederick, who has a very amiable countenance, came over from Nice with him. I made the poor broken down Maharajah take a seat and almost immediately afterwards he broke into a most violent fit of weeping. I took and stroked his hand, and he became calmer and said 'Pray excuse me and forgive my grievous faults' to which I replied 'that is all forgiven and past'. He complained of his health and said he was a poor broken down man. After a few minutes talk about his sons and daughters, I wished him goodbye and went upstairs again, very thankful that this painful interview was well over. He was to have some refreshments and then drive back to Nice.[7]

The Queen, a strict moralist, had however refused to receive Duleep Singh's second wife, his former mistress Ada Douglas Wetherill, on the grounds that he was living with her when he was still married to his first Maharani. The Queen had been very fond of Duleep Singh's first wife, Maharani Bamba, and disapproved of Duleep Singh's disregard for her. With the painful chapter of Duleep Singh resolved, the Queen spent a few more relaxed weeks in Grasse, even buying a she-ass for her donkey chair. The she-ass would travel back with her to England and give welcome relief to Pierrot, the Queen's Scottish donkey, who was getting on in years.

The Munshi's fame had by now spread in Britain. His name figured regularly in the Court Circulars as he accompanied the Queen and attended royal dinners, levees and theatricals. The circulars would always mention him as 'the Queen's principal Indian secretary', along with the rest of her suite. Muslims living in Britain wanted to see the man who walked in the charmed Royal circle and was so close to the Queen. It was a custom with Karim and the Indian attendants that after the holy month of Ramadan – throughout which they would observe their strict fast – they would go to the Shah Jahan mosque in Woking to pray at Id. The mosque in Surrey, about thirty miles west of London, had been built in 1889 by an orientalist named Dr Gottlieb Wilhelm Leitner, born of Jewish parents in Hungary, who had lived for several years in Istanbul, London and India and was a professor of Arabic and Islamic law. In 1883 he had acquired the site of the Royal Dramatic College, a large Victorian building in extensive grounds in Woking, and started the Oriental Institute there. With funding from the Begum of Bhopal, a purpose-built mosque was soon constructed on the site, complete with pillars and a dome. Designed to look somewhat like the Brighton Pavilion, it became the first mosque to be built in Britain, and the first outside Moorish Spain in Europe.

The custom of Id prayers at the Woking mosque was followed by Karim every year, and *The Birmingham Daily Post* observed in an article in May 1891 that 'they are met on the occasion by Mohammedans from all parts of England, who come to see the Munshi and join him in prayer'.

The Queen was a great traveller. She enjoyed nothing more than sitting in her train and watching the countryside go by. She loved her visits to Europe, despite her advancing years, and always managed to pack in several engagements and meet her extended family. Barely a month after returning from Grasse, she left for Balmoral. The entourage travelled from Windsor to Derby and then to Ballater on 21 May 1891. The Munshi now travelled in luxury, solely occupying the whole of the fifth carriage on the Royal train, according to the Court Circular in *The Times*. His pre-eminent position in the Court can be judged by the fact that the adjoining fourth carriage had in it only the four senior-most members of the Household: Dr Reid, Alick Yorke, Lord Edward Pelham Clinton, Master of the Household, and Maurice Muther.

At Balmoral, the Queen often took her Hindustani lessons in the Summer Cottage within the grounds of the estate, a short distance from the Castle. She would drive out in her carriage, the Munshi walking behind. The Queen enjoyed the company of the Indian Princes, like the Maharajah of Cooch Behar and the Maharajah of Kapurthala, who dropped in to see her over the summer in Balmoral. The Indian Royals always excited the reporters and locals on account of their exotic clothes. A reporter from the *Dundee Evening Telegraph*, who was going to see a production of *Mikado* at Balmoral, ran into one of the Royal carriages with outriders taking an Indian Prince to the station from Balmoral. He

A document showing the arrangement of the Royal train carriages.

wrote next day: 'The bright turbans of the Prince and his people are to be seen for a mile or so as we look back, adding their "iota" to the rich colouring.'[8]

The Queen had by now begun to plan an extension to Osborne House to accommodate a special Indian room to be named the Durbar Room. The sixty-foot long, thirty-foot wide and twenty-foot-high room was to be built adjacent to the pavilion and used as the much-needed Banqueting Room. It would be connected to the main house by a long corridor called the Indian corridor, where the Queen planned to have portraits of her favourite Indians on the wall, busts that she had commissioned and some of her prized Indian crafts. She had already met the architect, Bhai Ram Singh, Master of the Mayo School of Art in Lahore, who had been recommended to her by Sir Lockwood Kipling, Curator of the Lahore Museum and father of Rudyard Kipling. Lockwood Kipling had been commissioned by several Indian Princes to build an Indian-style Billiard Room in Bagshot Park, the Royal hunting lodge eleven miles from Windsor, as a special wedding present for Prince Arthur, the Duke of Connaught, and the Duchess, Princess Louise. The Queen had seen the Billiard Room and always wanted an

Indian room herself. The decorations for the room were all made in India and the walls and ceiling faced with wooden panels carved by craftsmen in Lahore. It was Bhai Ram Singh who had created and executed the designs at Bagshot and had travelled with Kipling to England to see the installation of the room. When the Queen contemplated the Indian room at Osborne, Lockwood Kipling suggested that she employ Bhai Ram Singh to supervise the work. Owing to the high cost of bringing in decorators from India, it was decided that Singh would create the designs and supervise their craftsmanship by British craftsmen, though both the Queen and Princess Louise privately had their doubts about whether they would be able to carry out the work to the same standard.

Eventually, the plaster decorations were made by George Jackson and Sons from London. Princess Louise suggested that the fireplace have as its centrepiece a peacock, as a direct link to the famous peacock throne of the Mughal emperors. By February 1891, Ram Singh had already prepared some 'brilliant drawings' and had shown them to Kipling. By April, work began in earnest to build the room of the Queen's dreams. Here in the Durbar Room, she recreated the India that she could not visit. The ceilings and walls of the room were covered in ornate plaster carvings that resembled the architecture of both Mughal India and the Hindu temples of Rajasthan. The minstrel's gallery was decorated with wooden *jali* (latticed) work completing the effect of a Rajasthani *haveli* or palace.

All the objects for the room, including the lamps, the light-fittings and chairs, were specially designed by Ram Singh and Lockwood. A large carpet from Agra covered the floor and the pottery was made from the Bombay Art School where Kipling had once taught. Even the curtain fabric was printed and embroidered in India. The room was completed by December that year and the Queen was so delighted with it that Ram Singh was invited to stay for five days over Christmas and given a signed photograph and a gold pencil case by the Queen as a Christmas present. The Durbar Room was now used by the Queen as a Banqueting Hall and she had the menu cards made with an Indian theme. With the ornate surroundings, the Indian attendants dressed in their turbans and the menu comprising the steaming hot curries that were always prepared in Osborne for luncheon, visitors would have had the complete oriental experience. The Queen enjoyed presenting this mini-India to visiting Indian Royalty. The Durbar Hall was always splendidly decorated at Christmas and the tableau vivant staged against the elaborate backdrop. Here, surrounded by her family and Indian servants, the elderly Queen lived out her Eastern fantasies.

In the kitchens at Osborne the Indian chefs were a small coterie working alongside, much to the amazement of, the European chefs. One of them, the young Gabriel Tschumi, who had recently arrived from Switzerland to join the Royal kitchens, was fascinated by the abundance of meat and vegetables in the Victorian kitchens as compared to the frugal diet in Europe at the time. Watching the Indian chefs at work left him in awe, and he recalled:

Menu card at Osborne, which shows a sketch of a pillar with a turbaned man on the top right-hand side.

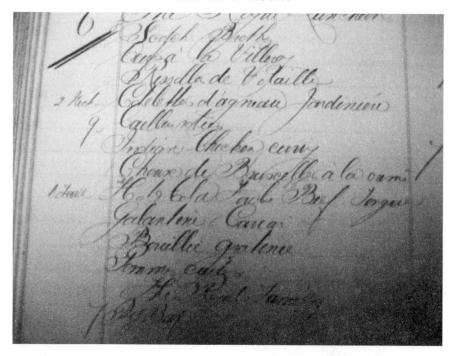

Menu at Osborne showing chicken curry.

For religious reasons, they could not use the meat which came to the kitchens in the ordinary way, and so killed their own sheep and poultry for the curries [halal]. Nor would they use the curry powder in stock in the kitchens, though it was of the best imported kind, so part of the Household had to be given to them for their special use and there they worked Indian style, grinding their own curry powder between two large stones and preparing all their own flavouring and spices. Two Indian in their showy gold and blue uniforms worn at luncheon always served the curry to Queen Victoria and her guests.[9]

Interestingly, curry was always served at lunch, never for dinner, as was the practice with the British in India after the Mutiny. To serve curry for dinner would definitely not be *de rigeur*. French or English cuisine would be the requirement for these occasions. However, it remained a tradition in the last decade of Queen Victoria's reign that curry would be cooked every day and served, regardless of whether or not her guests ate it. Her grandson, George, would later develop a taste for Madras prawn curry and insisted on always eating a curry with his meals.

The Queen continued to take a keen interest in Indian political developments and followed closely the trouble in Manipur in north-east India where the Senapati was overthrown and an English Resident put in control. She sent several letters through Ponsonby saying that the Prince should not be executed. The religious riots which had occurred in Bombay that year also concerned her. She met Lord Elgin, who had been appointed the new Viceroy of India, and discussed these matters with him before he left England to take up his post. She also told Lord Kimberley, Secretary of State for India, that the religious riots were rather threatening for the future of the country. Clearly under the influence of Karim, she felt that they were 'directed by the Hindus against the Mohamedans, whom we have to protect as much as we can'.[10]

The Queen had also sensed in her conversations with Karim that many of the Residents appointed to oversee the administration of the native states by the British government were overbearing in their attitude, and she frequently expressed her concern to Lord Cross about this. The Secretary of State wrote to the present Viceroy, Lord Lansdowne:

> I know not where she [the Queen] has got the impression that many of our Residents are rude and overbearing, and I took the opportunity afforded by seeing her constantly here [in Balmoral], of pressing for any instance that had been brought to her notice, but I cd. get no specific case. My own private opinion is that her Indian Munshi tells her that there is in India the greatest devotion to herself and all her family, but at the same time distrust and dislike of the Government, and that the Native chiefs think that the residents are rude and overbearing. I did not like to mention any case in which General Dennehy's name was concerned, as he is coming here as groom in waiting tomorrow. From former conversations, however, with her, I cannot help thinking that the names of Sir Griffin and Sir A Colvin find no favour in her eyes.[11]

In an earlier letter he had written:

> the Queen is constantly harping upon the manner in which she believes our residents to act in their respective posts, keeping the natives at a distance, showing no sympathy etc etc. I do not know on what she grounds such statements, unless it be from something which her Indian attendants may have said. Of course she does not know that I am writing this. She asks, by the way, if I knew what had become of the wives and children of the Senapati.[12]

The Queen was clearly concerned that the character of the Resident placed in Manipur should be scrutinised with care and a 'very judicious, firm, but a very conciliatory man' be put there.

Cross conveyed her concern to Lansdowne saying: 'I know she feels, rightly or wrongly, that the bearing of our Residents to the Native Princes is not what they should be, and that they are often rude and overbearing, their notion being that of governing India by fear and by crushing, instead of by firmness, joined with conciliation.'[13] It was clear that the Queen considered the latter two qualities as essential requirements of running a vast country like India.

While the Queen seemed to be listening to her Munshi on Indian affairs, his growing position in the Court continued to annoy the Household. To them, the privileges granted to him seemed endless and his demands ever growing. When the Munshi submitted a long list to Reid of medicines that he wanted to send to his father, Reid decided to put his foot down. He wrote angrily to Jenner:

> The Munshi came to me a day or two ago with a long list of drugs which his father has written to ask for; and he said the Queen wished me to get them for him. The list is too long to trouble you with: but it contains about 60 articles, and the quantities he asks for are enormous. For example he asks for 6lbs of Chloral Hydrate, 6oz Morphine, 12oz pf Nitrate of Silver, 3lbs of Chlorodyne, 6lbs of Laudanum, 2lbs Tincture. Of Belladonna, 2oz of pure Strychnine, 6lbs Paregoric, 6lbs tincture Iodo, 8oz Croton Oil, and so on. There are many other poisons besides those I have named, which he asks for in like quantities, and other drugs in correspondingly larger amounts. On thinking it over, I came to the conclusion that I could not take the dangerous responsibility of ordering in *my* name poisons (which I have calculated are amply sufficient to kill 12,000 or 15,000 full grown men or an enormously larger number of children) for a man I don't know, and whom I know not to be legally qualified in our sense of the word.
>
> H.M. has agreed to my suggestions that I should write to Sir J Tyler in India to get for the 'Doctor' what is required from some English chemist there, and send the bill here. The Queen says the Munshi must not in any way be annoyed or put about on the subject: so Dennehy is coming on Saturday to explain matters to him in a conciliatory way!!![14]

Dr Reid had to attend to the Munshi who suffered from influenza in the New Year, the Queen ever anxious about him. He recovered in time, however, to participate actively in the tableaux vivant that were staged at Osborne. The Munshi had the starring role in *An Indian Bazaar* which he helped direct as well, much to the Queen's appreciation. The tableaux were staged for the first time in the new Durbar Room, watched by the Queen and Prince Christian of Schleswig-Holstein. The Munshi was becoming quite familiar now with the Queen's extended European family, thanks to her annual visits to the Continent, and they with him.

While the Queen would not even think of moving around without her turbaned coterie, the Household clearly did not like the idea and made their dislike known to the Royal reporters in the newspapers, who were constantly looking for Court gossip. When it was learnt that the Queen's suite for the trip to the Continent in the spring of 1892 consisted of a retinue of forty-five servants, the papers were quick to report the unpopularity of the Indian servants. A report dated 3 March 1892 said:

> The officials who are responsible for all the arrangements would be delighted to dispense with the company of the Indian domestics, who are absolutely useless, and they give an enormous amount of trouble, and are execrated by everybody. These Oriental menials are as tiresome and exacting as the Irish servants who are so amusingly described by Lever in his capital story, 'The Dodd Family Abroad'.

The underlying racism in the article could hardly be ignored and the source of the stories is quite clear. The Queen chose to ignore the reports, as she usually did, and insisted on travelling with her beloved Indians.

After their return from the Continent, Reid had the opportunity to meet Sir John Tyler who was visiting Windsor. The doctor was determined to find out the truth about Dr Wuzeeruddin and quizzed Tyler about him. Tyler told Reid that the Munshi's father held no medical diploma and was not 'qualified' as understood in England and could not be put on the medical register.[15] Wuzeeruddin had, however, received instructions at the Agra Medical School, for which he held a certificate, and was 'qualified' in that sense for the post he had held for a long time – that of a hospital assistant – of which there were a great many in India. Tyler informed Reid that they were called the 'native doctors', though of course strictly speaking they were not entitled to the proper term 'doctor', not being M.D., or indeed holding any diploma that could give them such a claim.

'In the last circular he ought strictly to have been called Hospital assistant or native doctor, but of course to add the word native would have "taken the cream off it", and he would not have liked it so well, or the Munshi either,' noted Reid, who kept detailed notes of the conversation with Tyler in his diary.

Tyler told Reid that Wuzeeruddin was now made a great deal of on account of the 'high position to which HM has raised his son', and because the Munshi 'has the Queen's ear'. Tyler said that if it hadn't been for this fact, Wuzeeruddin was not a man with whom he would have any social intercourse. He confirmed, however, that Wuzeeruddin could prescribe and perform small operations and had managed a dispensary. He had accompanied General Roberts in his march to Kandahar in the capacity of hospital assistant and was anxious to have his position raised, 'now that his son is such a great man, and made so much of by the Queen', Tyler told Reid. All the while, the Queen remained oblivious of the fact that her Household were carrying out discreet enquiries about Dr Wuzeeruddin in order to embarrass Karim and expose him as a liar.

She fussed over her Munshi and was always keen to show him off to her European relations. In the summer of 1892, when her granddaughter, sixteen-year-old Princess Marie (Prince Alfred's eldest daughter), arrived in Windsor with her fiancé, Crown Prince Ferdinand of Romania, the Queen insisted they meet her Indian secretary.

Marie, already anxious that 'Grandmama Queen' might disapprove of the match, waited nervously for her in the Great Corridor at Windsor. The Queen entered on the arm of her turbaned Indian attendant, smiled at the shy young couple and spoke to Prince Ferdinand in perfect German, asking him about his father. The next day, the awestruck couple were told that 'the Munshi would like to make Ferdinand's acquaintance'. It was arranged that they would come to the Queen's private sitting room to meet him.

As Ferdinand entered he saw the Queen sitting at her writing table. On an easel beside her was an oil portrait of Ferdinand's mother, a beautiful Portuguese Infanta. '*Wunderschon*,' said the Queen. '*Wunderschon*,' replied the tongue-tied Ferdinand.

The young Princess recalled how the silence was broken by the click of the door handle and the tall figure of the Munshi who stood in the doorway. He was dressed in gold with a white turban. Without moving from the doorway, he raised 'one honey-coloured hand to his heart, his lips and his forehead. He neither moved into the room nor spoke.'

The young couple could only stare at this vision in silk and gold. No one spoke for several minutes. The Queen – evidently pleased with the effect the Munshi had had – continued to smile. The Munshi remained standing at the door, manifesting, as young Marie said, 'no emotion at all, simply waiting in Eastern dignity for those things that were to come to pass'. Ferdinand remained frozen and stared at the Munshi. Finally, Marie decided to take the initiative and walked over to Karim and shook his hand. Her fiancé followed her. The Queen, satisfied with the encounter, and pleased to have indulged her Munshi with a glimpse of the Royal bridegroom, finally allowed the couple, 'who were only too pleased to escape', to leave the room.[16]

In June that year, the Munshi's father came to visit him. A month ahead, the Queen had requested Alex Profeit to ensure that the rooms in the stables in Balmoral were comfortably furnished for him and the central heating checked. Profeit confirmed that these would all be looked into.[17] Dr Wuzeeruddin had expressed an interest in seeing the hospitals in Edinburgh and the Queen arranged for Karim to accompany him there, even organising their stay at the Balmoral Hotel in Edinburgh. The generosity towards the Munshi's father met with the usual murmur of discontent from the Household. Arthur Bigge wrote from Balmoral to Reid, who was on holiday in Ellon:

The A.B and Sohn went off this morning to Edinboro' and are going to visit the Infirmary, University and Jail, to the authorities of which, Dennehy has written saying exactly who and what the Oriental visitors are. They are to be put up at the Balmoral Hotel *coute que coute*. I am in hopes that they may find a happy and lasting retreat in the Jail!'[18]

Despite the best attempts of the Household, the Munshi continued to flourish. The Munshi's father became the first person to smoke a *hookah* in Windsor Castle, in a room usually reserved for the Prime Minister, Lord Salisbury. The Queen even urged her grandson, George, Duke of York, to sign two of his photographs and give them personally to her 'good Munshi for himself and his father (whom it will be sent to)'.[19]

In Osborne that Christmas season, the Munshi took the starring role in the tableau *King of Egypt*. Dressed in an elaborate Bedouin costume and crowned with the headgear of the pharaohs and sitting on a lion throne, the young Karim – now rapidly becoming portly – looked delighted as the King of Egypt, with the other Indian servants playing envoys from other African countries, paying homage to him. The Queen sat separated from the stage only by a strip of fern and palm and showed her appreciation of the theatricals.

The Queen's closeness to Karim meant that she remained constantly concerned for Muslims in India and never failed to convey this to the Viceroy or the Secretary of State. Having discussed at length with Karim the passing of the Indian Council Bill, which gave representation to Indians in the native assemblies, she was convinced that Muslims would not be adequately represented and urged the Viceroy to consult various bodies on this. 'The Mahomedans are undoubtedly by far the most loyal of the Indian people, and wd. be a great support in Council,' she said.[20]

The Viceroy replied that it would be necessary to fill a certain number of appointments to the Councils by direct nomination in order to safeguard the rights of minorities. 'This,' he said, 'would afford the means of securing proper representation for Mahomedan interests.'

The Queen's passion for Indian colours and ceremonials remained unquenched. For the inauguration of the Imperial Institute, she now wished for a guard of honour from the Indian Native Army and requested the Viceroy to send her a small contingent from India. The latest demand provided another headache for Lansdowne as bringing native soldiers to England on duty was illegal. The costs would also be quite high. The problem was overcome for the sake of the elderly Queen by sanctioning the travel expenses of eight officers, under the condition that their expenditure did not exceed £2,500, they stayed no longer than three weeks and it was clearly understood that they were there 'on furlough and not by orders on military duty'.[21]

The Munshi was due to go on leave in May, but the Queen wanted him to accompany her first to Florence where she was going for her European spring break. *The Times* reported on 24 March from Florence: 'The Queen's Indian attendants who followed Her Majesty's carriage excited great interest as they drove along.'[22] The *Birmingham Daily Post* had an intriguing article titled 'The Florentine's Impression of the Queen'. It remarked that the Florentines were apparently not 'particularly impressed' by the style of the Queen's cortege, but that her Indian secretary had intrigued them as he had sat in his carriage in 'solitary state, arrayed in a splendid Oriental costume, and blazing with gold lace'. The paper went on to report that on the box of his carriage sat one of the Indian domestics, who was attired in a sumptious dress. The correspondent wrote:

> The Munshi (Hafiz Abdul Karim) has fairly puzzled the Florentines of all classes, and also the Italian court … for it is reported that after King Humbert's visit to the Queen at the Villa Palmieri, his Majesty requested Lord Vivian to inform him who the Munshi is, and what is his exact position in the household, as the King did not understand why this magnificient and imposing Hindoo should have been formally presented to him. The popular idea in Italy is that the Munshi is a captive Indian prince, who is taken about by the Queen as an outward and visible sign of Her Majesty's supremacy in the East.

The reports only amused the Queen as she spent her mornings with Karim taking her lessons. She had nearly finished her fifth Hindustani Journal. 'This is my last lesson,' wrote the Queen, 'as the Munshi goes on leave to his own country tomorrow morning.'[23] She always missed him terribly when he was away.

Six months later, the Queen was beside herself with excitement. The Munshi was bringing back his wife and mother-in-law. The Queen told Ponsonby to spare no expense to ensure that they had a comfortable journey and ordered a cottage in Frogmore to be prepared for them. Ponsonby sanctioned £300 to the Munshi for his wife's expenses. He entered the extra funds under the head of 'extra ordinaries' in the accounts. The Queen went to visit them at the earliest opportunity. She wrote in her Journal:

> Abdul has just returned from six month's leave and brought his wife back with him from India. She and her mother are staying at the Frogmore Cottage, which I had arranged for them, and I went down with Ina McNeill [extra woman of the bedchamber] to see them. The Munshi's wife wore a beautiful sari of crimson gauze. She is nice looking, but would not raise her eyes, she was so shy.[24]

The Court circular of *The Times* newspaper covered the formal presentation of the Munshi's wife and mother-in-law to the Queen. The reporter wrongly wrote that one of the ladies was his daughter.

The wife and mother-in-law of Munshi Abdul Karim had the honour of being presented to the Queen yesterday.

The Queen's Indian secretary, the Munshi Abdul Karim, who has been visiting his native land returned to England on Saturday in order to resume his duties upon the arrival of the court from Scotland. The Munshi was accompanied by his wife and daughter [sic], both of whom were closely veiled, the lady being shrouded in a cloak of yellow stuff and the girl in a darker garment, the Oriental coverings completely concealing the features and figures of the wearers. During this journey every attention by command of her Majesty was shown to the Munshi and his family, who travelled from London in a south western saloon, with drawn curtains, and on reaching Windsor in the evening were conveyed in a Royal carriage to Frogmore Cottage, where apartments have been provided for them.[25]

The Queen wrote to her eldest daughter Vicky in great excitement:

I don't think I told you of the two Indian ladies who are here now, and who are, I believe, the first Mohammedan purdah ladies who ever came over … and keep their custom of complete seclusion and of being entirely covered when they go out, except for the holes for their eyes. They are the wife of my Munshi … and her Mother. The former is pretty with beautiful eyes … she was beautifully dressed with green and red and blue gauzes spangled with gold, very gracefully draped over head and body …[26]

The Queen had resumed her Hindustani lessons the very day after Karim returned, quickly making up for the time lost over the past four months. She wrote in her Journal that she had begun the sixth book and hoped it would be finished nicely.[27]

'*Aj yeh chhati kitaab shuruat hain. Umid hai ki yeh bhi bakhubiat tamam hogi*,'[28] she wrote. She also noted that this would be a little larger than the last book. The Hindustani Journals from now on were thicker, replacing the old smaller diaries which she had used for the last few years. Clearly the Queen had made substantial progress and had now graduated to writing full sentences. As always, Karim wrote the lines first in Urdu, followed by Urdu in roman script so the Queen could read out the lines, then finally the English translation. The language that had evolved largely during the rule of the Mughal Emperors in India, who had combined elements of Persian and Arabic with the Prakrit dialect of the locals, appealed to the Queen. Urdu was a rich language, suited to the Mughal courts. Well over seventy now, the Queen's enthusiasm for learning a new script was remarkable. She faithfully copied out Karim's Urdu writing and then read out the words to him. Karim patiently helped her along, encouraging her at every step. He enjoyed these lessons as much as she did, as it gave him both the chance to relax and a sense of fulfilment. Sometimes, in the English translation, Karim would make a grammatical mistake. The Queen would discreetly correct the English when she wrote it again, teacher and pupil now both learning from each other.

A leaf from the Hindustani Journal of 31 December 1892 shows how they worked together:

> Today I at all out not went, because cold worse was. I was uncomfortable, but I downstairs twice went and arrangements of the tableau saw. [Karim's entry in English]

> *Aj ham bilkul bahar nahin gae kuinke zukham zyadah raha. Ham ko taklif the, lekin ham niche do dafa gae aur taiyari tableaux mulazah ki.* [Karim's entry in Urdu in roman letters]

> Today I did not go out at all as my cold was worse and troublesome, but I went twice downstairs to see the arrangements (rehearsals) for the Tableaux. [Queen Victoria's entry with corrections].[29]

With the arrival of the Munshi's wife, the Queen now had two people to fuss over. She would often drive to see the Munshi's wife in her cottage, whether she was in Balmoral, Windsor or Osborne, and always noted her visits in her Hindustani Journals. She also liked to take her family, visiting foreign Royalty and ladies of the Household to meet her, as well as other Court officials. The Munshi's house soon became filled with gifts and memorabilia given to the couple by visitors accompanying the Queen. Victoria, now more than ever, became a mother figure to the couple.

Visitors to the Munshi's house included Duchess Helena, as well as Princesses Beatrice and Louise, Empress Frederick, Princess Henry of Prussia and the Empress of Russia, among others. The Queen would often take her daughters and her grandchildren to the Munshi's house where they would have cake and tea, the Munshi's wife and mother slowly losing their initial shyness and inhibition. Princess Victoria and Princess Maud were taken there, as were ladies-in-waiting like Lady Churchill and Lady Lytton. The Munshi often received a note from the Queen which informed him at short notice that the Queen was bringing a visitor.

'Would you and your wife prefer if I only brought Beatrice, or might Victoria who is so interested in India come at the same time or would she rather only see one at a time?' the Queen wrote to Karim in Osborne shortly after their arrival. 'Perhaps tomorrow mg. wd. do? P.S. Pcss. Louise w. also go some morning – perhaps later.'[30]

A few weeks later, she wrote again:

My dear Abdul, The Empress [Frederick] wd. much like to go – see your dear wife tomorrow (Friday) mg. at a little past 12. She says she is sorry she shd. trouble herself by dressing in her smart clothes for her, but I know you wd. like her to be seen in her fine clothes. Only I think the *large* nose rings spoil her pretty young face. Your loving mother, Victoria R.I [signed in Urdu][31].

Sometimes the Queen signed these hastily written notes as 'Your affectionate friend'. At other times it was 'Your loving mother'. She nearly always signed now in Urdu. The presence of Abdul Karim and his wife, and the knowledge that there was now a cosy domestic atmosphere in his cottage, gave the Queen a feeling of satisfaction. She was happy that he could have his family by his side and she appreciated his closeness to his wife and her extended family. Her own children, by contrast, were often troublesome. The Queen provided the Munshi and his wife with cottages in Balmoral, Osborne and Windsor. In Windsor the Munshi lived in Frogmore Cottage; in Osborne it was Arthur Cottage, which was extensively renovated and extended for him, and in Balmoral a special cottage was built for him on the estate. The Queen called it 'Karim Cottage' in his honour. Alexander Profeit reported to the Queen that he was trying his best to follow the Munshi's instructions on the furnishing. The Munshi himself spared no expense in decorating his house.

On the completion of the building of Karim Cottage, a delighted Munshi threw a house-warming party, inviting the ladies and gentlemen of the Household. At his party, Karim made a gracious speech thanking the Queen for all her kindness:

Ladies and gentlemen, I thank you most heartily for coming here today, and thus honouring with your presence this new home of mine which Her Majesty has been graciously pleased to name Karim Cottage. Your visit, I assure you, gives me very great pleasure indeed. There can be no doubt that the great majority of the people of Her Majesty's Empire are well aware of the position which I hold as Indian Secretary to the Queen Empress; and this position I have tried, and will always try by faithful service, to be worthy of. I do hope that my service here will ever grant me the sympathy of the Royal Family, the noblemen and the people of the British Empire. Ever since the year 1887, the year when first I came to Scotland (but especially the people of Balmoral) has been that of good faith and kindness, and I sincerely trust that as long as I and my family remain in this country and among you, this feeling may reciprocally remain unchanged.

The *Aberdeen Journal*, which faithfully reported the party, noted that the Munshi again thanked his guests after which Dr Profeit, on their behalf, 'thanked the Munshi in a few words for his hospitality, and hoped that he and his wife would be long spared to live happily in his new house and to serve our beloved Queen'.

The newspapers noted that the Queen and the Princess of Wales were among the first to visit Karim Cottage.

The Queen now took on the role of mother to Karim and his young wife. She very quickly learnt from Karim that they had been unsuccessfully trying to have children, and decided to get medical advice:

> I spoke to Dr Reid about your dear wife and I think he will understand easily what you have to tell him. It may be that in [sic] hurting her foot and leg she may have twisted (moved or hurt) something in her inside, which would account for *things not* being regular and as they ought.
>
> If this is so, it can only be found out by her being examined (*felt*) by the hand of this Lady Doctor. Many, many 1000 ladies have to go through this with a *Doctor,* wh. is vy. disagreeable, but with a Lady Dr there can be no objection, *and without* that, you *cannot find* out *what* is the matter.
>
> It may be something is out of its place which can be put right and then the *object* of your *great wishes* may be obtained.
>
> There is nothing I would not do to help you both, as you are my dear Indian children and you can say (any) thing to me. I have had 9 children myself, and have had daughters, daughters-in-law, nieces, grandchildren etc to look after and I can help you, Your loving Mother, VRI [signed in Urdu].[32]

Three days later, Reid was despatched to London to check out a lady doctor for the Munshi's wife. Reid called on Barlow to discuss this.[33] The next day he received Mrs Boyd at the station, who had come to see the Munshi's wife, and drove her to Frogmore along with the Munshi.

The Queen wrote to Karim: 'The Lady Dr. Dr Reid has heard about is very good and quiet and clever and … is a married woman.'[34]

Some time later, the Queen wrote again to Karim, giving him every possible advice about his wife:

> Your wife should be very careful not to neglect her bowels and never to let a second day pass without their acting. She should take a weak pill if necessary.
>
> She shd. be careful at the *particular time* every month not to tire herself or go on rough roads.
>
> If she has passed 2 of these times already the 3rd and 4th ought to be past before we leave for Windsor and the journey cd. be safely performed. If it would be safer to go a little sooner, you could, *by that time* consult the Doctor about it, for you cd. easily ask Dr Reid who *then might be told about her.* She ought in another fortnight or 3 weeks to increase in size.
>
> Lying down every day for a short time and for longer as time goes on, would be good for her. If her back hurts her she should lie down.[35]

The intimate details that the Queen wrote about showed how close she had come to Karim and how freely she discussed everything with him. Monitoring their love life and giving them suggestions on pregnancy and childbirth gave her a sense of matriarchy and fulfilment. The 'purdah ladies' were a novelty in the Royal Court and the Queen showed them off to her Royal visitors as if they were a collection of rare ornaments. The Munshi soon found that his days were getting very packed. Between attending on the Queen's innumerable boxes and letters, the Hindustani lessons and the supervision of the Indian attendants, there was now a steady supply of visitors to the house to deal with. The Queen herself visited regularly, every two or three days. The Queen wrote to him every day giving him instructions or advice or both. She wrote:

> My dear good Abdul, The Dss. of Roxburghe who goes away quite early on Thursday morning will come with me tomorrow morning at about 12 – she is very good and kind and has had many sorrows and trials within the of late years.
>
> Your dear wife must not *dress* and must not tire herself. She always looks so nice. We only will stop a few minutes as you know.
>
> Mr Bryce is anxious to see you again about the Pilgrims and other things.
>
> As the days will soon oblige us to be in before six (6) I should like to make another arrangement, viz, for you to come at 6 or ½ p. 6 to do what has to be done and then once more after 8 to see if my letters are ready to be put up – & to say good night.
>
> We might wait 3 or 4 days before making the change. God Bless you. VRI [signed in Urdu].[36]

Sometimes a note would be carried to his cottage at night by the pageboy. The Queen had probably had another idea:

> You spoke of coming back tomorrow and going out again in the afternoon, but you must not forget that I shall bring the Pss. of Wales at ½ p. 3 or ¼ to 4 to see your wife and you must be there.
>
> Mr Bryce told me *how* pleased he was with his talk with you. Ever your truly devoted and fond loving mother, VRI.[37]

The conversations with Karim kept the Queen up to date on India. Karim would often voice his concern that Muslims, being a minority, could be marginalised in India. Every report of a religious riot now convinced her that the Hindus were often the antagonists, hearing as she did the story from Karim. She always wrote immediately to the Viceroy about her worries: 'Distressed at terrible religious riots at Bombay. Believe that Hindoos are generally the aggressors. Cd. not some arrangement be made by which festival were not at same time, and each section agreed not to interfere in other's devotion. Cd not Moharum be altered?'[38] A few days later she wrote again:

> Can no sensible and reasonable Hindus of some influence and standing be spoken to as to the possibilities and necessity of putting a stop to this anti-cow killing practice which naturally enrages the Mahomedans? If leading and enlightened men on both sides cd. be spoken to – and the danger of stirring up such gt. strife which might lead to very serious complications – it wd. be a gt. thing.[39]

The Viceroy always replied on these occasions informing the elderly Queen that there was no question of changing the dates of Hindu or Muslim festivals. 'A change in the date of the Moharram, would be, the Viceroy believes, out of question. It would be like changing the date of Christmas Day in Great Britain ...'[40]

The Queen soon learnt that Lansdowne was to return to Britain and the new Viceroy, Lord Elgin, was to take up his post. Though she had been displeased with the Viceroy over what she thought was the heavy-handed dealing of the Senapati's revolt in Manipur, she was on the whole pleased with him because of the effort he had made to look after her Munshi and his father at her request, and for ensuring that Karim had received the plot of land she wanted him to have. She now begged him to stay another six months in office, as she felt the situation in India was still very uneasy.

She wrote to Lansdowne: 'She [the Queen] feels very uneasy at the state of India, lest these riots shd. increase and take a more dangerous form. The Native troops she believes to be faithful, the Native princes are very friendly, at least most of them and the Mahomedans generally support our rule.'[41]

The Queen felt that Lord Elgin was clever but inexperienced, and hoped he would be 'firm, prudent and cautious'. The Queen had been convinced by Karim that her Muslim subjects were far more loyal to the Crown than the Hindus. This was against the general line of the British administration's thinking at the time, as the Muslims were seen as the main agitators in the Indian Mutiny, since the uprising had been led in the name of the last Mughal Emperor, Bahadur Shah Zafar. The extent of Karim's influence on her is clear from her thoughts, which she expressed to the Viceroy: 'She thinks Mahomedans do require more protection than the Hindus, and they are decidedly by far the most loyal. Though the Mahomedans' cow killing is made the pretext for the [Hindus'] agitation, it is in fact, directed against us, who kill far more cows for our Army etc than the Mahomedans.'[42]

The Viceroy usually chose to ignore these inputs as he could not agree with the Queen's views. Instead, knowing Victoria's weakness for Karim, he tried to draw her delicately away from political comments and gave her some news that he knew would please her. He informed the Queen: 'The Viceroy had almost forgotten to tell your Majesty that while he was in Agra, he asked Sir John Tyler to bring the Munshi's father to see him. He is very well and full of devotion and gratitude to your Majesty.'

The Viceroy also informed her that he was shown at Agra Jail 'a large and very beautiful carpet which is being made for your Majesty. The design is extremely good and the Viceroy thinks your Majesty will be pleased with the carpet.'[43]

The Queen was delighted with this. She immediately informed Karim of the Viceroy's meeting with his father and replied that the visit had 'greatly gratified his good son', who wished his sincere thanks for the kindness to be conveyed to the Viceroy. She also added another request for the Viceroy:

The Doctor is about to retire from the service and to ask for his pension. He has served 36 years and has always borne the highest character, and was with the army under Lord Roberts on the celebrated march to Kandahar. The Queen would be very glad, were it possible, on his retirement from active and honourable service, to give him some reward, such as the title of Khan Bahadur.[44]

Before he left India, the Viceroy completed the last wish of the Queen. He wrote to tell her he had included Dr Wuzeeruddin's name in the list of New Year Honours.

Your Majesty's letter received just in time to include Dr W among the recipients of the honour which will be distributed on New Year's Day. The title of Khan Bahadur is one which under ordinary circumstances the Doctor cd not have ventured to expect, but it will be well understood in this country that he has obtained the distinction as much on account of the regard which yr Majesty feels for him and his family as for the services which he has rendered to the state.[45]

The Queen sent a delighted reply from Osborne on New Year's Day: 'Many thanks for kind wishes and reward to Dr Wuzeeruddin which is great pleasure to the son.'

The New Year had begun well for Karim. His father had received the equivalent of a Knighthood, and become Khan Bahadur. He broke the good news to his family and there were celebrations that evening in Arthur Cottage.

8

THE VICEROY RECEIVES
A CHRISTMAS CARD

That year in Europe the Munshi could be seen riding through the town in his own carriage with a footman on board. At the luxurious Villa Fabricotti in Florence, where the Queen stayed with her entourage, he was given a room on the first floor with large windows and sweeping views of the city's skyline. He shared the floor exclusively with the Queen, Prince and Princess Henry of Battenberg, Lady Churchill, Harriet Phipps and Dr Reid. Resentment for the Munshi grew in the ranks. The other Indian attendants were lodged in a detached tower in the grounds where they could enjoy complete seclusion and the privacy to cook their own meals. The Munshi moved in a different circle now. His name appeared regularly in the Court Circular and the Queen had allowed him to use the Billiard Room with the other gentlemen of the Household. They could not accept the fact that the Queen expected them to socialise with an Indian man who had once done menial jobs. John Brown had remained a servant till his last day, even though his closeness to the Queen was well known. But the Munshi had been elevated in rank and the Household found that intolerable.

Even Sir Henry Ponsonby, a man usually patient and tolerant, grew ballistic. 'The advance of the Black Brigade is a serious nuisance,' he wrote to Reid. 'I was afraid that opposition would intensify her [the Queen's] desire to advance further. Progression by antagonism.' The Royal family and the aristocracy that made up the Household had never shared the Queen's total lack of race or class barriers. With the Munshi, she was now pushing them to breaking point.

If the Munshi was aware of the deep-rooted ill-feeling towards him, he did not allow it to affect him. With the Queen as his protector and promoter, he continued to climb the social ladder. When the Queen's party arrived at Villa Fabricotti, the Munshi gave the Queen's courier, Dosse, an autographed manuscript which he asked him to publish in the *Florence Gazette*. He also gave him a photograph of himself taken by Royal photographers Byrne & Co. with instructions for the head to be made 'thinner and less dark'. The article, drafted by the Munshi himself, said that he 'belonged to a good and highly respectable family' and that all his family were in high positions in the government service, including his father who had been in the service for thirty-six years and a brother who was a City Collector. It also clarified that all the Indian attendants of the Queen worked under him.

The article was published in the *Florence Gazette* on 21 April 1894 with the brief that it had been requested by the Queen's Munshi to correct 'erroneous impressions being in circulation as to this gentleman's social status'. The Munshi also sent a large frame with ten cabinet photos to a shop in Florence to put up as a window display. It consisted of nine photographs of the Queen and the tenth one of him in the centre. Crowds of people looking into the shop window said he was a 'Principe Indiano' with whom the Queen was in love, hence the photo being put where it was. Once this was brought to the Household's notice, the Vice Consul, Placci, was sent to the shop and had the photo of the Munshi removed.

Reid decided it was time to go on the offensive against the Munshi. He wanted to show the Queen that Karim was resented not only by her Household, but by his own people as well. He prepared a nine-point dossier on him.[1]

The list of complaints included the fact that he had visited Rome for one night spending £22, that he had complained to the Queen about the position of his railway carriage from Bologna and that the Queen had given directives to Ponsonby that the Munshi could drive with the gentlemen of the Household on occasions. The Munshi had, moreover, apparently refused to allow other Indians in any part of the same railway carriage as himself and deprived Her Majesty's maids of the bathroom and insisted on having it entirely reserved for himself.

Reid also noted that the Queen's nurse and her dressers, Mrs Boyd and Mrs Keith, said that the Munshi's wife and mother-in-law were 'more degraded and dirty than the lowest labourers in England; spitting all over the carpets. Performing functions in the sitting room, etc.'

Another remark, heard by Arthur Bigge in the English Club, was also noted. Bigge reported that he had overheard a conversation about the Munshi where the gentlemen had remarked on his 'low appearance' and said that he was a man 'who in India would have no place anywhere but with menials'. The Englishmen were much astonished at his being with the Queen and surmised as to the meaning of it and who was responsible.

Reid recorded that when the Munshi had apparently complained to the Queen and to Dosse that the newspapers took too little notice of him, the Queen had responded by immediately sending her dresser, Mrs MacDonald, to Dosse with the command that 'he was to see that the newspapers took notice of and mentioned the Munshi more frequently!' The last point revealed more about the Queen than the Munshi.

Reid may have been peeved with the Munshi for personal reasons as well. A few months previously he had written to the Queen asking for a rise in his salary, saying he was quite overworked as he had to look after not just her health but also that of many of the members of staff and servants. The Queen in her reply made no mention of a salary increase, but told Reid that he should not listen to the constant applications made by the other servants as it would wear him out. She informed him that he still had to look after the Indians, who required him for they had 'different constitutions', but they were generally well and probably did not trouble him much anyway.[2] The Queen had asked him to reduce his extra duties rather than increase his salary. Reid might have felt irritated by the knowledge that the Queen would have reacted differently had the Munshi asked for something. She always put herself out for the smallest request made by him.

The problems with the Munshi carried on after the Royal suite left Florence for Coburg. The Queen was to attend the wedding of her granddaughter Victoria Melita of Saxe-Coburg-Gotha with the Grand Duke Ernest Ludwig of Hesse.

The Duke of Coburg informed Ponsonby that 'nothing would induce him to allow the Munshi to come to the chapel with the Q's suite for the wedding'. He instructed Ponsonby to tell the Queen this, putting it, if he wished, 'on the ground of his religion, if he needed to assign a reason other than the real one'.[3] This left the Queen 'most indignant' and she did everything she could to get a place for the Munshi with the Household. Negotiations continued for the whole day preceding the wedding and up to the forenoon, but the Duke remained firm. The Queen would not speak to the Duke, her son, personally about it, so the letters and pleas flew through Ponsonby. At last it was arranged that the Munshi would be taken to the gallery in the church by the son of one of the Duke's gentlemen, the Queen's condition being that 'there must be no servants there!' The Munshi, however, on reaching there, found that he recognised some of the grooms in the balcony. He stalked off in a fury and did not watch the ceremony, writing about it to the Queen who was given the letter after the couple left. She was greatly distressed by the episode and 'cried a great deal'. The incident became the main source of gossip for the servants and the Household, and Dosse spoke about it to Reid with glee, recalling the 'discomfiture of the Munshi, but of shame for the Queen'.[4]

The matter left the Queen more defiant and eager to protect her Munshi. She took the management of Karim's position out of Ponsonby's hands and gave it to Condie Stephen, the private secretary of the Duke of Coburg, with special instructions about how the Munshi was to be treated. Karim was now given his own Royal carriage with a footman on the box, and often had Bambridge sitting on his left. 'He was also invited to the State concerts etc, and was escorted in by Bambridge, but everyone avoided him,' recorded Reid in his diary.

While the Munshi did indeed invite some of the dislike of others by insisting on having pride of place at all events, it must have been fairly lonely and isolating for him to be the only brown man in a sea of white English aristocracy and European Royalty, all of whom made their opposition to him perfectly clear. The only person who stood by him was the Queen, and he in turn remained devoted to her. Every incident of the Household or her family revolting against her beloved Munshi would see the Queen only more determined to protect him.

Ponsonby, who had borne the brunt of the Coburg melodrama, went on holiday a few weeks later and wrote to Reid: 'I hope you like your holiday. I do very much and I have been able to forget the Munshi entirely.'

The campaign against the Munshi was spreading outside the close walls of the Royal family and Household. With leakages to the press and gossip in gentlemen's clubs, the matter was now beginning to appear in newspaper columns as well. The Munshi had a friend, Rafiuddin Ahmed, a lawyer and a journalist who wrote a piece praising the Munshi and the Queen's virtue of racial tolerance in the *Westminster Gazette*. It immediately evinced a response in the letters column:

Sir, – Rafiuddin Ahmed endeavours to show the cause why a native of India of the lower middle-class should be treated on an equality with the nobility of England. The Queen has an undoubted right to favour whom she likes, but is it not going too far when she expects her guests to associate with a man who is greatly their inferior, in rank at any rate? Perhaps Mr Rafiuddin Ahmed imagines that the unsophisticated and gullible radical believes a Munshi to be a prince or something of that sort in 'them foreign parts', but he knows, and I know, the intrinsic value of one in India. Mr Ahmad [sic] is perfectly aware of the fact that if his countryman was at this moment in his native city of Lahore he would most probably be sitting on a high stool in a government office, copying letters, or engaged in some such commendable but scarcely princely task on a stipend of 50s or 100s per mensem at the outside, and that if he ever had the good fortune to attend a Lieutenant-Governor's levee – leaving out of the question any Viceregal affair – his only means of doing so would be to enlist himself as a table servant.

I wonder what the Hyderabad nobles would say if the Nizam were to import a Board School assistant – whose position is far above a Munshi's – and expect them to play Tom, Dick and Harry with him. And the Nizam's in only a petty State. I am, Sir, your obedient servant,
Gore Ouseley Notting Hill April 5[5]

The Munshi was horrified at this public denunciation of his status and let the Queen know how he felt about it. The Queen, ever protective, scratched an angry note to Ponsonby:

The Queen wrote rather in a hurry when she mentioned to him the stupid ill natured Article or rather letter about the poor good Munshi and she wd. wish to observe that to make out that he is *low* is really *outrageous* and in a country like England quite out of place – She has known 2 Archbishops who were the sons respectively of a Butcher and a Grocer ... Abdul's father saw good and honourable service as a Dr. and he (Abdul) feels cut to the heart at being spoken of. It probably comes from some low jealous Indians or Anglo-Indians ... The Queen is so sorry for the poor Munshi's sensitive feelings.[6]

Ponsonby wrote wearily to his wife: 'As long as it was English or European work I got on fairly. But these Injuns are too much for me.'[7]

Though aware of the Household's antagonism to him, the Munshi had no idea that a dossier was being prepared on him. The complaints against him kept building up. In June, Ponsonby received a letter from Florence Hammond, a maid in Karim's household, who said that the Munshi had treated her 'unfairly' and that she was anxious to leave his service as soon as possible.[8]

Florence said she had agreed to work for the Munshi for £20 a year, a sum less than she had accepted before, but had taken the job after he told her in an interview that it would be increased after the first four months. However, when she reminded him after the period, he said he had no recollection of having said such a thing. She wrote:

I have to pay my own laundry expenses here, so my salary at the end of the year would amount to about £15 ... but the Munshi's code of honour being such a peculiar one that it not only allows him to break his word, but also open and read all through a letter addressed to me, and as he has also been very rude, I am naturally anxious to leave his house as soon as possible.

The letter was filed away by Reid as another example of the Munshi's unacceptable behaviour and unpopularity.

The Munshi's high annual expenditure on maintenance of Frogmore Cottage also became an issue, and the Master of the Household sent a memo to the Lord Chamberlain bringing to his notice the 'constant charge in excess of the usual expenditure ... on the furnishing and maintenance of Frogmore Cottage for the Munshi'. He pointed out that it had been agreed that after the initial expenses of refurbishing, the Munshi's residence would not cost more than £50 a year and that the housekeeper, Mrs Barnes, would receive £6 per annum for looking after it whenever Karim and his family were away.[9] This, however, was being clearly exceeded by the Munshi, who had spared no expense in redecorating his house and maintaining it at a high cost. He lived in style, decorating his house with exotic Indian artefacts and the numerous gifts that he had received from Royal visitors.

To the Queen, nevertheless, the Munshi remained faultless. She was delighted to receive his birthday card on 24 May 1894 and marvelled at how well his English had come along. He had written:

Munshi Abdul Karim presents his humble duty to your Majesty and humbly offers my best wishes for this day. I and my family pray for your Majesty's long life and happiness. They hope they will be able to see many many returns of this day.

I am your Majesty's most humble and obedient servant,

M. H Abdul Karim.

There were no spelling errors in the card. Either the Munshi's English had improved remarkably or he had a little help from his friend Rafiuddin in drafting the letter.

In August 1894 the Court Circular of *The Times* noted that Karim was invited in the Royal circle for a dinner party thrown in Osborne for the German Emperor, attended by the Prince of Wales, the Duke and Duchess of Connaught and several other dignitaries.

That October in Balmoral, Dr Reid found himself spending most of his time attending on the Munshi's wife. It wasn't easy for the doctor to treat the lady who remained in purdah. He recorded how he had felt her pulse for the first time, 'she being covered up in bed with hand projecting!'[10] For nearly three weeks the doctor walked to Karim Cottage twice a day to see her and reported later that she was finally improving. The Munshi's wife had a nurse in constant attendance. Reid also learnt from Alexander Profeit that the Munshi planned to publish two volumes of his memoirs in January the following year. He spoke immediately to Harriet Phipps about it, both of them agreeing that it 'must somehow be prevented'. The fact that no such volume was published meant the Household managed to successfully kill the project.

The Queen was a great letter writer. She liked to send written instructions to members of her Household and insisted that they write to her as well. All this meant a lot of paperwork for the Household, but they had no choice. She wrote regularly to the Viceroy, the Secretary of State for India and her extended family. Sitting at her desk – whether it was the brass-edged one in her sitting room which was always cluttered with innumerable trinkets, photos and memorabilia, or the field table under a tent in the gardens – the tiny figure of the elderly Queen could be seen writing endless letters on her black-lined notepaper, underlining some words for emphasis. Her plump fingers would move agitatedly over the paper when she was angry or upset, the rings and bracelets that she always wore glittering as she worked late into the night. She would never go to bed without completing her boxes and often worked for two hours after dinner. Sometimes she would sit late at night and look at the family photographs and those of her Indian servants, and arrange them in the velvet-lined albums. Her favourite was the blue velvet album with gold embossing in which she kept hand-coloured photographs of her Indians.

Over the years, the eyes grew dim and the handwriting virtually illegible, but her enthusiasm for letter-writing never ceased. Helping her with her papers, Karim became a letter-writer himself. He wrote regularly to the Queen and never missed congratulating her for a happy event in her life. Sometimes he would send her an ode, composed by an Urdu poet in India. When he travelled to India on holiday, he wrote to her every day, updating her on all developments.

When a boy was born to the Duke of York, Karim wrote the same night:

Munshi Abdul Karim presents his humble duty to your Majesty and beg [sic] to inform your Majesty that I am extremely pleased to hear this delightful news that the HRH Duchess of York safely delivered of a son tonight. I beg to offer my best congratulations to your Majesty for your Majesty's great grand child.

Also my wife and mother-in-law beg to offer their congratulations. They are so pleased to hear this good news. We all pray that God will grant this child long life, and all the happiness to his parents.

I am your Majesty's

Most humble and obedient servant

M.H. Abdul Karim[11]

That year, Karim decided to send a Christmas card to Lord Elgin, who had taken over as the Viceroy of India. He had had the privilege of meeting him at Balmoral the previous year when he came to call on the Queen. Little did Karim know that the card was going to cause a flutter. Karim wrote:

My dear Lord, Your Lordship was pleased to show me much kindness during my interview with you here last year. I hope your Lordship and Lady Elgin are quite well and have enjoyed your visit to the North Western Frontier of India.

I take the liberty of enclosing a Christmas Card, with best wishes for a happy new year and hope the same will meet your gracious acceptance.

With best respects,

I am your Lordship's,

Very faithfully,

M.H. Abdul Karim.

The card had a handwritten poem which the Viceroy considered most inappropriate. It read:

Flow'ers
Fair as the
Morning light
Wake for you
Tho' the earth
be white,

With hearts
Of gold,
And a breath of May,
And a wish from
My heart to yours
To day

The poem was by Ellis Walton and the inscription from Karim read: 'To Wish you a Happy Christmas, from M.H. Abdul Karim, Windsor Castle.'[12]

The Munshi had no idea that he had overstepped the limits of propriety. He informed the Queen that he had sent a Christmas card and she made enquiries about whether the Viceroy had liked the card, much to the embarrassment of officials at Whitehall, as Lord Elgin firmly refused to acknowledge it.

Meanwhile, there had been a change of guard in the Queen's Household. Henry Ponsonby had fallen seriously ill over the winter and Arthur Bigge had taken over as acting private secretary to the Queen. Bigge had never taken kindly to the Munshi and had already had a row with the Queen when she had suggested he be allowed to ride in the same carriage as the gentlemen of the Household. Henry Ponsonby's son, twenty-seven-year-old Frederick (Fritz) Ponsonby, had recently returned from India (where he had been ADC to the Viceroy Lord Elgin) to join the Household as junior equerry to the Queen.

Fritz Ponsonby, too, had had a bruising Munshi experience. He had gone into the Queen's black book after arguing with her over the official position of the Munshi's father in India. In 1894, when Fritz was still in India, the Queen had asked him to go and see the Munshi's father, the 'Surgeon General' in Agra. He called on Dr Wuzeeruddin and found that he was not the 'Surgeon General', but an 'apothecary at the jail', and repeated this to the Queen when he met her in London. The Queen 'stoutly denied' it and dismissed him saying he must have 'seen the wrong man'.[13] Fritz continued to insist that he was right. The Queen did not forgive him for several years, such was her passion for the Munshi and his family. She largely ignored him and did not invite him for dinner for a year. Both Bigge and Fritz Ponsonby now became part of the vocal anti-Munshi camp in the Household.

It fell to Fritz Ponsonby to find out about the fate of the Munshi's Christmas card to Lord Elgin. The junior equerry wrote to the Viceroy. The letter reveals how tangled the politics could get over something as simple as a Christmas card:

The Queen has sent to me and asked me to find out whether you had received the Xmas card from the Munshi. I thought this an excellent opportunity of telling her myself all about the Munshi, but Bigge, Edwardes and others strongly opposed my doing so as they thought that the Queen would be angry at messages being sent through me, that she would not listen to what I had to say and that it would take away from the effect of your letter.

The Queen's message to me was that I might find out through anyone on the staff or write straight to you so that if you think it best Babington Smith [personal secretary to the Viceroy] or Durand [also personal secretary to the Viceroy] could write to me a letter that I might show.

Miss Phipps, who is a sort of confidential secretary to the Queen, tells me that Lord Harris and Lord Wenlock returned the Xmas cards at least the Queen told her so. This makes it rather more difficult.

I only see the Queen after dinner when she chooses to send for me so that really I have no opportunity of talking to her. I am certain that if the facts of the case were explained to her by you she would understand.[14]

Fritz Ponsonby's plea was answered. A letter duly arrived from the Viceroy's office from his private secretary, A. Durand. It declared that the Viceroy had received the Christmas card and did 'not imagine that any acknowledgment was necessary, or that the Queen would expect him to send one'. He also stated that he need scarcely point out 'how impossible it would be for an Indian Viceroy to enter into correspondence of this kind'.[15] The matter simmered for a while, the Viceroy thinking that he should update an official of the India Office at Whitehall about the episode in case the Queen ever raised it again. Tearing himself away from matters of Indian administration, Elgin wrote to Henry Fowler, Secretary of State for India.

Dear Mr Fowler,

I asked Gadley to mention to you some time ago that I had received a Xmas card from the Queen's Munshi with a covering letter, and that I did not intend to answer, but had asked young Ponsonby, who had been my A.D.C., to say if asked, that I had received it.

I now enclose some correspondence from which you will see that H.M. is somewhat persistent and I ought to add that in a letter to Lady Elgin she enquired if I had received the card. I am quite ready to write myself if it will do any good. I am, however inclined to doubt it. H.M. would scarcely give up one of her favourite attendants because of anything I could say – and unless she did so little good would result.

If she writes to me direct, not being satisfied with the reply sent through Ponsonby I suppose I should have to speak out plainly, and it is in case this happens that I mention these circumstances – because I should be glad to know the

position you and Rosebery [Prime Minister] have taken up and be then guided
in my own.

Sincerely, Elgin.[16]

Though the Queen would have got an inkling of the Viceroy's reaction to the
card from the letter sent by his private secretary, she did not let the Munshi know
about these. He remained blissfully unaware that his card had caused such a furore
and had been sent back to Whitehall, where it lay in a government file marked
'Confidential'. As the year drew to a close, he made one of the first of his personal
entries in Urdu at the end of the Queen's Hindustani Journal:

> I owe gratitude to God that this auspicious year ended on an extremely happy
> note and, compared with all previous years, many more happy and memorable
> occasions took place in it. Firstly, the visit of Her Majesty to Coburg for attend-
> ing the marriage of Victoria Melita of Saxe Coburg Gotha and Grand Duke
> Ernest Ludwig of Hesse, and fixing of another marriage there itself, that of
> Princess Alice (Alix) of Hesse as Tsarevich of Russia which took place with
> great pomp and show on 26th of November 94. Secondly, the birth of the dear
> son of the Duke of York. The marriage that took place on 26th November this
> year occasioned the greatest joy as it led to more love between England and
> Russia. Her Majesty enjoyed good health in all respects, with the exception of
> some problem in hearing. But she did not change any of her daily routines and
> continued writing and reading of Hindustani which is evident from this book.
> Hence, I conclude this writing with the prayer that Allah may give Her Majesty
> as long age as that of Noah. Amen! Amen again!
>
> Humbly Abdul Karim.

It was as if the Queen and Karim had passed the year celebrating births and mar-
riages, the politics of the Court leaving them untouched.

On New Year's Day, the Queen began her eighth Hindustani Journal. 'This is
my eighth Hindustani lesson book which I began to keep and which I hope to
complete happily,'[17] she wrote in Urdu.

9

THE HOUSEHOLD
CONSPIRES

Knowing that the Queen would stand up for her Munshi at all costs, the Household and some members of the Royal family now began trying to discredit him for his association with fellow Muslim, Rafiuddin Ahmed. Ministers of the Crown and government officials soon became suspicious as well. Rumours were circulating that Rafiuddin had links to radical Muslim groups in Afghanistan and was a spy for the Amir of Afghanistan. Rafiuddin had surfaced in British politics in December 1892 as a journalist and a barrister. Born in 1865 in India and educated at the Deccan College, Poona (present-day Puné), he had travelled to London to study law at King's College. After a stint at the Middle Temple he was called to the Bar in 1892. He was a member of the Muslim League, a political organisation in India, and published several articles in the *Strand Magazine*, *Pall Mall Gazette* and *Black and White*.

An ambitious man, Rafiuddin had befriended Abdul Karim and through him won access to Queen Victoria. Through her offices and with the help of Karim, he had met the Lord Chancellor. He had managed to charm Victoria who gave him an example of her Hindustani Journal and a photograph of herself, which he published in the *Strand Magazine* in December 1892. The article praised the Queen for finding time to learn an oriental language and for making so much progress in the past three years that she could write a separate diary in the Hindustani language.

'For the first time in the history of Europe a Sovereign of a Great Power has devoted herself seriously to the literature of the Orient,'[1] wrote Rafiuddin Ahmed, describing how the Queen never failed to write her Hindustani diary no matter how much she was under pressure from work or personal anxieties and sorrows. The Queen, pleased with the young man, commissioned Swoboda to paint his portrait. When Britain was having difficulties with Turkey, she sent him as an ambassador to the Turkish Sultan, Abdul Hamid. She even recommended to the Foreign Office that he be appointed to the British Embassy in Constantinople and requested that the Prime Minister, Lord Salisbury, meet him, writing: 'I hear that Rafiuddin Ahmed is most anxious to see you. You know how serious for us in India wd. be injustice or supposed injustice on our part towards the Moslems, for I have more Mohammedan subjects than the Sultan. Pray see him as soon as you can.'[2]

The British establishment believed that Rafiuddin could be encouraging disenchanted elements in India in the freedom struggle. Discreet enquiries led to a report from the office of Charles A. Bayley, of the Thugee and Dacoity Department in India, who suggested that Rafiuddin may have been an informer who relayed messages to a contact in Calcutta, who forwarded it through various channels to the Amir in Kabul.

In April last, Sir A. Martin informed Mr Clarke, Assistant secretary in the Foreign Department, that Sardar Nasrulla Khan, when in England made an arrangement with Mr Rafiu-d-din of Gray's Inn, studying as a barrister, to forward information to Ghulam Miyyu-d-din of Bulbul Bazaar, Calcutta, who is general recipient in India of information for the Amir to whom it is forwarded through Abdu-r-Rauf Khan, Kotwal of Kabul, by whom in turn it is delivered over to H.H [His Highness]. Some of the most extraordinary stories thus find their way from English palaces to the Kabul court, and the dish, always more or less spicy, is obviously prepared to suit the assumed taste of the recipient. Hatred of everything English inspires the writer of these productions, who is well known to the Secret Police as a gentleman who is believed to make a good thing of trading on his friendship with the Queen's Munshi.[3]

The Household feared that the Queen was showing the Munshi her confidential papers from India and he was passing the information to Rafiuddin. Everything that the Munshi did was now closely observed and Rafiuddin's movements monitored. When Karim received an application from Messrs Nuthoo Ram and Sons of Agra to get the license 'By Special Appointment' for their shop, and forwarded it to Lord Carrington, the Lord Chamberlain, it was met with suspicion. After consultations, it was decided that it ought not to be allowed as it would 'strengthen the Munshi's position in India and give Rafiuddin and Co *increased* opportunities'.[4] Officials concluded that the Munshi had written directly to the Lord Chamberlain, instead of taking it up with Ponsonby, because he may have thought he 'would get round the thing without any communication with us'.

Fritz Ponsonby, who had been sidelined by the Queen over the issue of the exact rank of the Munshi's father, was one of the lead players in the move to discredit Karim. The young Ponsonby had not inherited his father's patience or diplomatic skills. A former Etonian and an officer in the Grenadier Guards, Ponsonby had enjoyed his term in India and wanted to serve in the North-

West Provinces, but he had been somewhat reluctantly recalled to England. His father's illness meant he had to take on the job of assistant personal secretary to the Queen and come into direct contact with Karim. Ponsonby went quickly on the offensive and wrote a long and confidential note to his former boss, the Viceroy, updating him on the affairs of the Munshi. He informed him that not only was the Household ranked against the Munshi, but also the Royal family, including Princess Louise, Princess Beatrice and Prince Henry, disliked his position in Court. They had all spoken to the Queen about it and Lord Rosebery and Fowler had done their best to explain to her the state of affairs, but she would not listen to any of them and it was useless to try.

'The Munshi occupies very much the same position as John Brown used to,' wrote Ponsonby. He also informed the Viceroy that both his and Lady Elgin's letters were apparently given to the Munshi to read and that he retailed all the news back to India. Ponsonby said there had been two rows in the Household lately, one when Edwards refused to go to tea with the Munshi and the other when Dr Reid refused to take the Munshi's father round the hospitals in London. In both cases the Queen refused to listen to what they had to say but was very angry, 'so as you see the Munshi is a sort of pet like a dog or cat which the Queen will not willingly give up'.

Ponsonby urged the Viceroy to explain to the Queen that it was not sensible to elevate the Munshi to the position of confidential adviser and also explain to her the feelings in India with regard to him, as this may be the only thing that would work. He informed the Viceroy that the Munshi took 'a very prominent part' at the tableaux and that a seat in the audience next to the lady-in-waiting (much to her disgust) was reserved for him by order of the Queen. 'The Khitmadgar on duty helps the Queen to walk into dinner and even into chapel here so you will see how great is her opinion of all the natives here,' wrote Ponsonby. 'I have now got to think it lucky that the Munshi's sweeper does not dine with us.'[5]

Ponsonby had fired the first salvos against the Munshi directly to the Viceroy's office. Elgin, already annoyed by the Christmas card fiasco, lent him a sympathetic ear. His dislike of the Munshi was further cemented when he received a letter from Mr Gadley at the India Office in Whitehall, who warned him that his letters to the Queen were likely to be read by Karim. Gadley said that Elgin had been perfectly right in declining to write to the Queen about the Christmas card.

Gadley informed Elgin that Fowler had suggested he 'take note of the fact that the Queen does show your letter to this gentleman', and that he should be careful as to what he put into them. He told him that Crosthwaite had been telling him some curious things about the Queen's correspondence with the Munshi, specimens of which he appeared to have seen. 'I suppose you know the sort of thing,'[6] warned Gadley.

A week later he wrote another letter to Elgin at the request of Fowler. He said that it was Mr Fowler's opinion that the matter was not serious. 'The position which this gentleman occupies is ... tiresome, and makes care and caution necessary, but he Mr Fowler, does not regard it as anything worse than this,' wrote Gadley. 'Of course, those who correspond with the Queen on Indian matters must reckon with the fact that he will *probably* see their letters. This is a bore, but if you and the Secretary of State know it beforehand, you can write accordingly.'[7]

Though Fowler had dismissed the Munshi as more of an irritant than an actual danger, the Household remained unconvinced. Members of the Royal family, like the Prince of Wales, Princess Beatrice and Princess Louise, were also up in arms against him. None dared tell their mother about him, so they put pressure on the Household and ministers. Their ire at the Munshi was understandable. The Queen never failed to tick off her children if she felt they had not been courteous to Karim. She wrote a stern letter to her granddaughter-in-law, Princess May, wife of George, Duke of York, after receiving a complaint from the Munshi that the couple had not acknowledged a present sent to them for their baby in the proper way. The Queen wrote angrily:

> The Munshi told me that he had heard from one of your gentlemen that the Indian gentleman who had sent this present to the Baby was to be thanked by the Secretary of State. This upset him a good deal, and I must say with *right* for it was a *private present* sent *through* his *father*, who is the *intimate* friend of the Indian gentleman who would otherwise *not* have offered it &, who sent it to *me* for the little boy through the Munshi's father, & the Munshi himself. Therefore, to have this private present thanked for, *ignoring* the person who was charged to send it would be a great offence.

She commanded the young Royals to have a letter written in their names and sent directly to her the very next day. 'I am sure you and Georgie will at once see that this is no *state* affair and would only hurt my good Munshi and his worthy father very much if they were ignored,'[8] she wrote.

Under the close scrutiny of everybody, the Munshi sailed with the Queen for her annual spring holiday to Europe. This year the destination was Nice. The Queen was returning to the French Riviera. The *Pall Mall Gazette* noted that the Queen's servants, horses, carriages, plates, household linen, furniture for her bedroom and other heavy luggage were sent ahead by special trains from Calais. A private telegraph office was also fitted up in the hotel for the Queen's house and separate quarters were arranged for the Indian attendants. A kitchen was to be built especially for the Indians in the grounds of the hotel. The Queen would always see to it that every need of the Indian attendants was met.

In an article titled 'Royalty at the Battle of Flowers', a local newspaper reported:

Nice, March 21:

The 1st Battle of Flowers of the season took place today and was one of the most superb known for many years.

The English royalties arrived at three o'clock ... and the Munchi [sic] in a carriage by himself. All took up their positions in a specially prepared tribune and joined the fight at 3.30. The Queen watched for one hour and many flowers were thrown to her.[9]

The Battle of Flowers held on the Promenade des Anglais in Nice was one of the Queen's favourite festivals. As young army officers in the crowds threw bouquets at her, she threw them back with enthusiasm. She also had her own bunch of flowers supplied by the Mayor of Nice and threw them at the crowds. She rode in her carriage to the nearby Villa Liserb where she saw two Indian jugglers 'perform some very clever tricks' and was 'very pleased'. The Munshi immediately arranged that they visit London and attend the Empire Exhibition, which was to be held in Earl's Court in summer.

When the Queen returned to her villa, there was slight excitement as there was an outbreak of a fire in the chimney of the apartment occupied by the Munshi. However, following the prompt action by Monsieur Paoli, Mr Greenham, the servants of the Household and the hotel attendants, the outbreak was quickly extinguished without damage. Reports of the fire were sent out by Reuters news agency and picked up by newspapers around Britain and France.

The Munshi enjoyed the trips to the Riviera and the special attention he inevitably attracted. Always prickly about his status vis-à-vis the other Indian attendants, he had been upset when a local newspaper wrote that he had helped the Queen out of her carriage and conveyed his hurt to the Queen. *The Galignani Messenger* immediately carried a clarification of the Munshi's position:

By telegraphic error it was made to appear that the Munshi assisted the Queen from her carriage on her arrival at Nice, which was of course not the case, as Her Majesty is always assisted by an Indian servant. The Munshi, as a learned man and the Queen's Indian Secretary and preceptor in Hindustani, is one of the most important personages '*auprès de la Reine*' having several men under him, and being often privileged to dine with his Royal Mistress and pupil.[10]

A few weeks later, much to the Munshi's delight, there was a piece on him in the local French newspaper complete with a sketch of his. The French called him 'Le Munchy' and described him as '*le professor de la reine*' (the Queen's teacher).[11] He was also described as being in charge of Her Majesty's correspondence and

C'est son portrait que nous publions ci-des-sous, dessiné par Douhin d'après une photo-graphie de M. A.-L. Henderson, photographe attitré de la reine d'Angleterre.

Le Munchy, secrétaire indien de S. M. Britannique
Voici maintenant quelques détails biogra-phiques qui intéresseront certainement nos lecteurs :

Article on Karim in a French newspaper, including a sketch of the Munshi.

classifying her documents on Indian affairs. The article said that his qualities had made the Queen appoint him her Indian Secretary and that he had been chosen because he could be trusted and relied upon.

The Household was incensed when the article appeared, not least because they themselves were hardly ever noticed or commented on by the European media. Fritz Ponsonby sent the cutting to the Viceroy, Lord Elgin, with the note: 'I send you a cutting from a French newspaper, apparently the details have been supplied by the Munshi himself.'[12]

When the Queen's suite moved to Darmstadt in Germany, she gave the Munshi a special note of recommendation to give to her daughter Vicky, Empress Frederick, asking her to show him around the Palace.

1. Portrait of Abdul Karim by Rudolf Swoboda. (The Royal Collection © 2009 HM Queen Elizabeth II)

Clockwise from above

2. Portrait of Abdul Karim by Heinrich Von Angeli.
(The Royal Collection © 2009 HM Queen
Elizabeth II)

3. Queen Victoria, 1887. (The Royal Collection ©
2009 HM Queen Elizabeth II)

4. Abdul Karim and Mohammed Buksh,
hand-coloured photo. (The Royal Collection ©
2009 HM Queen Elizabeth II)

5. The Household – Top row standing (*left to right*): Sir James Reid, Sir Fleetwood Edwards, Marie Mallet, maid of honour, Lord Cross, Secretary of State for India; bottom row (*left to right*) Emily Lock (Princess Helena's lady-in-waiting), Ethel Cadogan, Fritz Ponsonby (legs crossed), Hon. Alexander Yorke, Master of Ceremonies for Royal Theatricals, Lady Ampthill (Queen's lady-in-waiting); 12 June 1897. (Courtesy of Reid Archives)

6. Hand-painted photo of Abdul Karim, 1887–88. (The Royal Collection © 2009 HM Queen Elizabeth II)

7. Signed photograph of Abdul Karim in tweeds in Balmoral. (Courtesy of Reid Archives)

8. The Garden Cottage in Balmoral. (Author photograph)

9. Durbar Hall, Osborne. (Courtesy of English Heritage)

10. Arthur Cottage, the Munshi's house in Osborne. (Courtesy of Reid Archives)

11. Tableau of *An Indian Scene*, Karim and other Indians. (Courtesy of Reid Archives)

12. Tableau of *Empire*, with Princess Helena, Princess Beatrice, Abdul Karim and other Indians. (Courtesy of Reid Archives)

13. Tableau of *Rebecca At The Well*, Abdul Karim and other Indians. (Courtesy of Reid Archives)

14. Tableau of *Rebecca At The Well*, Abdul Karim and Minnie Cochrane. (Courtesy of Reid Archives)

15. Tableau of *King of Egypt*, Abdul Karim as King with Ghulam Mustafa, Sheikh Chidda, Khuda Buksh and others as envoys from Ethiopia. (Courtesy of Reid Archives)

16. Tableau of *Semiramis*: Princess Beatrice, Lady Katherine Meade, Ethel Cadogan, Abdul Karim with Ghulam Mustafa, Sheikh Chidda and Khuda Buksh and others. (Courtesy of Reid Archives)

17. Study of portrait of Abdul Karim, 1891. (Courtesy of Reid Archives)

18. Riding in Scotland – Abdul Karim on horseback behind the Queen's carriage. (Courtesy of Reid Archives)

19. The Queen's tent at the Highland Games, with Indian servants on side, Balmoral, 8 September 1898. (The Royal Collection © 2009 HM Queen Elizabeth II)

20. Widow's Cottage at Glassalt Shiel, Loch Muick, 1895. (The Royal Collection © 2009 HM Queen Elizabeth II)

21. Abdul Karim at his desk with photo of Queen Victoria. (The Royal Collection © 2009 HM Queen Elizabeth II)

22. Queen Victoria with her Indian attendants, Sheikh Chidda and Ghulam Mustafa. (The Royal Collection © 2009 HM Queen Elizabeth II)

23. The controversial photograph published in *The Graphic* of Queen Victoria and the Munshi in the Garden Cottage in Balmoral, 1895. Note Karim looking at the camera. (The Royal Collection © 2009 HM Queen Elizabeth II)

24. Abdul Karim, signed photograph. (Courtesy of Reid Archives)

25. The Munshi and his nephew, Mohammed Abdul Rashid, 1897. (The Royal Collection © 2009 HM Queen Elizabeth II)

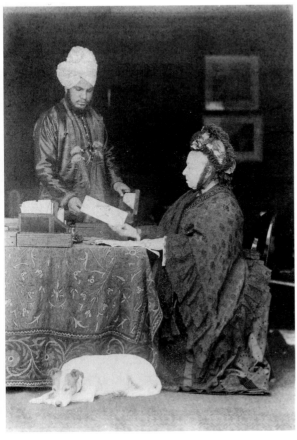

26. Queen Victoria and the Munshi in the Garden Cottage, Balmoral, 1890. (The Royal Collection © 2009 HM Queen Elizabeth II)

27. Balmoral Castle. (Author photograph)

28. Windsor Castle. (Author photograph)

29. Queen Victoria's Diamond Jubilee Portrait. (The Royal Collection © 2009 HM Queen Elizabeth II)

30. The Munshi's grave in Agra (centre), his father's grave to the left and wife's to the right. (Author photograph)

31. The mausoleum over the Munshi's grave in Agra. (Author photograph)

If the *Munshi* is able to go tomorrow, you wld. kindly remember that he is my Indian secretary and considered as a gentleman in my suite and that as you kindly proposed Herr Walter would show him about & especially let him see the charming House. He can take no meat and only a little milk and fruit cld. be offered him. If Herr V Reischach shld. happen to be at home perhaps he wld just see him for a minute, I hope I am not troublesome?[13]

On their return from Nice, the Queen decorated the Munshi with the CIE (Companion of the Indian Empire). He now wore several medals on his chest at Court functions, including the Star of India (1890) and the Order of the Red Eagle given by the Kaiser in 1890. The Household disapproved thoroughly and tried their best to dissuade her, but the Queen rarely listened to their opinions on the Munshi. Instead, she gushed over him in her usual way, taking a stream of visitors to call upon his wife. When the Munshi's cat had kittens, the Queen was most excited and informed her ladies-in-waiting. Lady Churchill was interested in having one of them and the Queen scribbled a note to Karim:

Lady Churchill and Miss Phipps wd. like to call on 'Mr Munshi' between *12 and one* and the former choose a kitten. This cd. then be sent over to Lady Churchill's place near here as soon as it can leave its mother.

If the weather is like today – please come up here at 1/2 p.10.

If it shd. be *hot* I wd. telephone down to you not to come up, but to join me at the Tea Cottage.

Your affte Mother, VRI.[14]

In June the Munshi's mother-in-law fell ill and Reid had to attend to her. Reid once commented that every time he visited the Munshi's house, a different tongue would be stuck out for him from behind the purdah. Later, Tyler, who was visiting England, was also sent by the Queen to look her up and feel her pulse. 'He knows the family well and their peculiar nature,' the Queen wrote to Reid, to explain the visit.

Reid took the opportunity of Tyler's visit to have another conversation with him about the Munshi. Even though Tyler had a somewhat tainted reputation following the revelations by the Viceroy and the controversial business of his promotion, Reid took his views on the Munshi seriously and kept detailed notes in his diary:[15] Tyler was clearly jealous that Karim – a humble clerk chosen by him – was rapidly going from position to position in the Royal Household and had now been honoured with the CIE. While seated next to Reid at a Household dinner Tyler told him that the Queen had a made a vital mistake in giving the Munshi the CIE, that he was a man of very low origin and of no education and that he was never anything but a 'Khitmadgar' in which capacity he was sent to London. Tyler said that the idea of Karim being considered a gentleman was most ludicrous to those who knew him. He also informed Reid that accounts of him published by Rafiuddin Ahmed in *Black and White* and other magazines were false, and that Rafiuddin was a clever but unscrupulous and dangerous man 'who ought never under any pretext to be admitted into any of the Queen's houses'. Tyler said that Rafiuddin used the Munshi as a tool for his own purposes, and that when he had served his purpose, he would be the first man to expose him and turn him into ridicule with the public.

Fritz Ponsonby, meanwhile, wasted no time in relaying to the sympathetic Elgin the adverse reactions in the government and the Household to the Munshi's new honour. 'Mr Fowler [Secretary of State for India] and Lord Rosebery [Prime Minister] tried very hard to persuade the Queen not to give the Munshi the CIE but she wouldn't listen to them.' While running down the Munshi, Fritz Ponsonby had no qualms in requesting the Viceroy in the same letter to consider his elder brother, John Ponsonby, for a job at his office in India, saying his brother had spent the last two years at the Cape and though he had a 'slight impediment in his speech, this did not in any way prevent his being able to run Govt House at the Cape single handed'.[16]

It wasn't everybody who was opposed to the Munshi's CIE, however. The Munshi received a congratulatory letter from Lord Breadalbane, who belonged to the Campbell clan, one of Scotland's great landowning families with their baronial estate at Taymouth Castle, and was the Lord Steward of Her Majesty's Household. A copy of the letter was sent to Reid.

Harcourt House
Cavendish square
23/6/95

Dear Munshi,

I was so very sorry I did not have the opportunity when at Balmoral of congratulating you on your well earned honor Her Majesty has conferred upon you. A CIE, CSI or CB are all distinctions any one should be proud to possess as they are only given for service and were I ever fortunate enough to have any one of them offered to me, I should feel as I have no doubt you do, proud of such a mark of our Queen's favour.

I send you a photo of myself and would much like if you would have some time or send me one of yourself.

Yr truly
Breadalbane[17]

The Queen and the Munshi remained unfazed by the criticism around them. Both were unaware that Reid was compiling a dossier on Karim and that Fritz Ponsonby was complaining about him to the Viceroy and the Secretary of State, and that letters concerning them were circulating in Whitehall. They were pre-occupied with other things that summer. The Empire of India Exhibition was running through the summer at Earl's Court in London. The Munshi had organised for the two Indian jugglers, who the Queen had enjoyed seeing in Villa Liserb, to come to London for the exhibition. He also arranged for the entire party of 112 members, who had arrived from India and Burma for the exhibition, to visit the Queen at Windsor. One Sunday morning in July, the whole troop came to Windsor. They were conducted across the quadrangle to the Victoria Tower and assembled in a group beneath the windows of the Oak Room, where the Queen acknowledged their presence with a gracious bow. Princess Alexandra and Princess Ena of Battenberg, the Queen's granddaughters, stood with them in the courtyard. Victoria stood at the window and asked the Munshi to tell her the names and the different castes of the visitors. She then received one of the natives, a resident of Bombay called Ardesher, who presented her with an exquisitely carved silver rosewater bottle and a bouquet of roses, carnations and maiden-hair fern. After offering his gift, Ardesher pronounced an Indian blessing on the Queen. The delegation were then conducted to St George's Hall and given a tour of some of the state apartments. The Queen was said to be very pleased with the rosewater bottle and the devotion of her subjects.

Early in September, the Royal train wound its way to Scotland as the Queen journeyed to her Highland home. The *Aberdeen Journal* reported the arrival of the party:

> The black attendants were, as usual, turbaned and smiling. The Munshi Abdul Karim's lady arrived in a saloon by the ordinary forenoon train. She was closely veiled, and on her arrival was quickly bundled into a closed carriage. Last year this lady had her first taste of Balmoral, and as may easily be supposed, the climate did not suit her. She had also her first taste of a male doctor, Dr Reid, as he then was, who found some difficulty in diagnosing the case from the hand extended through a curtain for his inspection.[18]

The Munshi was not the only one who had been honoured that summer. James Reid had been made a baronet and was now addressed as 'Sir James'. Over the next few years, 'Ask Sir James' became one of the Queen's constant phrases as the doctor was drawn into various Court issues regarding the Munshi, all quite beyond his duties as a doctor.

Lady Lytton, widow of the former Viceroy to India, Lord Lytton, now took up employment in the Palace as the Queen's lady-in-waiting, and she too arrived in Balmoral to take up her duties. As was customary, the Queen wanted to take her to Karim Cottage to see the Munshi's wife.

The hills of Scotland reminded Lady Lytton of the mountains in India and she told the elderly Queen this. The Queen spoke to her about her favourite Indian, the Munshi: 'Her Majesty spoke of the Munshi for the first time, and wished me to see him and his wife,' wrote Lady Lytton. The Munshi had once been presented to her late husband, Lord Lytton, at Grasse. The Queen had a detailed discussion about India with Lady Lytton and told her that she wished the Muslims would be left alone by the Christian missionaries. Lady Lytton did not quite agree with this view and it left her concerned about whether the Queen discussed these things with the Munshi, which she felt was 'a risk'.

Her account of the first meeting with Karim is recorded in her diary:

The Queen wished me to go and see Mrs Karim and the Munshi at their house, so Miss Phipps came with me. She is a nice little woman and had such a pretty native dress and jewels. He came in very jauntily after a bit and put out his hand á l'Anglaise, so of course we took it, but we did not sit down and we did not stay long.

I wrote my name in his book where many Royalties have written. I wonder what he writes home to his country?[19]

The Munshi's guestbook was a truly exotic collection of names of various European Royals, diplomats, officials, lords and ladies. His cottage was decorated with many gifts given to him by visiting Royals from the Continent and included an exclusive gold and enamel tea set presented by the Emperor of Russia. He was now very much part of the Queen's close circle. At a dinner for the King of Portugal in Balmoral, he was included in the Royal circle with the gentlemen of the Household.[20] Lord Wolseley, who had succeeded the Duke of Cambridge as Commander-in-Chief, recounted how on being summoned to Balmoral after his appointment, he was riding up from Ballater station in a hired carriage when he was astonished to see 'the Munshi drive by taking the air in a Royal carriage'.[21]

Back in India, the Munshi's father was also moving in quasi-Royal circles. As a recipient of the honour of Khan Bahadur, he was invited to the Viceroy's Durbar in Agra and brushed shoulders with local gentry and Maharajahs. The Munshi's family members were also promoted, causing a ripple in the Viceroy's office and annoying Elgin.

'How did it happen – by whose authority that the brother became a *tahsildar* without examination?' thundered Elgin, who was already irritated with the Munshi following the Christmas card fiasco and the reports from Ponsonby.

Of course they will become rich: that doesn't so much matter: but I feel from the danger lies chiefly in the fact that in India more than anywhere else, the supposed possession of influence may be used to get money out of more or less important people, as that this may be worked not only by the Munshi but by the Munshi's friends, about whom there is some uneasiness.

It must be a bother, I am afraid and an anxiety to you, but I hope as have said before, that Sir H Fowler's view that it is a troublesome but not a serious matter may be verified.[22]

Lord Hamilton had barely taken up his new job as Secretary of State for India replacing Henry Fowler when he was being flooded with letters and complaints about the Munshi. He replied briefly to Elgin that he was disturbed to learn about the exaltation of the Munshi's family and the fact that they had been given promotions.

In November 1895 Sir Henry Ponsonby died, succumbing to his long illness. The Queen wrote to his daughter Magdalen:

There is one person who feels your beloved Father's loss more than anyone, and whose *gratitude* to him is *very deep*, and that is my good Munshi Abdul Karim. Your dear father was kinder to him than anyone, always befriending him, and the loss to him is, as he says, that of 'a *second* Father'. He could not well go to the funeral tomorrow to his regret, but sends a wreath, and I enclose what he wrote on it as I fear in the multitude of similar wreaths this tribute of gratitude might be overlooked.[23]

Magdalen wrote to Reid, enclosing the Queen's letter, asking: 'If you think I ought to write to the Moonshi [sic], I will if you think it is expected of me, and that the Q. wishes it. I don't want to start him as a brother.' Reid told her not to, saying that the wreath was made in the garden on the Queen's special command and that she dictated what was to go in it. Yet, there was no doubt that Henry Ponsonby had been kinder to the Munshi than his successor, Arthur Bigge, or his son Fritz Ponsonby would ever be, and the Munshi was aware of this.

As Karim continued to be decorated, rewarded and protected by the Queen, the media became fascinated by him and soon the Munshi featured in lengthy newspaper articles. On 19 December 1895 *The Times* newspaper carried an article on Karim titled 'The Queen's Munshi Follows his Sovereign to Osborne'. In the flowery language of the Royal reporter, it covered the journey made by Abdul Karim and his family, their cat and the canary, across the Solent to Osborne House, describing his unique semi-regal position in the Royal Court.

The Munshi Abdul Karim came to England as the Queen's personal attendant and instructor in Hindoostani. Her Majesty, having acquired the language, has promoted Abdul Karim to be her private secretary for India, and he now occupies a position as regards India corresponding to that held for the United Kingdom by the late Sir Henry Ponsonby. He has his own apartments, his personal staff and is admitted to the drawing room with the gentlemen of the court. No longer does the Queen rest upon his arm when moving from room to room, but she rests upon his judgment when she is in communication with the subject princes of the Great Empire beyond the seas and Abdul Karim Knows His Own Importance.

Yesterday the Queen traveled from Windsor to Osborne. So did AK. For the Sovereign, the *Alberta* was the detailed yacht, for the dusky secretary the *Elfin*. Like his Sovereign he is a stickler for secrecy and like her, too, he is very human. He never travels without his Scotch attendant, he has a horror of salutes; and though he courts ceremony it must not be ostentatious. The Queen has her animal attachments and the donkey is her favorite; the Munshi takes a lower ground, but his cat and his canary go with him wherever he travels.

The Munshi stands some six feet in height, speaks broken English in a melodious voice, and interprets to his wife and mother in law who are so veiled and draped as to resemble moving automata, and as they pass down the *Elfin* they vanish out of sight of the porters, who are the only spectators of the passage of the singular Oriental who has a rooted antipathy to the gaze of the vulgar. Yet to look upon his face and hear his voice one would think that the Munshi could tame lions and silence tigers. But he has an exalted position and fully recognizes his own importance. For the Munshi is the only member of the Queen's personal staff who is allowed to travel in semi-regal state.[24]

The Munshi could not have asked for more.

There were other articles on the Munshi in the newspapers and magazines. Never had an Indian been so profiled in the media. The Munshi pasted one of the clippings from *Black* in the Queen's Hindustani Journal as part of his annual year-end entry. The article carried a picture of him and the cottages given to him by the Queen: Frogmore Cottage in Windsor, Arthur Cottage in Osborne and Karim Cottage in Balmoral.

The article concluded: 'By the decoration of the CIE just conferred by her Majesty upon the Indian Secretary, is marked the value placed upon his services.'[25] The article eulogised Karim and said he was a well-wisher of the people and helped his relations, orphans and the poor, mixed with people of other religions in London and still kept his own faith.

Karim ended the year on another high note. He wrote:

Now at the close of this eighth volume of Her Majesty's Hindustani lessons, her humble teacher the Munshi would again lift up his voice in thankfulness to His God for his mercies.

To tell of all the kindnesses & honours received of God through Her Gracious Majesty is quite beyond his power. Their name is legion. But the Munshi must chronicle with deepest gratitude and humility how that his father has been made a Khan Bahadur by the Govt of India for his 40 years of able and faithful service, and how that Her Majesty recognizing the increasing duties of her Munshi in taking the charge of various important papers & in undertaking the arrangements for the service of Indian Attendants, has been fit to honour him with the title of CIE and this she did on her last happy birthday, the 77th of her age, and the 58th of her reign.

The past year like all years, has had its joys and its sorrows, but on the whole I think it has been a happy year for Her Majesty. There has been it is true the death of the mother of Prince Henry of Battenberg and likewise the death of the old Highland Attendant of Her Majesty, Francis Clark, but these events sad as they were have been outweighed by the joyful news which has come of the betrothals of Princess Alexandra of Coburg and of Princess Maud of Wales. This last engagement has been eagerly looked for and it is certain was hailed with great pleasure by the Queen.

In the future English history will tell us of an important event of the past year viz the visit of H.H Nasrullah Khan, son of the Ameer of Afghanistan as the guest of the Queen and the Royal Family. Again we shall read with interest and pleasure of the visit of Don Carlos, King of Portugal, as the guest of Her Majesty at Balmoral. Scotland indeed is glad and proud to receive this friendly visit of a foreign potentate.

The Munshi prays for the long life and happiness of Her Majesty and the members of the Royal Family through whom he had the honour of being presented to the Royal guest from Portugal.

Lastly, happy was the day that brought the glad tidings to Her Majesty of the birth of a daughter on the 18th of November last to the Empress of all the Russians.

The last sorrow also was a great, the loss of Her Majesty's good, kind and true friend, Sir Henry Ponsonby's death on the 21st November last.

I am my readers, obedient servant, H. Abdul Karim.
December 2, 1895[26]

Remarkably free of spelling or major grammatical errors, the entry in English in Karim's handwriting showed that the Munshi had made great progress and had nearly mastered the Queen's language.

10

REBELLION IN
THE RANKS

The Munshi was to be shadowed. Though opinion was still divided in the government on how dangerous he was, he was visiting India, and the Viceroy wanted his movements carefully tracked.

'The Munshi is coming out. I am not sure about the exact date, but about this time,'[1] an excited Lord Elgin wrote to Lord Sandhurst, the Governor of Bombay. He advised him to be cautious in following the Munshi and asked him to report back if any of the 'intriguers' in the native states and elsewhere who were 'generally watched by the British government' made any attempt to approach him.

Elgin had received the clearance from Whitehall to follow the Munshi, but advised extreme caution. He was clear that while no steps were to be taken that could be seen to 'show a dislike for the Munshi personally', general information about visitors and the like could be easily obtained. The whole matter was conducted in hushed tones and confidential telegrams. Elgin wrote personally to Sandhurst so that 'no written instructions need issue to any police officer'. He informed Sandhurst that the Munshi could be contacted by 'the certain gentleman' he had mentioned while in Bombay. 'My object therefore is to ask you to do what you can with as little stir as possible,' the Viceroy said. 'You will understand that mistaken zeal in this case might do more harm than good and would be capable of any amount of misrepresentation.'

Earlier, in February 1896, Hamilton, who had just taken over from Henry Fowler as Secretary of State for India, had told Elgin that he did not think the Munshi was 'as dangerous' as some believed and that the Prime Minister, Lord Salisbury, concurred with that view. 'He [the Munshi] is a stupid man,' wrote Hamilton. 'And on that account he may become a tool in the hands of other men.'[2] However, Hamilton clearly thought it worthwhile to ask for surveillance orders on the Munshi, but he clarified that this would have to be done with extreme caution as it could backfire if the Queen got to know. He wrote:

> I think that you would be justified in keeping such general notice of his pro-
> ceedings as to enable you to determine whether or not anything unusual is
> going on and if there are signs of a proper agenda of intrigue to have recourse
> to closer supervision. I should be inclined to restrict at first to a very general
> and unobtrusive supervision … It would be better to err on the side of laxity
> than of vigour of watch at first.

Elgin, too, was worried that if it was discovered they were unnecessarily trailing the Munshi, it could do more harm to the authority of the Indian government than 'any amount of underhand intrigue'. About the Queen, he felt: 'The older anyone becomes the less reasonable they are to argument in anything effecting the personality of a favourite.'[3]

Meanwhile, the New Year had begun gloomily in Osborne House. Prince Henry of Battenberg, husband of Princess Beatrice and the Queen's youngest son-in-law, died of fever on 20 January. He had gone to West Africa to join the Ashanti expedition just over a month ago, but had contracted high fever and died at sea on his way back. His death left the Queen distraught. She had been very fond of her son-in-law, called Liko by the family, who had lived under her roof after the wedding. She relied on him much more than she did on her son and heir, Bertie. With two of her daughters widowed, the Queen felt helpless. The body arrived at Portsmouth and, after the funeral on the Isle of Wight, the Queen sent Beatrice and the four children to Cimiez to recover at the Villa Liserb. She would join them later in the spring.

The Munshi, who always stood by her side like a rock on these tragic occasions, was also to go on leave soon. He was granted annual leave every two years. The Queen would miss him terribly as he would be away for six months. It was with a mournful heart and without Karim that she set out for Europe to revisit Cimiez. Both were unaware that the Munshi was to be watched.

Karim landed in Bombay in March carrying the sword and two rifles given to him by the Queen. He sailed through Customs without any encumbrances, as the Queen had ensured that all permissions were given beforehand. By the time Lord Sandhurst got the telegram from Elgin, Karim had already left Bombay and was on his way to Agra.

On 20 March, two days after the Munshi had landed, a confidential memo from Government House Bombay to the Viceroy reported: 'The visitor from enquiries I made apparently passed through and I don't know where he has gone, but I shd. think most likely to Agra.'[4] The Munshi, it seems, had not tried to communicate with any 'suspicious person'. He did not call on Sandhurst, either; something the Governor General had been secretly dreading. He told Elgin he was relieved he did not have to meet him and that he was sorry that the Munshi and his brother were causing trouble. Sandhurst, however, felt that it wasn't a 'serious' matter at present.

The close watch on the Munshi continued, but he was always ahead of the powers that were tailing him. He relaxed in his family home in Agra, drove around like a nawab in his carriage and made enquiries about purchasing the land adjoining the vast stretch that the Queen had already bestowed on him. The land ear-marked by him was 143 acres of prime government land. It would make the Munshi and his family wealthy landowners in Agra, adding property to the already swelling number of honours being bestowed on him by the Queen. His wife and mother-in-law visited the Agra jewellers and ordered jewellery. Karim was never one to deny his wife her indulgences. Local Muslim groups approached him for charity contributions and favours, and the Munshi delighted in this as it added to his sense of self-esteem. With the Queen as his chief patron, the Munshi was considered extremely important and visitors flooded through his doors to hear firsthand the stories from the Royal Palace.

When Karim delayed his departure and failed to board the *Peninsular* back for England on 26 June, the officials went on full alert. The Thugee and Dacoity Department stayed hot on his trail and S. Bayley of the department wrote immediately to the Inspector General's office in the North-West Province (NWP). He received the reply that the Munshi was not likely to leave India until he knew whether the NWP government was going to 'let him buy at his own price a plot of govt land adjoining and equal in size to the plot given him in *jagir* some time ago'. The Munshi was reported to have left Agra for Kashmir on the night of 27 June. Messages were relayed to Gulmarg in Kashmir and officials there replied that the person believed to be the Queen's Munshi had passed Baramula in Srinagar and intended to stay two days.[5]

All networks of the Thugee and Dacoity Department from the North-West Provinces to Kashmir remained on alert and another telegram was posted to Babington Smith at the Viceroy's office on 24 July: 'Col Lock, PA Eastern states, Rajputana writes on the 22nd. Passing through Agra, I heard that the Munshi had obtained a further extension of three weeks. I think this is reliable. Donald Franklin.'[6]

A full report on the Munshi's travels was prepared by the department on 14 September 1896 and transmitted to London by Bayley, and a copy marked to Lee Warner at the India Office.

Confidential telegram 30.3.97
Report on Munshi

Munshi Abdul Karim, C.I.E came to India by the mail steamer which arrived in
Bombay on the 18th March 1896, and went to Agra.

His real object in returning to India is said to have been to purchase, at his
own price, a plot of government land adjoining and equal in size to the plot
given him in *jagir* for two lives some time ago.

The *Muslim Chronicle* (Calcutta) of the 25th April 1896, had a paragraph stating that the Munshi had earned the thanks of the Muhammaddan community
by handing over a building worth Rs 14,000 to the *Anjuman Hamdard-i-Islam* of
Agra for the purpose of opening an orphanage. No confirmation of this statement has been received.

He remained in Agra till the 27th June 1896, when he left for Kashmir. He
arrived at Baramulla on the 2nd of July and went on to Srinagar where he
arrived on the 5th and left again on the 7th idem. He stayed, while in Srinagar,
with Azizu-d-din Kansa, *alias* Samad Shah, but took his meals at the house of
Babu Sham Narain, Munsif, who gave him a *nach*. He visited some of the places
of interest near Srinagar. On his way back he paid a flying visit to Jammu and
stayed for one day in the dak-bungalow there. Is not stated whether any one
visited him at the dak-bungalow. Pundit Bhag Ram was told of the Munshi's
visit by Pandit Sham Narain, assistant judge, Srinagar, who is a friend of the
Munshi and had heard of it from him.

The papers mentioned that the Munshi visited Delhi on his return from
Kashmir, but enquiries made failed to elicit any particulars regarding his pro-
ceedings there.

He left Bombay with his wife and his son [sic] by the mail steamer of the 21st
August 1896.

During his stay at Agra he is reported to have received visits from Captain
Ahmed Husain of the Nizam's personal Body Guard and Rahim Baksh, a pensioned Deputy collector (formerly a hospital assistant) from Bhartpur.[7]

Further confidential memos were exchanged between political agents, the
Thugee and Dacoity Department, the Viceroy's office and Whitehall right up to
mid-October. By then the Munshi was back in Balmoral unaware of the hullabaloo that he had caused. The Queen even sent a messenger to receive him and
his family in Calais. The gossip columns of *Reynold's Newspaper* reported 'the great
event' of the 'Munshi's return to Deeside' in an article boldly headlined: 'John
Brown's Successor'. The Munshi brought back with him his nephew, much to the
delight of the Queen who immediately went to visit the young boy. The familiar
routine was re-established, the Hindustani lessons resumed and the Queen realised even more how much she missed the Indian when he was away.

Marie Mallet, the Queen's maid-in-waiting, described a visit to see the Munshi's wife in their cottage in Balmoral in November:

> I have just been to see the Munshi's wife (by Royal Command). She is fat and not uncomely, a delicate shade of chocolate and gorgeously attired, rings on her fingers, rings on her nose, a pocket mirror set in turquoises on her thumb and every feasible part of her person hung with chains and bracelets and ear-rings, a rose-pink veil on her head bordered with heavy gold and splendid silk and satin swathings round her person. She speaks English in a limited manner and declares she likes the cold. The house surrounded by a twenty foot palisade, the door opening of itself, the white figure emerging silently from a near chamber, all seemed so un-English, so essentially Oriental that we could hardly believe we were within a hundred yards of this Castle. Do not repeat this, it would not be safe, but in days to come it will be a curious bit of history.[8]

Unknown to Queen Victoria, her Diamond Jubilee year in 1897 would be known by her Household as the 'Year of the Munshi'. As the Queen sorted her mail with Karim, discussed guest lists for the event and made future plans, a mutiny was being plotted in an adjoining room.

A major row was brewing behind the heavy oak door. Marie Mallet, maid-in-waiting, paced up and down, her face blazing red as she directed her anger at the tall figure of James Reid. The doctor stood motionless, his eyebrows knitted in a frown which, when combined with his dark sideburns, complimented his fierce expression.

Jane Churchill, lady-in-waiting to the Queen, stood by the table in the corner of the room, her fingers picking nervously at the dark velvet fabric of an arm-chair. Beside her was Fritz Ponsonby, the young equerry and forceful anti-Munshi campaigner, protesting fiercely and supported by Sir Arthur Bigge, the Queen's personal secretary, who looked furious, even distraught.

The news just broken by Reid had provoked this collective display of raised tempers. It concerned the Munshi. The doctor revealed that he had been treating the Munshi for gleet and a relapse of venereal disease. The Queen, said Reid, nevertheless wished to take him to Cimiez on her annual spring visit. This meant the Household would have to dine with him, which they were determined not to do. If Karim went, they would strike. Despite his best efforts, Reid could not quell the revolt. Her Majesty would have to be informed and Harriet Phipps, lady of the bedchamber, was picked for the job. Phipps was a slim lady with golden hair, who liked to dress with many trimmings and ribbons and always wore dozens of bangles that rattled so loudly that at times it even 'worried her Royal Mistress'.[9] She was the Queen's private secretary and informally the head of the ladies of the

Household. Phipps had a reputation as a tactful intermediary, but never before had she carried such an extreme ultimatum, the awesome task of relaying to her Queen the Household's message. She would have to choose between them and her Munshi.

Phipps gathered her stiffly starched skirts around her, thrust her chin out in a defiant mood, and walked briskly across the courtyard towards the Queen's sitting room. Her heart was racing as she strode out, her bangles rattling even louder as she mounted the flight of steps in the Tower and approached the door. She knocked and entered. The Queen was sitting at her desk looking through a large pile of papers. Almost instinctively she knew that something was amiss.

No sooner had Phipps spoken the words than the seventy-eight-year-old Queen flew into a violent rage, dramatically sweeping off the contents of her desk. Books, pens, papers, memos, boxes and mementoes went crashing to the floor as the Queen threw them down, shattering several glass objects in her fury. Never had Phipps seen her in such a state. She fled the room and tearfully conveyed the scene to the shocked Household. They had not expected the Queen to back her Munshi over them. For the incandescent Household, the Cimiez trip was a step too far.

The Queen won the argument, the Household did not resign and on 10 March the Royal suite started for Cimiez. The Court Circular noted that the Munshi was part of the suite along with Phipps, Arthur Bigge, Lieutenant-Colonel W. Carrington, Lieutenant-Colonel Davidson and Reid. The mood was decidedly grim.

A report in *The Times* newspaper from Cherbourg on 12 March rubbed further salt into their wounds and it carried the usual praise for the Munshi: 'In a twinkling the platform between the two trains became animated and the somber tones on the twilight hour of a gray day were quickly relieved by the scarlet coats of the servant and the picturesque dress of the Scotch attendants. The colors and style of the dress worn by the Munshi and Indian secretary, Hafiz Abdul Karim, added to the effect,'[10] wrote the correspondent.

That year, Cimiez simmered like a cauldron with tension over the Munshi. Though the Excelsior Hotel Regina had been renovated to a high standard and even provided electric lights and sweeping views of the Mediterranean, the break was ruined by the tension. The Household was on the warpath and they were now joined by the Prince of Wales. Matters were made no better by Princess Beatrice, who had a selfish streak in her and often made the Queen very unhappy. Reid recorded in his diary a day after reaching Cimiez: 'HM came and sat with me for sometime in my room to tell me about her health and Princess Beatrice's unkindness to her.'[11]

Reid was then called to Bigge's room where he had a meeting with the Prince of Wales about the Munshi and the crisis which the Queen's relations with him were bringing on. Bigge, Carrington and Davidson had already been discussing the matter with the Prince. 'I told HRH much that I know and how serious I think it. He was much impressed and promised to support us in any action we take,' wrote Reid.

To the fury of the Household, Rafiuddin Ahmed joined the Munshi. He had not been invited to Cimiez, and within forty-eight hours of his arrival the Household expelled him, something that angered the Munshi. The Queen too found it 'disgraceful' and wrote to Lord Salisbury that he should apologise for the expulsion and tell Rafiuddin that this had happened only because he was a journalist. She also asked Lord Salisbury to invite him to at least one ball in the Royal Court. The Munshi remained in Nice, enjoying the weather in the French Riviera. The locals, who saw him drive around the town in his carriage, would never have imagined the storm in the Court. *The Galignani Messenger* reported: 'As for the Munshi Abdul Karim, although every deference is paid to him, and he is generally seen following the Royal carriage in a separate carriage drawn by splendid horses, each Nicois is firmly convinced that he sees in him a captive Native Prince, attached, as it were, to the chariot wheels of the Empress of India.'

The atmosphere in the Household continued to get heated. On 27 March Reid held several meetings with Bigge, Carrington and Davidson about 'acting together in the Queen and Munshi question'. Their resolve to close ranks on the issue was strengthened even more when the Queen drew Prince Louis of Battenberg into the matter and asked him to tell Davidson that the Household 'must associate more' with the Munshi.

'We all agreed to stand together and resign if HM presses the matter,' wrote Reid in his diary.[12] The daily conferences went on, the expedition to Cimiez getting totally hijacked over the question of Karim. Bigge, Carrington and Davidson were joined now by Prince Louis who had been charged by the Queen to find out the reasons for the Household's objections to the Munshi. Late at night, Reid visited the Queen and stayed for an hour. He recorded: 'Told her *all* I knew about the Munshi.'[13]

Reid's diary at this time has a daily entry on the 'Munshi affair'. He had meetings on the issue as early as seven o'clock in the morning to well past midnight. The Queen would send for him several times during the day to discuss Karim. He went through the various points he had been keeping in his dossier with her. On 30 March Reid noted that she admitted 'she had been foolish by acceding to his constant requests for advancement' but yet tried to shield him. Reid told the Queen about the comments he had heard about her and the Munshi both outside the Palace and by her own family, and how he had 'been questioned as to her sanity'. After a particularly stressful day, when the Prince of Wales, the Duke of Coburg and Princess Beatrice rounded on him about the Munshi, the doctor wrote: 'Saw Queen twice again about Munshi – sick of it.'[14]

Despite the endless rounds of stormy meetings, nothing was being resolved. The Queen remained stubborn, protecting her Munshi, and the doctor bore the brunt of complaints from both the Household and the Royal family. 'Another killing day with the Queen about the Munshi,' he recorded on 31 March. After a particularly tempestuous meeting one night, when the Queen accused Reid of being in 'league against the Munshi', he finally lost his temper and said he was ready to resign. The Queen was being worn out by the pressure on her, but she remained firm. In her defence of the Munshi, she felt she was taking on a fight for the underdog against the racism and snobbery of the upper classes. After her showdowns with the Household, she would sob to the Munshi about her troubles with her family, especially Princess Beatrice and the Prince of Wales.

The Prince of Wales now tried another approach. He asked the Household to get details of the Munshi's family so he could be discredited in the Queen's eyes. A telegram was despatched to the Viceroy requesting 'particulars regarding birth, parentage and history of Queen's Munshi, giving exact social position at time of engagement in his present place, also particular as to wife or wives', with instructions that a reply was required 'as soon as possible'.[15]

Once the details were collected, the Viceroy sent a telegram to the Secretary of State, Lord Hamilton, on 3 April 1897.

Your telegram of Mar 30. Munshi's father Sheikh Mohammed Waziruddin is subordinate Medical service as Hospital Assistant. Pay Rs 60.00 reported. Respectable and trustworthy. Native of Agra. No record of ancestry but position of family humble. Eldest son served in jail department, promoted tehsildar in 1893 at Her Majesty's wish. Four daughters, married. Husbands in jail departments or constables. One of them Harmat Ali, formerly in Queen's service. There are other relations but of no mark or education.

Munshi was Mohurir or vernacular clerk in Agra jail at ten rupees a month till he left Indian to become household servant to the Queen. No information about wife or of there being more than one. Will enquire if desired.[16]

The enquiries revealed nothing that the Household or Secretary of State did not know already. The meetings and rows, however, continued at Cimiez.

Reid remained at the centre of the Munshi controversy. When not seeing the Queen, he was locked in discussion with the Prince of Wales or Prince Louis. After an 'excited interview' with the Queen and her dresser, Mrs Macdonald, Reid had to telephone Lord Rowton, former private secretary to Disraeli, to visit the Queen as she wanted to discuss the Munshi with him. The Queen often sought Rowton's advice.

At one meeting the doctor decided to tell the Queen in no uncertain terms that people thought she was losing her sanity:

It seems to me that Your Majesty is only thinking of the Munshi's feelings. But that is of infinitesimal importance compared with the gravity of the situation as regards Your Majesty. As I said to Your Majesty before, there are people in high places, who know Your Majesty well, who say to me that the only charitable explanation that can be given is that Your Majesty is not sane, and that the time will come when to save Your Majesty's memory and reputation it will be necessary for me to come forward and say so: and that is a nice position for me to be in. I have seen the Prince of Wales yesterday and he again spoke to me very seriously on the subject. He says he has quite made up his mind to come forward if necessary, because quite apart from all the consequences to the Queen, it affects *himself* most vitally … Because it affects the throne.

Reid's words had the opposite effect on the Queen. Far from being cowed down by her doctor's charges of insanity, she went on the offensive. Torn between her loyalty to the Munshi and upset by the pressure from her Household and family, she concluded that the Household was being racist, and her own son, selfish and mean. She summoned Reid yet again 'in a most violent passion' and said they had all 'behaved disgracefully'. The doctor stood his ground and the Queen broke down again, apologising for her harsh words to him. The doctor did not have any more unpleasant scenes with the Queen after that ('the first day since the 28,' wrote Reid) and the Prince of Wales thanked him for all he had done and assured him of his full support. The ceasefire lasted a few uneasy days, to be broken the moment the Queen heard that another member of her Household, John Carstairs McNeill, had said something disparaging about the Munshi. The Queen was confiding in the Munshi about her family and the strain was becoming almost unbearable for her as she found herself fighting a lone battle against her sons and youngest daughter.

Reid, meanwhile, decided to tackle the Munshi himself. He rounded on him and told him that he had created a situation which could no longer be permitted to exist.

The Queen has believed all the lies you have told her and in her kindness has given you all you have asked for up to now; but she is beginning to find out what everyone in England and India knows, viz., that you are an imposter. On the subject of your origin we have a certificate from India about your Father, your wife and yourself. You are from a very low class and *never* can be a gentleman. Your education is nil. To be called 'Secretary' is perfectly ridiculous; you could not write either an English or an Indian letter that would not disgrace the name of Secretary. You have a double face, one that you show to the Queen, and another when you leave her room. The Queen says she finds you humble and 'honest' and kind to everybody! What is the reality? The Queen says the other Indians like and respect you. What do they tell me? And what would they say if they were not afraid of you and the old ones were brought back to give evidence? You have been deceiving the Queen in other ways … You have told the Queen that in India no receipts are given for money, and therefore you ought not to give any to Sir F Edwards [Keeper of the Privy Purse]. This is a lie and means that you wish to *cheat* the Queen. The Police know this and other things. The Queen's letters in your possession are asked for by H.M. Where are they? Why have you not given them up at once? You had better do so now or it will be the worse for you. If the Queen were to die and any letters of hers were found in your possession no mercy will be shown you. The Queen does not know *all* I have told you because it would shock her greatly to know how completely you have deceived her and what a scoundrel you are, and she hopes it may be possible for you to stay with her still. But this can only be if your 'position' is altogether taken away.[17]

Reid told the Munshi that none of the Queen's gentlemen would recognise the Munshi's position and that it would be impossible for him to remain in England if they informed the Queen of everything they knew about him and how he had 'deceived' her. He also advised him that Prince Louis was being sent by the Queen to speak to him, but he had come instead. That would be much more serious than the doctor speaking to him, but it would be done next time.

Though some of the allegations made by Reid were true, the rest were exaggerated. The Munshi had never claimed that his family was from the upper classes. He had merely said his father was a doctor in Agra Jail and he himself had been a clerk, which was true. He had rightly told the Queen that he had never done menial jobs and had never been a servant. Regarding the position of his father, perhaps some of it was lost in translation. A hospital assistant was a native doctor with some medical qualifications and allowed to do minor operations. His father was in charge of a clinic in Agra, which had been confirmed by Tyler. It was true that the other Indian servants had complained about the Munshi, but this was natural as none of them had been rapidly promoted by the Queen in the manner that Karim had been, leading to inevitable jealousy and resentment. Karim had not helped matters by being somewhat high-handed with them and preening about his closeness to the Queen.

The outburst from Reid left Karim in shock. The force of the ill-feeling towards him became clear to him. The threats of police action would have also frightened the man, who was, after all, a brown man in a white country, with only the elderly Queen prepared to stand up for him. He had told the Queen that he had been so distressed by the hostility towards him that he had not been able to eat or sleep.

The doctor turned these words against him as well.

The Queen says you tell her you are in great distress and can't sleep or eat and Her Majesty in her great kindness is sorry to hear it. But if you do this again, and try to humbug the Queen, the Q. will be told everything about you, and then her pity will be turned to anger when she finds out how you have deceived her and you will only hasten your ruin.

The Munshi retreated into silence after this. He did not know what the police had against him, unaware that it was his friendship with Rafiuddin that was putting him in the firing line. He had no idea that Rafiuddin was suspected of being a spy for the Amir of Afghanistan and for fuelling discord among the Muslims in India by his association with the Muslim Patriotic League. Though all these charges were dismissed later, the mud had come to stick on Rafiuddin and, indirectly through him, on the Munshi.

The rest of the fortnight in Cimiez passed tediously with frayed tempers, jumpy nerves, a sullen Munshi and a distraught Queen who was still having long meetings with Lord Rowton and Reid on the affair. The Munshi complained to the Queen that he had seen a Frenchman ask Bigge who he (the Munshi) was, and that he was sure Bigge had told him 'something bad about him'. Everybody, it seems, was disgruntled. The Queen's own children, being too frightened to approach her directly, passed everything through Reid, who became the lightning conductor for all parties. He wrote in his diary on 14 April: 'The Q still constantly speaking to me about the Munshi and trying all she can to get me to hedge and agree with her. And when she sees I will not is rather angry.'

The Queen was adamant to defend her Munshi. On 23 April she sent a defiant memo to the members of her Household.

Excelsior Hotel Regina
Memo from Queen April 23, 1897

I wish to be assured on the foll points viz
1. That the gentlemen here shd not go on talking about the painful subject either amongst themselves or with outsiders and not *combine* with the Household agst the person.
2. That while I know that they do not wish to consider him at all as an equal which I never considered him, they shd treat him with common civility, which good breeding must prompt.
3 Give him his carriage at home which Sir H Ewart thought it right he shd have for himself and wife. His name will only appear when all the others of the suite are mentioned and he has been there, and in the same way he will be invited to plays and parties, as he has been for several years past, and will come in with the others when all the others are asked.
4. His friend will not come to the castle unless specially asked by the queen. He will also occasionally when there are addresses and receptions come in if there are members of the Household, and as I may wish, as heretofore, occasionally on India.

5. Great care can be taken to avoid all special and separate mention of him excepting on the occasion of going for several months to India, when as is often the case with other people who are in my office, to prevent people (photographers, booksellers etc) from writing to him.[18]

She also clarified that the much talked about carriage the Munshi used was a hired one, just as the dressers used. The Queen had reclaimed her Munshi. The Household were now told firmly that they could not gang up on him and that he would continue to be invited for Court occasions. They were not prepared to give up so easily. Lord Rowton told the Queen that the conditions of her memo were dependent on 'the person' respecting them.

Not prepared to waste any time, Fritz Ponsonby immediately wrote to the Viceroy's secretary, Babington Smith, from the Hotel Regina, urging him to treat his letter and its contents as '*strictly confidential*' and to treat it 'like the confessional'. He recounted that they had been having a good deal of trouble lately over the Munshi and although they had tried their best, they could not get the Queen to realise how very dangerous it was for her to 'allow this man to see every confidential paper relating to India, and in fact to all state affairs'. Ponsonby said he did not know where the Queen would stop if it was not for their protest. 'Fortunately he happens to be a thoroughly stupid and uneducated man, and his one idea in life seems to be to do nothing and to eat as much as he can. If he had been kept in his proper place, there would have been no harm done,' said Ponsonby. He said that the real danger lay in his friend, Rafiuddin, who supplied the brains that were deficient in the Munshi, and he tried to extract all he could from him. Ponsonby said the Munshi was allowed to read the Viceroy's letters and other letters of importance that came from India. He said the police had supplied interesting details on Rafiuddin, but it was of no use, 'for the queen says that is "race prejudice" and that we are all jealous of the poor Munshi!'

Ponsonby requested Smith to send him cuttings from the native or European papers carrying any details on the Rafiuddin question. 'I got hold of some from the Hindoo papers before I left India, & had them read to the Queen, but their contents did very little good. Now however as the question has arisen with such force, it would be of the greatest use to be able to quote Indian papers,'[19] he added. Fritz Ponsonby was not accepting defeat yet.

While the Household carried on trying to discredit the Munshi, the Secretary of State, Lord Hamilton, was beginning to grow weary of the Munshi issue and the constant flurry of letters and telegrams on the subject. When nothing substantial was pegged on either the Munshi or his friend Rafiuddin, despite the surveillance on them, he wrote to the Viceroy, Lord Elgin, saying Karim had done nothing wrong and could not be charged with anything. He also felt that the Household was overreacting on the friendship of Rafiuddin and the Munshi and over-representing it to the Queen.

Hamilton wrote to Elgin that there was some 'commotion going on as to the position and conduct of the Munshi'. The Secretary of State felt that the Household generally, and especially the private secretaries, resented the social and official position accorded to the Munshi in the Court Circulars and in all occasions by the Queen. He, however, added that as far as he knew, 'the Munshi has done nothing to my knowledge which is reprehensible or deserving of official strictures'. Hamilton acknowledged that Karim was close to the 'Mohamedan intriguer named Rafiuddin' who was known to the reactionary police in India as an 'untrustworthy adventurer' and 'the agent of the Amir'. Nevertheless, he disapproved of the fact that under the pretext of investigating Rafiuddin, it was the Munshi who was being subjected to scrutiny by the Thugee and Dacoity Department in India on the request of Lee Warner. Clearly annoyed, Hamilton wrote:

> I did not see the letters till after they had gone. This I do not want done. I do not want to get mixed up in any court matters unless the Queen directly asks me. Enquiries shd be made as regards Rafiuddin ... If he is a fellow making money out of his association with the Munshi, then it might be seen to make such a statement to the Queen. I do not however want any fishing enquiry to be made in connection with the Munshi as such enquiries wd not be right, unless they were in connection with some definite statement or accusation.[20]

Hamilton had made his disapproval of the enquiries against the Munshi clear. The Royal suite returned to Portsmouth on 30 April, a sober and weary group of people. The Queen said she had taken a dislike to her room in Cimiez on account of the 'scenes' she had there with the doctor and from the pain she suffered. The Munshi, firmly back in the Queen's favour, now asked her to honour him with the rank of KCIE (Knight Commander of the Indian Empire) in the Jubilee honours. He quite fancied the thought of being called 'Sir Abdul'.

The Household, though chastised, would not go quietly. The Prince of Wales continued to meet Reid and urged him to carry his messages on the Munshi to the Queen, leading to more painful interviews with her. General Dennehy visited Windsor and also spoke to Reid saying he was 'resolved to be firm' on the Munshi question. Dennehy and Reid went over all of Karim's letters to the Queen and found that the chief one was 'written by the Hindu'. They did not remember that Rafiuddin was a Muslim. The Munshi's own letters were apparently full of 'vile spelling and composition and very insolent'. Reid wrote: 'HM getting shaken about him.' The four-way talks between Dennehy, the Munshi, the

Queen and the doctor continued for a few days and the Queen complained that Karim was being sulky in her presence.

When the Munshi went to London in an ordinary train rather than the Royal train, the Queen was very upset. Reid wrote in his diary on 12 May that he had a long and unpleasant discussion about him with the Queen before dinner and quoted to her the opinion of members of her own family. The doctor learnt from Dennehy that the Munshi had asked to be made KCIE. When he was last in India he had apparently written to the Queen and asked her to make him a nawab, a title which gives regal dignity. The Queen wrote to Dennehy to ask him what he thought and when the latter explained to the Queen what it meant, she said it could not be done. The meetings with Dennehy had troubled the Queen and she wrote to Reid:

All you shd say to Sir T Dennehy wd be to say how troubled and distressed I have been and how anxious I was that he shd help me. That nothing has happened but tittle tattle of outsiders which had not been properly put down and too much talked.

That unfortunately a remark of mine had led to misunderstanding and people had behaved very ill. However that is passed and I will explain that to him – the ill nature and spite came from India – but all can be set right with a little tact – no alteration in treatment is required – he can help me as you can say how troubled I am.[21]

The Viceroy's office and the Thugee and Dacoity Department in India were still continuing their investigations on the Munshi and the reasons behind his trip to Kashmir the previous year. They reported that Sham Narain, whom the Munshi stayed with in Srinagar, was a sub-judge and a friend of the Munshi's. They also reported that the Munshi had probably written to Sham Narain about Lord Breadalbane, who was visiting Srinagar, and the latter had therefore been put up in the government house. Lord Hamilton wrote to Lord Elgin that two Indian officials in the Queen's Court had spoken frankly to her about the official position accorded to the Munshi and his social standing in India.

'This does not concern us here but indirectly and is too delicate a matter for me to interfere with, so when I am affected I shall sit still,' wrote Hamilton. 'But the result of this row has been to put him more into his humble place, and his influence will not be same in the future, what it has been in the past.' Hamilton also told Elgin that he thought he could write freely on general matters to the Queen. 'So far as I know nothing I say or write to her is committed to the Munshi. He may of course get hold of papers, but I doubt if he does. Where care has to be exercised, it is officers or individuals,' said Hamilton.

Elgin had been firmly told by Hamilton that he should not pursue the Munshi. But when he heard that the Munshi was asking for a knighthood, the Viceroy could not take it lying down. He immediately wrote to Hamilton that the Munshi was 'wholly unsuitable for a place in an order of knighthood' as it would offend the Indian nobility and Royalty. The Viceroy emphasised:

> I should be the last to desire to appear to interfere with her Majesty's prerogative, but I shd. fail in my duty if I did not represent to you that the idea of promoting him to one of the higher grades might raise very serious political questions. The distinction of KCIG is bestowed on men of the highest rank and cover to Ruling Chiefs and yet precedence in the order is determined by seniority. What wd. be the feelings of the Rajputana chiefs who found himself in a chapter of the order placed below a man of the Munshi's social status?[22]

The Viceroy was determined to block any chance of a knighthood for the Munshi. He suggested that the Secretary of State ask the Queen to give him the MVO or the Victorian Order, an honour which was granted to those who had served in Britain, and therefore would not have too many ramifications in India.

Later that month, the Viceroy wrote to Lord Hamilton again. He too now wanted to distance himself from an enquiry into the Munshi's affairs. He explained that he had written to Bayley to make a few enquiries and Bayley had written to the agents in the North-West Province to see if they could provide information, but had not received anything.

> I told him you did not want fishing enquiries and that I shd say to you that I was myself satisfied from enquiries made in 1894 and from what occurred when the Munshi came to India on wh. I took steps to be informed ... there really was nothing more to learn. As to the other gentleman, I asked him if he could be shown in your words 'that he is disreputable fellow making money out of his connection with the M.' He said No – there was absolutely no proof. There was not even a pool to fish in – we certainly believe that you rightly describe him, but we have no facts.[23]

Both enquiries into Rafiuddin and the Munshi had come to nought. The Munshi had emerged triumphant. On his return from the Continent, he went salmon fishing in the River Dee in Balmoral 'with much success', according to the *Pall Mall Gazette*. It was as if nothing could touch him now.

11

'MUNSHIMANIA'

The Queen's Diamond Jubilee was rapidly approaching. It would be ten years since Abdul Karim had joined her Court. The Queen remembered the first day he had presented himself, a shy youth of twenty-three with a serious expression on his face. He had now grown portly, the wealth and fine living in the Queen's palaces adding to his girth. The Queen gazed at the photograph of Karim hanging in her Dressing Room in Osborne House. He looked like a Prince in his turban and fine clothes. The studio had coloured in the black and white photograph, filling in the rich colours of his Indian clothes. It hung just below a photograph of John Brown and was placed near her dressing table. Above her bed was a photograph of her beloved Albert. The Queen had chosen to be surrounded by the memories of the men who had been closest to her in life.

In the ten years that Abdul Karim had been by her side, the Queen had travelled in a different world as the Empress of India. She could now talk to her Indian servants in Hindustani and even say a few words to the Indian Princes who visited her. She had tasted Indian food, learnt the language and endeared herself even more to her Indian subjects. The large number of Jubilee presents from Indian Princes, committees and individuals showed how the Queen was revered as a mother figure in India. Yet what should have been a glorious celebration for Victoria, in the achievement of her milestone Diamond Jubilee, was soured by the 'Munshi affair'. The world outside witnessing the glorious Diamond Jubilee celebrations of an iconic Queen did not know the anxiety and distress that she was going through and the trouble brewing in her Court.

Having been persuaded against the knighthood for Karim, the Queen wanted to grant him the MVO (Member of the Royal Victorian Order) as a Jubilee honour, but this too brought her once again into a headlong clash with the India Office and her Household. A letter from Sir Fleetwood Edwards, Keeper of the Privy Purse, about the Munshi threw her into a rage and she wrote to Reid to inform Edwards that he could not treat the Munshi as a servant. Reid, as always, was her first stop for all complaints. She angrily sent him a copy of a memo drafted by the late Henry Ponsonby, in which he had clearly stated the position of the Munshi in the Household, and asked that it be forwarded to Edwards. The Queen wrote:

> Though I certainly do not want to revive the subject wh. for 3 months has so painfully impressed me and upset my nerves and peace of mind and though I don't want you to give any message to Sir Edwards – but I think you shd. show him these papers. He must see what I was afraid of and how wrong I think the conduct of others has been ... after this they cannot attempt to treat him as a servant. It is impossible and wd. be a breach of faith with him and me. I send them to you and hope this is the last I shall hear of conduct in no way creditable. Yrs. truly VRI. [1]

The tension of the last few months had taken its toll on the Queen and she wrote to Reid that she was 'feeling very tired and somewhat depressed'. The Queen felt she had so much to do, so many questions to answer and that she had no rest. The Queen by now was seventy-eight years old and her eyesight was failing her. She insisted that Fritz Ponsonby, who copied her telegrams for her, should use a darker ink as she could not read the letters. Her own handwriting had become a spidery scrawl and her letters and memos were consequently also difficult to read. Yet she unfailingly carried on her daily correspondence and her Hindustani lessons.

The Jubilee preparations were in full swing, with Indian Princes lining up to pay their respects to the Queen. Even Captain Ahmed Husain, who had been packed off to India because of his frequent complaints about the Munshi, had returned for the Jubilee. The Queen, characteristically generous, was happy to have him back. Ahmed told the Queen that he would like to stay back with her for some time.

Reid took centre-stage in the Munshi affair. With the Queen relying on him to find a solution, he had no choice in the matter. The doctor took Sir Pertab, ADC to the Prince of Wales, into his confidence and held further talks with Fleetwood Edwards, Davidson and Bigge. He advised the Queen that Davidson was so upset that he was thinking of resigning and warned her that she would lose 'One of the very best men she has'. Bigge, meanwhile, declined the KCVO and tempers were frayed over the Queen's determination to give the Munshi the MVO.

The Queen continued to clash bitterly with Edwards, who had become a vociferous anti-Munshi campaigner. When he wrote to the Queen that a decision to honour Karim would be 'most unfortunate', the Queen wrote another angry letter to Reid on 28 June saying she was very 'indignant' at the 'unnecessary letter from Sir F Edwards'. She said he threatened her in such a way that he almost made it impossible for her to do what she needed to do as she had given her word. 'I think that I might have been spared this unkind and uncalled for expression,' she wrote. 'This set at me makes my position a very painful and cruel one, and I really

The Queen's photo signed in Urdu by her (1899).

shall never get over it with the Gentlemen or the pain wh. it caused the poor Munshi.'[2] The elderly Queen said she was crushed and annoyed by the hatred and determination to 'treat a man whom I have no reason not to trust', and that Edwards' attitude amounted to 'a shameful and unjust interference'. The Queen was clearly distraught. The constant confrontations with her Household were tiring her out and she felt they had begun to bully her.

Jubilee Day passed with the customary processions and fanfare, and the Queen drove – as she had done for her Golden Jubilee – in an open landau to St Paul's Cathedral with the Princess of Wales and Princess Helena by her side. The sun was shining again as it had that day on 22 June 1887, and the Queen was moved to tears by the cheers and ovations from the crowds. The Indian Escort led her carriage, the sight of the colourful uniforms and turbans once again raising a cheer from the crowds. The Queen – despite her seventy-nine years – looked in fine form. She had now ruled longer than any other English sovereign, having overtaken the record of George III. Telegrams flooded in from all over the world. She was the grandmother of Europe and enjoyed a tremendous following both on the Continent and in the colonies. Despite a crippling famine in India, the native Princes came to London to participate in the Jubilee and brought exquisite presents. Many of them – the Maharajah of Kapurthala and the Thakore of Morvi – were now well known to the Queen. The women of the Empire presented a statue of Prince Albert which had an inscription in Sanskrit and was installed in Windsor Great Park. The Queen was overcome with all the love and affection she received.

'*Ham ko bahut khushi howi ke aaj sath sal bakhuriyat khatam howi. Sab bachche aur aligar bahut ikhlak se pesh ai,*' she recorded in her Hindustani Journal on 20 June. (I am very happy that I have finished sixty years well. All the children and the pageantries were very well presented.)[3]

A day later she wrote: '*Aj hamari sawari ka jalsa bahut khoshi aur umdagi se khatam howa. Mausam bahut achcha tha.*' (Today my procession passed through the city and the celebrations ended with a lot of joy and happiness. The weather was very good.)

Throughout her Jubilee celebrations and the parties, the Queen carried on her Hindustani lessons. The hullabaloo over the Munshi's MVO would not go away, however. For Reid, there was no time to relax, even at the Jubilee garden party, as he spent half an hour discussing the issue with Lord Salisbury. He even consulted Lord Rosebery and Lord Rowton, all of whom, he said, deprecated the Queen's proposal.[4]

It took the Prime Minister, Lord Salisbury, to finally convince the Queen. He diplomatically put it to her that an honour for the Munshi may enrage the Queen's Hindu subjects, as she may be accused of showing partiality towards the Muslims. The Queen relented, but wrote to Reid on 29 June to emphasise that it was not under pressure from Edwards that she did so. 'Pray take care that Sir F Edwards knows that it is *not* because that he wrote that rather impertinent letter that she does not at present include the Munshi amongst those who are to receive the 4th class of order, but on Lord Salisbury's advice.'

Still hurting from the actions of Lord Edwards and the recent omission, she wrote again a week later to Reid on the subject:

> Tho' I shall see you soon, I wish to say that … I am so angry or at least so hurt: it was not that Lord Edwards had left the Munshi out … but that he believed *I* could ever have desired other names to be crossed and the unfortunate perse-cuted M's name to be put in that place. Such a thing is utterly preposterous. It is this that has so hurt me and the way in which he insisted on doubting my word about it. One of those representative officers is known to the Munshi and wrote to him – I believe it is all Hindoo jealousy … I think it is very possible that they may try to agitate against this poor harmless man.[5]

The Queen was convinced that it was the Hindus who were jealous of the Munshi and this had led them to influence Sir Pertab Singh against him. She wanted Reid to get to the bottom of it.

The Munshi was a prominent figure during the celebrations. Ten years back he had arrived as a humble servant. Now he strode confidently among the visit-ing Indian Princes. When the Queen inspected the officers of HM's Imperial Service Troops and Indian Cavalry Corps on the east lawn of Windsor Castle, the Court Circular mentioned that the Munshi Abdul Karim was among the guests. The Indian troops served as a Guard of Honour during the Jubilee celebrations and the inspection was attended by the native Princes in all their regalia. Despite all the ill feeling towards him, the Munshi was rubbing shoulders with Indian Royalty and enjoying every moment of it.

The Royal party soon moved to Osborne, but the Munshi affair kept burning. For over three months the doctor's diary had been filled with nothing but the Munshi issue and he was clearly tired of it. 'In the afternoon, again talked to for a long time by the Queen about the eternal Munshi,' wrote Reid. 'She evidently realizes what he really is but is resolved to stick to him – told her Lord Salisbury said to me that she has a right to keep him however bad his character may be!'[6]

As the days crept by at Osborne, the doctor heard from the Queen that the Munshi 'had been bullying her' and offered to take him to task, but the Queen would not sanction it. The next day Reid received a sixteen-page letter from the Queen on the Munshi. The Queen had been writing it over several days. She told Reid that 'the feeling that poor M is distracted and anything that can be invented against him and that he is suspected by jealous people of being dishonest is extremely trying and painful to me. She has known him for 10 years intimately and certainly has never had any reason to suspect or doubt him.' The Queen had received a complaint that a footman named Bagley had not been promoted because the Munshi objected to him and was at pains to dispute the charge. 'The

M never mentioned Bagley,' said the Queen, 'or ever has mentioned any one of the footmen or any other servants, but he is kind in trying to help others in trouble.' She thought the attack on the Munshi showed how ready everyone was to injure him.

> The queen has constantly, long before the M, chosen people herself on inquiry. But these gentlemen wish to have it all in their own hands, and in their hatred of the unfortunate M, put all down to him. It is very offensive to me that I should always be supposed to be *made* to do things ... I began this letter some days ago but go on today after the very painful conversation I had with you this afternoon. I must go on – if people believe the story about Bagley which is *completely false* they may not believe any shameful story bought against this poor defenseless man.
>
> Orientals intent and are of the most unbounded jealousy – the hatred of Hindu against Mahomeddan only adds to this – they talk to the officers, AOLS, and Anglo Indians who readily believe and retail everything – I do think it very shameful of people connected with the government or the country to give ready evidence to these stories of a person in their service. The position of *doubt* is becoming quite intolerable to me. I *must* have it out with my poor friend – it would be very wrong if Sir E Bradford had spoken about what was not to be mentioned and what is long ago – as you told me at Cimiez it was *not* to be spoken of – I am quite certain that when the Duke of Connaught was in India he never knew anything against him as he praised the son to the father and wrote to me as did everyone including Sir E Bradford. But jealousy is rife in India as anyone knows, and everything has already been believed about the Viceroy etc ...
>
> If there have been imprudences to faults, it may, I should hope, be possible to put a stop to this and let the poor M redeem his character. It is irresponsible for the host to feel the position as most offensive towards the guest. I can't bear it. VRI.[7]

The Queen was clearly in great distress and had now decided that she would stick up for her Munshi against all odds. Reid spoke to Ahmed Husain about Karim and the former attendant spared no detail in running down the Queen's favourite. Husain, clearly suffering from jealousy, was on his way back after the Jubilee and fired a last salvo at Karim, his fellow resident from Agra. He said the Munshi had boasted to him that he always saw the Queen's papers.

Husain obligingly put down his complaints against the Munshi in writing for Reid. In his broken English he wrote:

> Munshi always want more, and every day ask Queen plenty things. Queen give him too much and plenty present and too much luxury. India rajah very angry Munshi get CIE, when Rajah and big Indian man not get, and Munshi very little man like footman and some Queen footman better man.
>
> He talk me all Englishman cross, but he say I fight all and Queen always tells me, I tell Munshi much better you quiet – you only ten year servant, very little

man India. And your father very little doctor, and your brother and sister husband very little servant man and policeman. Queen give you plenty money and everything plenty give – Queen give so much English servant or English footman. Plenty English servant or English footman with Queen 15–20 years and get nothing. But Queen give you very much money and the recommendation for the brother and sister husband and big house and the land. You better quiet and not always ask Queen and want to be big officer.[8]

The Queen was not moved. She simply informed Reid to tell Ahmed Husain that she hoped he would always remain a true, kind friend to the poor Munshi, giving him good advice and standing by him. She said she had heard that his 'poor dear old father', Wuzeeruddin, was much troubled about what had been said.

The strain of the events of the Jubilee had also affected the Munshi, and he fell ill in August. Reid had to attend to him, much to his distaste. Though the illness of the Munshi put a temporary cover on all his issues, and the Queen was calmer after she had unburdened herself in her lengthy letter, Reid continued to hold discussions about the Munshi with the Household. He also spoke to Lord Breadalbane about the affair and heard how the Queen had asked the former to write to the Munshi and be his friend.

On 9 September the doctor received another lengthy letter from the Queen about Karim and had a long and stormy interview with her. 'I told her that the general belief is that she is entirely under the Munshi's influence,' Reid told the Queen. 'The tendency is at once to think of the M's influence in *every* thing that happens in the house, for there is a very general feeling, not only in HM's family and household but also among all the servants that HM is entirely under the influence of the M and that he knows it.' To add to his anger and weariness, the Queen asked Reid to postpone his holiday so he could meet Dennehy and 'talk over Munshi matters'.

If the Queen was having stormy meetings with Reid, the rest of the Household was rounding up on anyone who was seen to be friendly with the Munshi. One evening Fritz Ponsonby met Lord Breadalbane, an alleged sympathiser of the Munshi, at a gentleman's club in London and nearly came to blows with him over the Munshi.

On spotting Ponsonby at the club, Lord Breadalbane walked up to him and complained bitterly that he had been quoted as 'having backed up the M', though he had never been brought in contact with the Munshi and therefore had no decided line on him. Ponsonby, always aggressive when it came to the Munshi, and fuelled that evening even more by a liberal cocktail of champagne and whisky, was not prepared to tolerate the accusation.

'You are a blot on the Queen's Household,' he shot back. 'Because you let the Queen think you are a supporter of the Munshi.'

'Prove it,' challenged Lord Breadalbane, not taking kindly to the taunt.

'You praise the Munshi to the Queen in order to please her and you have even been rewarded with the Hessian Order for it,' continued the drunken Ponsonby. 'Even the Prince of Wales knows you are a supporter of the M.'

'I absolutely deny backing the Munshi,' replied the incensed Breadalbane. 'It is Sir Carstairs McNeill who has been spreading stories about the M and me.'

'McNeill has nothing whatever to do with it,' said Ponsonby, as the exchange got more heated. 'It is the Queen who always quotes you as being kind and good to the poor M.'

This was all too much for Breadalbane, who had indeed written to the Munshi once congratulating him on his promotion. His pride hurt, he hit back at Ponsonby: 'The Prince of Wales told me that the gentlemen had been very rude to the Queen at Cimiez. The Queen told him [the Prince of Wales] that she wished she had accepted their resignations when they had tendered it.' Breadalbane continued: 'When the Prince of Wales told the Queen that he had never heard anything about the Household's threat to resign, she replied, "Oh of course they would not tell you about it, they are too much ashamed of themselves ever to talk about it!!!"'

Ponsonby, by now equally furious at Breadalbane's aspersions that the Queen would have been happy to accept his resignation, warned him that he could still redeem himself and make the Queen understand that 'he disapproved of the M'.

By then it was nearly 2 a.m. and Ponsonby confessed that the two had nearly come to blows. Breadalbane left in a rage saying he was sorry to think that Ponsonby was heading a dead set against him, but that he was glad to know who his enemies were.

The next morning, Ponsonby met Breadalbane again at the Traveller's Club. Both were considerably sober now and Breadalbane said that he had not slept a wink all night. Ponsonby felt that though Breadalbane did not outwardly appear to bear him any malice, he wasn't quite sure where the latter stood.

'How can I show you that I do not wish to be a Munshiite?' Breadalbane finally asked, anxious not to alienate the Household. 'Shall I tell the Prince of Wales and other members of the Royal Family about my thoughts on the Munshi?'

Ponsonby, however, told him that was not good enough, for as long as he allowed the Queen to think he approved of the Munshi, it mattered very little what he told the others. Ponsonby advised him to write to Reid explaining his views on the Munshi and suggested that the letter could on his request be read to the Queen. 'He did not appear to like this idea, but said that he would think it over,'[9] Ponsonby told Reid.

The incident shows the extent to which the Munshi was now dividing opinions in the Household and official circle. Ponsonby's attempt to browbeat Breadalbane into writing to the Queen to express his feelings against the Munshi showed how desperate the Household was getting in their attempt to smear him.

Meanwhile, the Munshi continued to get eulogistic press coverage, much to the wrath of the Household. *The World* newspaper carried a small profile of the Queen's trusted Indian secretary:

The Munshi Abdul Kareem, who now occupies his own snug abode in the grounds of Balmoral, has received extraordinarily rapid promotion since he came to Windsor in the capacity of personal attendant to Her Majesty in 1887 ... So delighted is Her Majesty with her oriental teacher that when the Munshi went to India on leave, they were continued by almost daily correspondence. About seven years ago the Munshi was joined by his wife, and his father Waziruddin is certainly the only man living who has been permitted to smoke a hookah in the room usually tenanted by Lord Salisbury when he visits Windsor Castle. Frogmore Cottage has been assigned to Abdul Kareem as a residence and it is full of souvenirs and presents of all sorts, including a gold and enamel tea service, the gift of the Emperor of Russia. His place as 'personal attendant' is now filled by his compatriots Mustapha Khan and Chota Khan of Agra, and Aziz Khan of Moradabad, and when her Majesty dines, lunches or breakfasts *en famille*, no other servant is present but her faithful Indians, with whom she can speak in their own language.[10]

The Queen was always ready to rise to the defence of her 'shamefully persecuted Munshi' and told Reid not to believe the stories he was told about him, or in fact allow people to tell him these stories. She felt clearly tormented by the strain of taking on her entire Household single-handed in the protection of the Munshi. In the middle of the crisis, the Munshi threatened to resign, telling the Queen he would return to India. He told her that he would not remain beyond the year as he was not used to enduring the sort of treatment he had received. He also said he would forward all the receipts for his expenses, as he had heard allegations that he had not supplied them and was cheating the Queen.

The Queen was distraught. She told Karim that she could not let him go, that she felt '*deeply hurt*' and that it would harm both of them if he left. 'He wd. appear to admit to accusations and I to have yielded to very shameful pressure,' she wrote to Reid.[11]

The Munshi's wife was also suffering from headaches and he now told the Queen that he was worried and anxious that his 'poor father and brother seemed to be greatly troubled' since they had heard reports that he had resigned.[12]

The Queen wrote to Reid saying she had 'told the poor M' that it had all passed and he should not be anxious or alarm himself. She said she trusted and really thought that the stories and gross exaggerations were being gradually disposed of, but the shameful mischief which nameless people had done was quite severe and had produced a most unfortunate effect on the Munshi.

Reid replied defiantly: 'I am sorry to hear that HM is still having concern about the M: but judging from his robust appearance and undiminished stoutness

I do not think that, although no doubt his feelings may be considerably hurt, he can be worrying so much as HM fears, or it would certainly lead on his health and appearance.'[13] He added that any action being taken by the Household was out of concern for the Queen.

The Queen, embarrassed at her harsh words to the doctor, wrote to him again: 'I think I must have expressed myself badly about the M – I did not mean that he was worrying himself so as to make himself ill – only that the poor Father was distressed to write painful letters. More and more, I see by various things and inquiries that the whole thing was the grossest exaggeration and willful acceptance of stories.'

The rest of the days would have probably passed calmly at Balmoral, but the Munshi could rarely stay away from a little bit of self-publicity, causing another storm in the Palace.

On 16 October, to the shock and horror of the Household, an article appeared in *The Graphic* headlined 'The Queen's Hindustani Tutor'. It carried a photograph of the Munshi and the Queen cosily working together in the cottage in Balmoral. The Munshi was looking directly at the camera giving the impression that he was the one in control. The photo carried the caption: 'The Queen's Life in the Highlands, Her Majesty receiving a lesson in Hindustani from her Munshi Hafiz Abdul Karim C.I.E.' One of the Queen's dogs sat at her feet and the table was covered with a cloth showing distinctly Indian motifs.

The Household was furious. Reid discussed the article with the Queen and recorded that she was 'uncomfortable'.[14]

Two days later, determined to come to the bottom of the affair, Reid cycled eight miles in the afternoon to Ballater and saw Milne the photographer, who told him that the Munshi had met him on 16 June at Ballater Station and ordered him to have a photograph of the Queen and himself published in the Jubilee issue of *The Graphic*. 'Told the Queen what Milne had said and had 3 painful interviews,' recorded Reid in his diary.

The next two days involved long and 'trying talks' with the Queen on the 'Munshi business'. Several tense interviews, a fourteen-page letter, a painful boil in his right leg and non-stop worrying about the Munshi affair had wearied Reid to such an extent now that he seriously considered resigning. He didn't, however, get round to giving the letter as the Queen was suddenly 'gracious and nice', realising that she might lose the services of a trusted confidant.[15] Perhaps the Queen also agreed for once that the Munshi had overstepped his limits, but she resented being dictated to by the Household.

In sheer frustration, she wrote to Reid on 20 October from Balmoral saying she was terribly annoyed at the publication of the article and thought she was to

The Queen's Hindustani Tutor

THE Munshi Hafiz Abdul Karim, C.I.E., who teaches the Queen Hindustani, came to Windsor in 1887. He was then only twenty-three. He soon began giving lessons in Hindustani to the Queen, who now not only speaks that language fluently, but can write it with more than average correctness in the Persian character. Frogmore Cottage has been assigned to Hafiz Abdul Karim as a residence, and he has been joined there by his wife and his father. Abdul Karim is the second son of Khan Bahadur Dr. Hajee Mohammed Waziraddin, first-class hospital assistant in the Indian Medical Department. He was for some time in the service of the Nawab Jadia, as assistant Wakil to the West Malwa Political Agency at Agra. In 1886 he became an India Government clerk. In the following year he was appointed Munshi and Indian clerk to the Queen, and in 1892 became Indian Secretary to Her Majesty.

Article on Karim – 'The Queen's Hindustani Tutor' – from *The Graphic*.

blame for it. Yet she could not forgive the Household for continually trying to find fault with the Munshi and felt that Reid also sided with them. She wrote:

> I feel continually aggrieved at my gentlemen wishing to spy upon and interfere with one of my people whom I have no personal reason or proof of doubting and I am greatly distressed at what has happened. I have suffered enough from having suspicions put into my mind and if I am put into a still further difficulty I shall be unable to talk as I did before even to you whose kindness I should most gratefully acknowledge.

Torn between her Household and the Munshi, the Queen ordered Reid to see Milne and explain that there had been some misunderstandings. She said she would talk to the Munshi about the affair herself, adding that she felt 'dreadfully nervous'.

> He is so furious against you all that I do not advise any interview at present – I fear, however Milne will say one thing to you and another to him – you say there is no intention or wish to drive him away – But how painful it will be for me to have a person whose veracity is disbelieved. I am feeling dreadfully nervous – I thought you stood between me and the others and now I feel you also chime against me with the rest.
>
> I must add that the M has never complained of any of the gentlemen who now seem to doubt my word. Better put an end to this story and not try to

bring about a possible scandal. I shall see him now soon and write how matters stand. But my peace of mind is terribly upset. I fear I have made great
blunders in this business – I should not have repeated anything to the M that
night – I can't read this through and would beg you to burn it as well as say
nothing.[16]

The Queen met the Munshi that evening and had a tearful exchange with him.
He was furious to learn that Reid had made enquiries behind his back and contacted Milne. He informed the Queen that he had written to Milne in this regard.
To the Queen's dismay, he threatened once again to return to India. The Queen
wept and begged him to remain. After the painful meeting she wrote to Reid
urging him not to see Milne if he called, as the Munshi had apparently written
to him. The troubled Queen appealed to the doctor to let it all pass: 'Pray let the
whole thing alone which would have been better. Do nothing more. Don't see
Milne. The Munshi is very angry and threatens to leave at once if he is troubled.
Written in post haste. Pray burn it all.'

The next day she wrote again:

Pray do not enter into discussion with the gentlemen about the M now. It is
becoming a regular habit and should not be. I am very sorry you did go to ask
the photographer for it was for me to inquire and no one else to do so – I think
the intention was good. But it has made it awkward. Please burn this and all
long letters on the subject.[17]

As the Queen veered between backing her Munshi and accusing her doctor
of ganging up on her, and then apologising to him for her action, she cut a
sad and lonely figure in the Court. Reid, too, had fallen ill under the strain
and retired to Ellon for a much-needed break. The Queen, sorry to see her
trusted doctor ill, wrote to him expressing her concern. She wanted all discussion on the Munshi, which was putting everybody under strain, to be
brought to an end.

Reid replied that it was true he had worried much from the thought that he
had incurred the Queen's displeasure, but he had done what he felt was right,
however much he had suffered for it. He said he was happy to learn that she did
not think he had acted 'from any unworthy motive' and that she appreciated 'the
difficult and painful position I have lately occupied in standing between your
Majesty and others'.[18]

The Household were also concerned about Reid. The Queen's personal secretary, Arthur Bigge, wrote to him saying he was sorry to hear about his illness. 'Yes,
you have simply become poisoned with Munshimania,' he joked, trying to make
light of the situation. Bigge reported that 'Everything (black and white) quiet as
far as I know!'

Though it had been a turbulent year at the Court, and one the Queen and her doctor would like to forget, the Munshi had not really been tamed. His Hindustani lessons with the Queen took place exactly on time, her visits to see his wife with any visiting Royalty or family carried on uninterrupted and she was also enchanted by the Munshi's young nephew, Abdul Rashid, who frequently played with the Royal grandchildren and great-grandchildren. Young Rashid was admitted to a school in St Andrews and the Munshi was given time off to take him there. The Queen kept track of his welfare and noted with satisfaction in her Journal that he was happy at the school.

As the autumn days drew to a close, Abdul Karim recorded his thoughts in her Hindustani Journal, not making any reference to the storm that the Household and the Court had seen that year, but lamenting instead for the suffering the famine had caused in India. He wrote in English:

I am extremely glad to record that Her Majesty has now finished the No 10 book of her Hindustani lessons today evincing great interest. I have found Her Majesty becoming more and more eager and proficient in her Hindustani. There were but a very few days out of the whole year that Her Majesty was unable to devote the usual daily time for study. This is all the more remarkable owing to this year being such an important and busy one. Throughout the year, Her Majesty's health has been extremely good and her reign of sixty years has been a great retrospective pleasure. I pray that Her Majesty's health may long continue good and that she may live for many more years to come. Unfortunately, I have to note that this year has been a most unfortunate and evil one for India.

No country or people in the world has shown so much kind feeling and loyalty to its Ruler than people of India have done. Yet India has been in the midst of great difficulties and disasters such as famine, plague, fever, and most unfortunate of all a severe war on the frontier. I hope God will never again bring so unlucky days to India.[19]

At the end of his sober entry, he pasted a copy of the article from *The Graphic* and the offending photograph that had so incensed the Household. To the Munshi, the picture of him and his Queen sharing their precious moments together was a fitting end to the Jubilee Journal and a record of ten years of his service. He was also having a private laugh.

The Munshi left Balmoral that year confident in the knowledge that he had triumphed against the opposition. A report from the local newspaper about the departure of the Queen's party from Ballater showed how he still managed to grab the headlines, the media being oblivious of the storm in the Household.

Her Majesty's train from Ballater to Windsor on Friday 12th and Saturday 13 Nov 1897
Arrangement of Carriages

It is getting on to two, and the arrivals are growing fast and furious. The Queen's Indian secretary, the Munshi Abdul Karim, is one of the first of the inner circle of officials to arrive, looking as dignified as can be, and as one who was indeed a trusted servant of the Empress of India. His dignity – he is an absolutely self made man, a giant as the old Greeks called your 'filius terrae', and he therefore looks neither to the left nor to the right – will not allow him to tarry a sight for sore eyes. In that peculiarly hued turban of his, he strides magnificently over the red carpet and buries himself in his own special saloon.[20]

The rest of the Household were barely mentioned in the article.

12

REDEMPTION

The Queen did not want to hear any more complaints about Karim and made this clear to Reid. After what had been a stormy few months, she decided to reclaim her Munshi. 'I have in my Testamentary arrangements secured your comfort … and have constantly thought of you well,' she wrote to him. 'The long letter I enclose which was written nearly a month ago is *entirely* and solely my *own idea, not a human being will ever* know of it or of what you answer me. If you can't read it I will help you and then burn *it at once.*'[1]

The urgent letter was signed 'your faithfully true friend, VRI'. The Queen was determined to ensure that Karim would be looked after when she was gone. Her family and the Household, she knew, would not be kind to him. The letter she wrote to him was one of the many that her son Bertie destroyed after her death.

Meanwhile, the Royal family and the Household were beginning to get frustrated with their attempts to expose the Munshi. The Prince of Wales approached the Prime Minister twice, but he told him that 'he did not see it was his business'. Since the Prince could not speak to his mother directly, he turned to Reid to help him on the Munshi issue. The doctor found he was once again becoming the hapless intermediary between mother and son. The Munshi did not make things easier for himself either. He seemed to have alienated most of the Indian servants as well. Ghulam Mustapha, the Indian attendant, apparently complained to Reid that he felt compelled to return to India because of the Munshi's tyranny and described him as a 'bad man' and 'a debbel'.

The Household made another attempt to discredit the Munshi through his association with Rafiuddin. Much was made of the fact that in January 1898 Rafiuddin had chaired a rally of the Muslim Patriotic League (MPL) at Chancery Lane. His presence at another 'disloyal' meeting at Bloomsbury was also confirmed by none other than Dadabhai Naoroji, the first Indian to be elected to the House of Commons, who wrote a letter to *The Standard* about it. The latter's statement, quoted by the media, was immediately picked up by the Household, and the Chief of the Metropolitan Police, Sir Ernest Bradford, thought it reason enough to keep Rafiuddin under further surveillance.

As with most things to do with the Munshi and Rafiuddin, the event turned out to be nothing more than a lot of hot air. The MPL rally had not actually passed any 'disloyal' resolutions, but had in fact resolved to stand by the Queen's government. A newspaper report quoted Rafiuddin Ahmed as saying that at a time when serious attacks were being made on Imperial India, 'it was the duty of all loyal subjects of the Queen, who sincerely appreciated the government, to come forward and freely bear testimony to the beneficent character and impartial spirit of that government'.

The resolution passed at the meeting clearly called on Indians to support the British government saying: 'That this meeting of the MPL has no sympathy with the revolutionary resolution recently passed at the conference held in Bloomsbury, and reaffirms its loyal support to the British rule in India because situated as India is at the present time it is under that rule alone that the peaceful progress of the country is at all possible.'

When Dadabhai Naoroji wrote that Rafiuddin had earlier attended the conference in Bloomsbury where a 'revolutionary resolution' had been passed, it gave the Household fodder to accuse Rafiuddin of disloyalty. Rafiuddin stated that he had attended the Bloomsbury conference merely as an observer and vehemently denied stoking any revolutionary feelings among fellow Indians. But it was enough for the surveillance on him to continue and for Reid to seize the opportunity to have a word with the Prime Minister. Reid wrote to Lord Salisbury personally, warning him once again of the association of the Munshi and Rafiuddin, and the fact that the Munshi would probably wish to take Rafiuddin to Cimiez as his companion.

'Should he [the Munshi] urge this on the Queen, I believe Her Majesty might consent, as she has of late been getting you to think well of Rafiuddin, and is believing that all suspicions about him are groundless,' wrote Reid. He went on to inform the Prime Minister that Ernest Bradford 'knew something of Rafiuddin' and entertained an unfavourable opinion about him and his capacity for mischief. He suggested that he meet Sir Ernest sometime and hear what he had to say on the subject, so he could get 'an unbiased and unprejudiced opinion from an authority of conspicuous probity'.[2]

Reid continued to have long conversations with Salisbury about Rafiuddin, trying to persuade the Prime Minister to take pre-emptive action against him. He even told Salisbury that Rafiuddin could at any time support the revolutionaries and make a case for weapons, and that he was 'quickly accumulating them'.[3] His attempts to convince the Queen about Rafiuddin, as always, came to nought as she simply dismissed him saying: 'But he does not sympathize with them.'

Salisbury decided to deal with the Rafiuddin issue in his special diplomatic way. He tried to dissuade the Queen from allowing Rafiuddin to go to Cimiez, suggesting that it would be 'unfortunate' if the French press got word of any-thing on him and treated her with ridicule. The Queen found this reasonable and agreed to the exclusion of Rafiuddin from the European trip. 'She saw this and seemed impressed by it, and I am quite sure that this is the argument to use with her,' Salisbury told Reid.

Reid tried to tell the Prime Minister that the Munshi was bullying the Queen, but did not get far with that. Salisbury told him he did not agree with this as she could always get rid of him if she wanted. Salisbury told Reid that he believed the Queen 'really liked the continual excitement, as he [the Munshi] is the only form of excitement she can have'.[4]

The Queen went to Cimiez alone that year, but the Household was premature in celebrating their victory as Karim joined her within days. The Queen had apparently written to him to do so. Before his arrival she sent a thirty-two-page memo to Reid and warned her Household that there should be no recurrence of the 'lamentable and unnecessary occurrences of last year', and they should be '*buried in oblivion*'. She forbade her gentlemen to indulge in any gossip and put down strict instructions: 'I *cannot* allow any remarks *about* my people being made by my Gentlemen, or any gossip and reports or stories being listened to by them; but [they] are at once to be stopped.' The Queen also said that the Munshi would have his carriage as usual and have his name mentioned in the circulars on arrival.

In her Journal she recorded that she had immediately resumed her Hindustani lessons as she had missed these while Karim was away. Though the Household fumed at his return, the Queen and the Munshi went about their walks and lessons simply as if nothing had happened. She would often take her lesson in the grounds in the donkey chair (the donkey being taken out) or the pair would sit in the gardens of the Hotel Regina and enjoy the Mediterranean sun. With Abdul by her side, the Queen would look through her boxes and fill her Hindustani Journal with sprawling Urdu letters, recording the weather and the day's events. Satisfied in the knowledge that she had not been browbeaten by her family, the Queen was calm and composed. Her family did not dare question her anymore. Their discussions on the Munshi continued in private. Princess Christian and Beatrice and the Prince of Wales all consulted Reid and had several discussions with him, but they did not confront the Queen. She would be entering her eightieth year soon, had lived longer and seen more Prime Ministers than any British monarch and was not to be taken lightly. The bitterness against the Munshi remained on the boil. One day, when the Household was invited to the Queen's Drawing Room to hear a Hungarian band from Monte Carlo play, the Queen warned Reid beforehand that the Munshi would be present and that he was to be 'civilly spoken to'. Reid recorded that 'no one did, but Clark' (Captain Clarke, the Prince of Wales's equerry).

The Munshi simply put up with the obvious hostility from the Household, but the Queen had had enough of it. Having spent a few pleasant weeks with Karim at Cimiez, she decided to let her Household know exactly how she felt about

their behaviour towards him. She sent a lengthy memo to Reid accusing the
Household of racist feelings and jealousy towards the Munshi.

> The bitterness feeling and nasty racial feeling can only have produced extraor-
> dinary behaviour and injustice which led to it last year. What could have
> recently caused this enmity to the poor man who injured no one, interfered
> with no one, never put himself forward and the very few occasions he appeared
> is credible.
>   He may have given himself airs or boasted in India but not more than others.
> He very most likely was misled into publication and let his name appear with-
> out reflection, but that has happened to others … More and more does the
> plot of Indian and English jealousy show that stories utterly unfounded to have
> appeared and were told by people out of sheer spite and jealousy behind every-
> thing and a tissue of falsehoods were believed which must be put a stop to. VRI.

She added a postscript:

> I have added to this long yarn as such numbers of things come to my mind. But
> one thing I have outlined which is the attack on Abdul Karim's position. It is
> not a high one and it's not in England that we should speak of this. Archbishops,
> bishops, generals and peers have risen from the lowest and as Lord Salisbury and
> I remember, Sir William Jenner who the Queen chose to raise a chimney sweep.
> They have no right to say a word. It is all very disgraceful, I must repeat.[5]

The Queen had chastised her Household. Despite their best efforts, her opinion
of the Munshi or Rafiuddin had not changed.

The Queen was nearly eighty, frail, but still enjoying an active life. The Aga Khan,
who had an invitation to Windsor for lunch, marvelled at her appetite, noting that
she ate and drank heartily 'every kind of wine that was offered, and every course,
including both the hot and the iced pudding'. She had given instructions to Reid
about who was to look after her when she was ill. Not surprisingly, these were her
'regular gentle nice Indian servants' who were to do 'whatever may be required to
lift or help me and in any way moving me'. The Queen remembered that when
she was ill in 1871, her 'excellent servant and friend J Brown' used always to lift
her in and out of bed and on to the sofa and saved her pain. This would now be
done by her trusted Indians, who looked after her reverentially.
   Thoughts about what would be done with the Munshi after the Queen's death
were now crossing the minds of the gentlemen of the House. Colonel Arthur
Davidson, one of those actively involved in the anti-Munshi campaign, set up a

meeting with Sir Edward Bradford, Chief of Police at Scotland Yard, to discuss how to secure all the Queen's letters from the Munshi. Davidson told Reid that he had had a long talk with Bradford and discussed the suggestions made by the Prince of Wales about what action would be taken after the Queen's death. His own idea was that Lord Salisbury's approval of the discussion should be obtained first and that a responsible legal adviser should act for them. Bradford, however, thought that discussing the legality of the action would lead to a 'tangle of difficulties' and he was prepared to 'do anything when the moment arrived' and worry about the legal implications later.

Davidson said that Bradford also felt the Prince of Wales should be kept in absolute ignorance of anything that they discussed and any decision that was made so that if 'errors were made and there was a row' then they would bear the blame and the Prince of Wales would not be mixed up in it in any way.

With regard to simultaneous action being taken in India, he thought it would be sufficient if the Prince of Wales insisted on the Secretary of State wiring the necessary instructions to India when the time came. Bradford told Davidson that secrecy was of the utmost importance. He was, however, a little worried that Dennehy, in his blundering way, may have given the Munshi a hint of what to expect and this may have put him on his guard and he may have put the letters away safely. The Prince of Wales had agreed to these arrangements.

He also had an update on Rafiuddin, who he constantly referred to as 'the Ruffian': 'Of course, the Ruffian enters largely into the business and to my mind the danger lies in papers and letters being with *him* but Bradford said he did not see how we could well get at him,' said Davidson.

Davidson had gone to the British Library and looked up the newspaper reports on the MPL meetings and the letter in *The Standard* by Dadabhai Naoroji and had come to the following conclusion:

29 Dec 1897 – Report of Naoroji's meeting (no mention of Ruffian being there) at which disloyal sentiments were enunciated and similar resolutions passed.

10 Jan 1898 – Meeting of Muslim Patriotic League. Ruffian in chair at which loyal resolutions were passed.

12 Jan 98 – Letter from Dadabhai Naoroji with reference to Ruffian's championship at this meeting. He was present at 29 December meeting and took part in the disloyal manifestations which he now pretended to deplore.

14 Jan 98 – A long and wordy reply from the Ruffian. Saying he was only present as a spectator and not a participator at meeting. After which the matter apparently dropped.

I have sent Bradford this data and we will get the papers referred to but I don't really think there is much in it except as showing the interesting underhand nature of the Asiatic generally.[6]

On receiving the enclosures from Davidson, Bradford admitted there was nothing much in it except that it showed the duplicity of Rafiuddin who had tried to make capital of his presence at the conference. The case against Rafiuddin was ending in a whimper.

A year later, the Queen wrote to Lord Rowton:

> Lord Salisbury had a very satisfactory conversation with the Muslim Rafiuddin Ahmed, whose loyalty is now beyond all doubt and uncertainty and the contrary which was believed 2 years ago by some of the ill-disposed and misinformed people at the India Office and elsewhere and was eagerly believed and used against the poor shamefully used Munshi.[7]

Nothing was unearthed on Rafiuddin and the accusations against him gradually fizzled out. It was clear that the whole business had been a case of overreaction and an attempt to discredit the Munshi.

The Munshi affair seemed, for the time being, to be under control. The Household had begun to accept that they could do nothing about him during the Queen's lifetime and were prepared to draw up a secret plan with the police chief to deal with him after her death. Meanwhile, the Munshi travelled to Balmoral and invited the usual media attention. On 23 May 1898, the *Aberdeen Journal* reported the 'Arrival of Queen's Indian Secretary' to Balmoral.

> The Queen's Indian secretary, Munshi Hafiz Abdul Karim, arrived in Aberdeen station from Windsor in a special saloon carriage by the 7.15 West Coast route train, and after having been served with breakfast in the carriage by Mr McDonald, station refreshment rooms, left by the 8.05 train for Ballater.

While at Balmoral, the Queen, with the Munshi, watched a performance of Lord George Sanger's Circus Company, which featured the elephant 'Prince' on which Prince Albert Edward rode through India. The local newspaper reported that the Queen was 'exuberant and laughed at the clown's jokes'. Karim was also invited to the opera *Romeo et Juliet* by the Royal Opera Company from Covent Garden at Windsor Castle on 27 June, according to *The Times* newspaper.

The Queen had finished her eleventh Hindustani Journal that year. Karim wrote the end-piece in Urdu. For the first time he noted the hostility he had faced in Court.

> Thanks to God that today this book No 11 of Her Majesty's lesson in Hindustani was completed well and nicely, which is a small sign of her exalted honour and

dignity. And Her Majesty's readiness and interest in this Urdu language is evident as fondness for it did not cease in the face of contentions and difficulties which I have often faced since the previous year because of the persons jealous of me. Since the charges have no stability and firmness, they faced humiliation. By God's grace, Her Majesty enjoyed good health during this period except for occasional complaints of indigestion which was cured by administering purgatives. Though Her Majesty did not like that but had no choice and agreed to it. The demise of Duchess of Teck [mother of Princess May of Teck, later to become Queen Mary] and especially His Highness the Prince of Wales's hurting himself in a fall were sad, otherwise there was peace and safety in all respects. In this very auspicious month, the future destiny of India began to take shape. After much effort and search, Mr Curzon, was appointed the new Viceroy of India. May God show His mercy and everything may end well! Amen! Humbly Abdul Karim, 13th August 1898.[8]

The Munshi left for India at the end of the year, mainly with the aim of sorting out the purchase of his land in Agra. He had been negotiating the sale for over a year, having identified a large plot of land adjacent to what the Queen had gifted him in 1890. The land consisted of 147 acres, three roads and ten poles in the Mauza Sarai in the heart of Agra, close to the jail where his father worked.[9] Several letters had been exchanged, as the land was considered government land and the formalities had to be dealt with by the Collector of Agra. The Munshi had paid Rs 7,032 for the land early in 1897 and was liable for the land revenue of Rs 335 per annum with immediate effect. However, the deeds took a long time to get finalised. On completion, he showed a clever head for figures, asking to be relieved of some of the taxes that would be assessed then or in the future as he had paid the full amount two years back on a high interest loan, but had not been able to benefit from the yearly profits from the land in that period.

The polite request was immediately agreed to, as it was considered very reasonable. The handwritten letter from Balmoral reveals the progress the Munshi had made in English as it was flawless. Karim was eventually handed the papers at the end of 1898 and joined the ranks of Agra's landed classes.[10] So famous was the Queen's Munshi that he apparently considered keeping a guestbook at his home in Agra, but soon abandoned the idea.

When the registration forms entered his name as the son of 'Munshi Waziruddin, Khan Bahadur', Karim immediately wrote to the Collector of Agra: 'Please note that my father's name should be written either Dr Waziruddin or Mahommed Waziruddin & *not* Munshi.' He remained proud and fussy about the title given to him by the Queen. The final land deed was made in the name of 'Munshi Hafiz Abdul Karim, C.I.E, Her Majesty the Queen's Munshi'.[11]

When the Munshi arrived in Nice in April 1899, a French newspaper referred to him as 'Le Prince'. It also said the 'Prince Munshi' was very well known in Nice where he visited every year with Queen Victoria.

The Queen was calmer now, the rebellions she felt had been contained, and she knew Karim had a secure future after her death. She took her Hindustani lessons in the landscaped gardens of the Hotel Regina and in her favourite donkey chair which always travelled with her. The French were used to seeing the two together. While in Cimiez, the Queen received the news that Mohammed Buksh had fallen seriously ill and died in Windsor on 24 April. Buksh had come with Karim to England for the Jubilee and remained an attendant while Karim had moved upwards. He had been 'the stout and jovial one', who had meticulously served his Queen, never once complaining that he had not been hand-picked by her for further promotions as Karim had been. Some years ago, Buksh had been devastated by the death of his young daughter. The Queen remembered how he had broken down and wailed in front of her and she had tried to console him. The Queen knew how heartbreaking it was to lose a loved one. Karim, too, felt the loss of Buksh, a man with whom he had shared the excitement and thrill of travelling to England for the first time, and who had been one of the few who had remained remarkably free of jealousy towards him.

The Queen's eightieth birthday passed in a sea of celebration, following as it did just two years after her Diamond Jubilee. In India the occasion was marked by the issue of a special medal of honour, the *Kaiser-e-Hind* medal, and the Queen took a keen interest in the recipients of the honour. The Munshi gave her a brass jar decorated with scrolling foliage and a handmade card. Despite opposition from the Household, the Queen honoured the Munshi with the CVO (Commander of the Victorian Order).

On 29 May 1899, five days after her birthday, Karim made one of the lengthiest entries in the Hindustani Journal. The three-page entry, written in Urdu, was a record of his time at the Court and a frank assessment of the attitudes towards him. It was almost as if it was written for posterity, secretly recorded in the Journal to which only his Queen and he had access.

Sir Henry [Ponsonby] died and after him there is no one who can be called your adviser or who can be said to be a worker as per your dictate, in the same manner as he was. Once he died, the persons jealous of me got a chance to defame. But all such persons had to repent and fall down just in the same way as their thoughts were mean. I have often heard you telling the stories of Henry Ponsonby and this too that he was more attached to the city of Delhi.

Dimanche 2 Avril 1899

ÉCHOS

LA REINE VICTORIA A NICE

La reine Victoria a reçu, hier après-midi, Mgr Chapon, évêque de Nice.

A 4 heures, la souveraine britannique est sortie en voiture en compagnie de la duchesse d'York. La voiture royale s'est rendue à Tourettes-Levens.

Ont été s'inscrire, hier, sur le registre de la reine :

M. Pollonnais, maire de Villefranche ; M. Henry Racine, vice-consul d'Autriche-Hongrie à Menton ; Sir Clarence Smith ; M. J. Charlton Parr ; M. Roger Charlton Parr ; capitaine V. Petetin ; lieutenant Dugrais ; lady M. Murdo ; comtesse Waldegrave ; lord et lady Brougham and Vaux ; amiral sir John Hopkins ; M. A. Laroute ; M. L. Paoli.

Hier soir, la reine Victoria a donné un grand dîner auquel avaient été priés : le duc Georges de Leuchtenberg, prince et Dawson Douglas, attaché militaire.

A l'issue du dîner, M. Leoncavallo, répondant à l'invitation de la reine, est venu jouer des fragments de ses opéras, « La Bohème » et « I Pagliacci ».

princesse d'Essling, Mlle Violette d'Elchingen, duchesse de Mouchy et le colonel

---

Le prince Manshi-Abdul-Hamin, secrétaire particulier de la reine Victoria pour les affaires des Indes, est arrivé à Nice hier matin, à 10 heures.

Le prince Manshi est très connu à Nice où il vient chaque année avec la reine Victoria.

Article in a French newspaper showing the French referring to him as *Le Prince*.

It is due to him that you have so many other well meaning servants, for example William Sahib etc. Otherwise, in this cunning world, really well meaning servants are few and far between. This is why none of your work or assignments have come to a halt. It is just another thing that it is too difficult to create a place for oneself in your heart. But still, if you have more faith on and believe more in the servants of other nation; then it is certainly a result of your Highness' inborn certitude and great faith.

Today, you are 80 and still your health, by the grace of God is better than youths. You take good meals and there is no change in the daily life of yours; it goes on as ever. Your morning and evening outings have stopped just for now and you travel just a little less. Nevertheless, your health and sight is still excellent by the grace of God. Because having such a nice health despite such exercising work and tensions of so many nations and issues of capital, can be nothing but a grace of God.

Apart from above-mentioned blessings, your highness is blessed with one more thing and that is wisdom and fine senses or alertness. So on this date, I would like to end this letter with a good wish that you may be graced by one hundred years and may always enjoy further happiness with your family. Also, like to thank God, that since you have punished those who were jealous of me, I would not be forced to face them. May God, make your sense of justice more and more robust day by day.

The Munshi did not end there however. He seemed to be in full flow and continued for another two pages:

But there has been an increase in jealousy and prejudice against Muslims and Islam; and in comparison with other religions, they [Muslims] have suffered greater pain and losses. Apart from this after 28 years, people of Sudan have been made part of some other nation.

Again in 1891–98, you defeated the jealousy and pride of my enemies and they got nothing but humiliation and remorse. Nevertheless, I would now like to tell something about myself unto you, the Queen of India (Kaiser-e-Hind).

You are wholly honest, good and truthful. I was given a chance to serve you despite the fact that hundreds of others are always eager to serve you. You have been gracious enough to take me in your service. And have been gracious during all these years. I swear that you are entirely a truthful and solemn personality. Your name will always be there, and more particularly from the time your rule was established in India.

I had quite a strange experience in this country (England). That is true to your being an Empress of multi-cultural empire, I have always found you quite free from the fire of jealousy born out of religion. All your subjects are one in your eyes. Secondly, wherever there was some contention, despite being ill advised by jealous persons, you never gave up your commitment to truth. Sometimes you did not heed even your own child. Thirdly, you have earned such a great goodwill and empathy from your empire that it will certainly be of a great help to our young Prince. Not to lose heart and that too in this age is a great thing. I have never seen your highness idle and have been witness to the fact that you almost always completed your daily work and never left it for tomorrow.

You never signed any document without going through it and whenever a signature was not needed, and such letters were also despatched same day and you also acknowledged the letters coming from all over the world the same day.

By the grace of God, I have been in this country for thirteen years (as per Islamic calendar) and for twelve years as English (Julian) calendar.

I have written my entire experience in the book. But it goes without saying that serving the Empress of India (Kaiser-e-Hind) has been a very taxing and ever vigilant work. I have never had an hour of idleness or a day of leave. On the day of General Holiday, often more work is to be done as thousands of letters have to be acknowledged the same day. Nevertheless, it is a matter of great joy that at least twice or thrice or four times a year, we have to go for hunting. And I like this much more than dance or other games. In January, the hunting of *barasingha* [stag] and fishes is pretty difficult. In the month of November and December the hunting of birds is quite absorbing and interesting.

But despite the whole day's work and tiredness there is nothing like rest for you in the evening. You perform all the necessary work and do all the work related to court. And whatever the writer and readers have to bring forth before you, they must bring that also. You never like to be absent. This is proved by the twelfth book. For ten years we have been given various gifts like books and photographs on Christmas. Apart from this, I have been also made the chief of all the servants. Apart from all these works, the works related to the management of Indian servants is also there. So anyone can guess that in the court of the Empress, there is no let up in work, even for one hour.

It is only when you go outside for some travel, your servants like me also get some respite and enjoy that. Only this much is possible.

Now I would like to mention something about the end of 1898 because I have been in the habit of saying something at the end of every year. The year 1898 has left many memorable things. And they were quite revolutionary. This is most unfortunate that in comparison to other religions, Islam and the Muslims have not been given their due. This is what I think. Nevertheless it is a matter of gratitude for me that I have been promoted to the great consternation of the persons jealous to me. It is also a grace of God that on your 80th birthday you are so happy and fortunate and full of command.

But since the world is always full of happiness as well as sorrow, this year saw the demise of the son of Koburg *sahib* [Duke of Coburg]. But it is a matter of solace that before his death he was able to come up to your expectation and did the work well, which was assigned by you to him. I am my dear readers, Your most humble and obedient servant, M.H. Abdul Karim, CIE, CVO. [12]

The three-page entry left little doubt of the Munshi's sincere regard for the Queen and the high estimation in which he held her. It was almost as if the Munshi had unburdened himself before the Queen and any future reader who may follow his account.

The Household had stopped him from publishing a journal some years back. The Hindustani Journals became the space where he gave his account without any censorship. His praise for Henry Ponsonby and genuine concern for the health and future well-being of the Prince of Wales is quite touching, given that the future King had no love lost for him.

In August that year, James Reid married Susan Baring, maid of honour to the Queen, surprising the Court who had presumed he would remain a bachelor. The Queen was upset with the marriage since she did not like losing any of her ladies-in-waiting, but soon came round to the idea.

The Munshi returned to India in early November 1899. The Queen wrote in her thirteenth Hindustani Journal that she would be having her last lesson for some time as he was going away. She went to see the Munshi's wife to say good-bye and 'to give her my little Christmas present'. [13]

In December that year, the new Viceroy – Lord Curzon – wrote to the Queen that during his visit to Agra he had the pleasure of meeting Dr Wuzeeruddin, the Munshi's father. 'He was a courtly old gentleman and had many interesting experiences to relate. Unfortunately the Munshi was too unwell to accompany his parent,' said the Viceroy. [14] Clearly the strain of the Court politics and the long sea journey had caught up with the Munshi.

13

⟨∞⟩

DEATH OF A QUEEN

The Munshi's father died in June. The Queen received the news from Karim and her heart went out for the old man whose son she had got to know so well and from whom she had learnt so much about India. She wrote immediately to Karim and to the Viceroy, who sent a feeling response:

> I had already heard with great regret of the death of the Munshi's father. The Viceroy recalls with much pleasure his interview with the old gentleman at Agra in December last, when he was much struck at the courtly manner and interesting conversation of the Khan Bahadur. He was a most devoted subject of your Majesty.

The Munshi's father – once a humble hospital assistant – died a titled man, living in a grand house with acres of land. The Queen and Karim had provided well for him. The Munshi remained in India following his father's death winding up the affairs of his estate.

It was a year of heartbreaking news for the Queen. She had lost her grandson, Alfred (young Affie), in the Boer War. In July she received news of the death of her son, the Duke of Coburg, to cancer. She was given the news after breakfast and got up slowly, saying, 'My people will feel for me'. Her maid-in-waiting, Marie Mallet, recalled how she wept silently and remembered his early days. The Queen had buried three children and three sons-in-law – all of whom had been in their prime – and this last blow was more than she could bear. A pall of gloom hung over the Royal palaces as news of the ravages of the war came in. In October the Queen received the telegram informing her of the death of her grandson, Prince Christian Victor, in South Africa.

The Munshi returned in November. It had been nearly a year since he had left. Marie Mallet was not particularly welcoming: 'The Munshi has also returned after a year's absence in India, why the plague did not carry him off I cannot think, it might have done one good deed!'[1] she wrote.

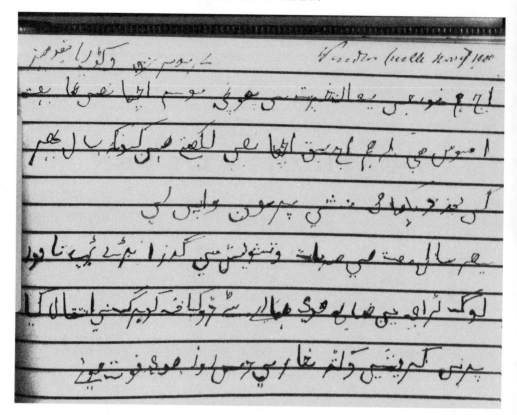

The Queen's last entry in Urdu in her Hindustani Journal.

The Queen – frail and lonely as she had become – was delighted to have her dear Munshi back. Both had lost their loved ones in the last few months. Karim was shocked to see how pale she looked. The Queen had made her last journey from Balmoral the night before, requesting that there should be no one at the platform at Ballater. The weather had been gloomy, a grey drizzle visible from the waiting room at the railway station, where she had sat by the fire and had a cup of tea with her daughter Beatrice. The Queen slept badly that night, knowing she would not be returning to her beloved Highland home. Back in Windsor, with her Munshi by her side, the Queen felt better and resumed her lessons immediately. On 7 November 1900, she wrote in Urdu:

Today, I reached here safely from Balmoral. The weather was not good. It is a matter of sorrow that we do not write the lesson well today because we paid attention to it after a year. The Munshi returned the day before yesterday.

The whole of this year we faced grievous shocks and concerns. Many a famous man was wasted in war. My son, Duke of Coburg, passed away. Prince Gracious Victor died of fever ten days ago.[2]

It was the Queen's last entry in her Hindustani Journal. She was soon to become seriously ill.

Osborne, 22 January 1901

The Queen died in my arms at 6.30, the Kaiser on the other side of the bed, helping me and supporting her.

James Reid made the entry in his diary and wiped a tear. A whole era had ended and the anxiety and stress of the last few days was just beginning to sink in. The Queen had died surrounded by her family in her favourite holiday home in Osborne. She had been confined to her bed for the last few weeks, showing signs of dyspepsia, impaired nutrition and brain fatigue. The doctor diagnosed it as 'periods of insomnia and mental confusion, brought on by damaged cerebral circulation after years of constant brain work through a long life of Royal responsibilities and Imperial events, domestic sorrows and anxieties specially in her later years'.[3] She drifted in and out of sleep, the doctor constantly by her side. Even in her semi-conscious state she asked Reid what her people would think because she had not ridden out for several days and wondered if they were getting anxious.

The Prince of Wales was summoned to Osborne and the Kaiser of Germany came to see his 'grandmama' before she died. He had troubled her during her reign with his hostile attitude to Britain and his uncaring attitude to his mother, the Queen's eldest daughter Victoria, but now came to make his peace. The Kaiser's arrival caused a stir and journalists started gathering around Osborne House as it came to be known that the Queen was dying. Regular updates on the Queen's health prepared by Reid were posted outside the gates of Osborne House. The sight of reporters dashing to the post office at Cowes to telegraph their copies to the news desks was becoming familiar. Mr Mott, postmaster at Cowes post office, had to lay on more staff to cope with the demand.

The day before her death, the Queen had been given oxygen frequently and in the afternoon asked for her favourite dog, Yuri. He was out for exercise, but on his return was taken and put on the Queen's bed. She patted him and seemed pleased to have him beside her. In her drowsy state, the Queen asked for the Prince of Wales and asked him to kiss her face.

On the morning of 22 January, the Queen started sinking after breakfast and the doctor nearly thought it all over by ten o'clock, but she rallied again after the last prayer was read. Regaining consciousness, she asked for the clergyman, Mr Smith, and recognised the Kaiser. She was left alone with her grandson for five minutes. Reid remained by her side all day and she murmured his name several times. Her last words to her doctor were, 'I will do anything you like', a sad testament to how helpless and vulnerable the wilful Queen suddenly felt. The end came at 6.30 in the evening and was peaceful and dignified, the Queen dying in the arms of her trusted doctor, with the Kaiser holding her other hand.

'All day long, the Angel of Death has been hovering over Osborne House,' reported *The Times*. 'One could almost hear the beating of his wings. But at half past six those wings were folded and the Queen put to rest.' At Cowes post office, Mr Mott laid on forty extra people to man the wires, working through the night on shifts, as the press sent out the story to the world.

The Queen had left detailed instructions regarding the procedures to be followed after her death in a sealed letter, which she had given to Reid on 9 December 1897, three years back. With the help of her faithful dressers, Mrs Tuck and Miss Stewart, the doctor laid out all the things she had requested – photographs and mementoes of all the people she had held dear to her through her life – even the sprig of Balmoral heather that she so loved. He then packed the sides of the coffin with bags of charcoal in muslin. But he still had a final duty to perform.

The Queen was already wearing her own wedding ring and the wedding ring of John Brown's mother, which was given to her by Brown in 1875, and which she had always worn after his death. The doctor now wrapped two items in tissue paper and placed them in the Queen's left hand. They were a photograph of John Brown and a lock of his hair in a case. He discreetly covered these with the flowers given by Queen Alexandra so that the family could not see them.[4] The loyal doctor had taken care to keep his Queen's last request; it was one of the secrets she carried to her grave.

Once the coffin was arranged, Reid called in the family and members of the Household to see the Queen for the last time. The Munshi was summoned at the very end. He was allowed to spend a moment with his Queen and was the last person to see her alone. As he left the room, the members of the Royal family entered and the coffin was closed by Mr Wardford, the Osborne carpenter and his two workmen. The Munshi watched silently as the coffin was covered with a white pall and carried downstairs by the Blue Coats (sailors) into the dining room, which had been prepared as the *Chapelle Ardante*.

'My duties were over with the Queen after 20 years of service,' wrote Reid in his diary. 'I am exhausted.'

The Munshi sat in Arthur Cottage that night, the tears silently pouring down his face. He prayed for the friend who had stood by him for the last thirteen years and changed his life. To him, she had been more than the Empress of India and Queen of England. She had been a friend, a mother and an inspiration. He gazed at a photograph of the Queen on his desk and read the inscription in her familiar writing: 'Dear Abdul, Merry Christmas, Your loving friend VRI.' The Queen had written 'VRI' in Urdu.

A rich Indian shawl with a border of golden sequins was spread near the foot of the wrought-iron staircase in Osborne House. On it was spread a beautiful cushion of violets, from which rose a huge cross made of moss. The Queen was making her last journey from her beloved Indian rooms in Osborne, with its ornate carvings, collection of memorabilia and paintings of her Indian subjects.

In Calcutta the news of the Queen's death had spread like wildfire. One of the Viceroy's staff, who was out shooting early in the morning in the countryside, was surprised to find a native running out of the village across the fields to ask 'if the Great Queen was dead', such was the speed with which the news travelled to even the rural areas. Soon all of India knew the Empress was dead and the day was declared as one of general mourning.

The Viceroy, who had been woken at 3.45 a.m. to be told the news, wrote to the Secretary of State:

> No one who has not been to this country, can well realise the extent to which the British government, the monarchy, and the Empire did loyalty assume a more personal and therefore, a more passionate form ... The virtues of the Queen, her domestic character, her homeliness, the old fashioned simplicity of her sentiments and sayings, the fact that she was equally revered as Queen, mother, and wife, have all combined to produce an overpowering effect upon the imagination of the Asiatic, and not until some time has passed and the new regime is started shall we realise, in all probability, to what a degree the contested incorporation of India in the British Empire has been facilitated by the character and attributes of the late Sovereign ... No successor to the Queen, however genial, tactful and popular, and the new King is known to be all these, can ever win from the Indian people the feeling of personal devotion which assisted by her gt. longevity, and the glory of her reign, Queen Victoria aroused.[5]

One hundred and one guns were fired at sundown to mark the death of Queen Victoria in Calcutta.

On 1 February the Queen's coffin was taken down to Trinity Pier and carried on board the *Alberta*, the Royal yacht on which the Queen had made the same crossing so often over the years. The massed bands, their drums muffled, played Beethoven's funeral march. King Edward followed the *Alberta* in the *Victoria and Albert*, and the Kaiser behind him in his own yacht, the gleaming *Hohenzollern*. Thirty British battleships and cruisers – proud evidence of Britain's naval

power – lined the eight-mile route from Cowes to Southampton, providing an escort to the *Alberta*. They stood in formation, barely 500 yards apart, the sailors linking hands on the deck and the officers saluting as the *Alberta* sailed past. It was late afternoon when the *Alberta* turned into Portsmouth harbour. The sun set on the Solent in a blaze of red and gold, as the ships sailed out in a fitting farewell to the Queen.

Next morning her coffin was taken from Portsmouth by train to Victoria. Nearly 1 million people, dressed in mourning black, lined the streets in London to watch the funeral cortege on its way to Paddington Station. The Queen – the proud daughter of a soldier – had wanted a military funeral and decreed that her coffin would be carried on a gun carriage. On the coffin was placed the Imperial Crown, the orb and sceptre and the collar of the Order of the Garter. The crowds filled Hyde Park – standing sixty deep – to catch a final glimpse of the Queen who had become a legend in her lifetime and taken the country into the age of steam, telegraphs, industrialisation and Empire. Four European Kings followed the gun carriage on horseback: King Edward VII, Kaiser Wilhelm II, King George I of the Hellenes and King Carlos of Portugal. King Leopold II of Belgium rode in a separate carriage. The Crown Princes of Denmark, Norway, Sweden and Romania rode in the procession along with other Royals. The Archduke Franz Ferdinand of Austria represented the Austrian Emperor. Thirteen years later, his assassination would trigger the First World War. Victoria had spread her family by marriage across Europe and her Empire covered one-fifth of the globe. At her death they had gathered from around the world to pay their respects.

From Paddington the funeral procession moved by train to Windsor, as the Queen had done countless times over the years. Once again the crowds gathered in Windsor to get a last glimpse of their Queen. A slight mishap occurred: the horses had got cold waiting outdoors and had got out of hand when being harnessed to the gun carriage, breaking the splinter bar and nearly causing a serious accident. As confusion reigned, Ponsonby suggested that the horses be abandoned and the gun carriage be manually pulled with ropes through Windsor and up the Castle's Long Walk to the St George Chapel for the funeral service. After the service, an eighty-one gun salute was fired, one for each year of the Queen's life.

Far away in Calcutta, in the capital of the Queen's Indian Empire, the city rang out with the sound of eighty-one guns, which were also fired there to remember the *Kaiser-e-Hind* and Empress of India.

The next day the coffin was taken to the mausoleum at Frogmore, where the Queen was buried beside her husband, Prince Albert. Standing in the funeral party was the Munshi, who watched as his Queen was buried in her own Taj Mahal. The Queen had left instructions that he would be one of those walking in her funeral procession along with her family, the Household and European Royalty. She had not forgotten him even in her death.

It was all to end soon for the Munshi. The King sent Princess Beatrice, Queen Alexandra and some guards to Frogmore Cottage where they demanded all the letters written by the Queen to the Munshi; they then burnt them in a bonfire outside the house. The King wanted no trace left of the relationship between his mother and the Munshi. Abdul Karim, the Queen's companion and teacher for thirteen years, was ordered to leave the country and packed his bags like a common criminal. All the other Indian servants were also asked to go home. After the Queen's funeral, Lord Esher noticed that the Indians were 'wandering about like uneasy spirits'. The new King did not want to see any more turbans in the palaces or smell the curries from the Royal kitchens. The Edwardian era had begun.

———∞———

14

LAST DAYS IN AGRA

T he division of the spoils followed soon after. Days within the departure
of the Munshi, Sir James Reid and his wife, Susan, went to see Arthur
Cottage in Osborne, the Munshi's former home, to see if it was suitable for them.[1] The Munshi's houses in Balmoral and Windsor were also quickly
occupied. Every effort was made to deep clean the memory of the Munshi. 'The
Black brigade', as the Indians were dubbed, were finally no longer occupying the
centre-stage of life in the Royal palaces.

In April a son was born to Reid. Fritz Ponsonby jokingly wrote to him asking,
'Is it true his name is to be Karim Reid!' In fact, King Edward VII became the
godfather of the child and he was christened Edward James.

The Household had been openly hostile to Karim and were keen to restore the
old order speedily. They had never understood what the Queen had seen in him.
To Henry Ponsonby, the Munshi was like 'a sort of pet, like a dog or cat which the
Queen will not willingly give up'. The Dean of Westminster, Randolph Davidson,
thought she was 'off her head' over the Munshi. Lord Salisbury was of the opinion
that the Queen enjoyed the spats over the Munshi with her Household because
'it was the only excitement she had'.

What her family could not comprehend was that the Queen was a born romantic. Beneath the trappings of the monarchy, the formalities of Court life and the
prudence she often displayed, the Queen was never afraid to love and show her
affections. The death of her beloved husband had left her lonely and heartbroken.
As a Queen she lived in a man's world and could have few women friends. Her
own daughters – Princesses Beatrice and Helena – kept their distance, not even
coming to see her through the night or nursing her when she was on her deathbed, a fact noted with disapproval by Reid. Princess Beatrice was often selfish and
the Queen had frequently been reduced to tears by her behaviour and demands.

Her sons, and grandsons too, gave her endless problems and she had no one to turn to or confide in after Albert's death. It fell to John Brown to draw her out of her self-imposed isolation, and the Queen soon leaned strongly on him. Brown was devoted to her and she could talk freely to him. More than anything else, he treated her like a woman rather than a Queen, something neither her family nor her Household could do. His death once again robbed her of a companion.

When the Munshi arrived during the Jubilee, his presence lifted her spirits. The Queen took instantly to the handsome twenty-four-year-old Indian and was soon roller-coasting into an Indian wonderland of fragrant curries, bright turbans and the sensuous sound of the Urdu language on Karim's lips. The Queen sensed a certain depth in Karim and found she could talk to him comfortably despite the language barriers. Karim brought her closer to India, the country that she had always longed to visit. A skilled raconteur, he told the Queen about his country, the religions and the culture. Soon these discussions became more political.

The Queen's maid of honour, Marie Mallet, observed that the Queen gossiped more with the Munshi than she did with the other ladies in the Household. 'He is ubiquitous here,' she noted, 'and I am for ever meeting him in passages or the garden or face to face on the stairs and each time I shudder more …'[2]

The Queen's Munshi was described by the Household as 'repulsive' and 'disagreeable'. Even Henry Ponsonby described him and his relatives as the 'Black brigade', forcing the Queen to decree that the word 'black' was not to be used with reference to the Munshi and the other Indians.

Lady Curzon, wife of the Viceroy, while on a visit to London, made a few deductions about the Household and the Munshi. She wrote to her husband six months after the Munshi had been banished: 'The Munshi bogie which had frightened all the household at Windsor for many years proved a ridiculous farce, as the poor man had not only given up *all* his letters but even the photos signed by the Queen and had returned to India like a whipped hound.' She also missed the presence of the Indian servants and wrote: 'All the Indian servants have gone back so that now there is no Oriental picture and queerness at court.'[3] Lady Lytton, widow of the former Indian Viceroy Lord Lytton and lady-in-waiting to the Queen, was also perhaps one of the few to be fairly sympathetic to the Munshi. Her granddaughter, Mary Lutyens, later edited her diaries and concluded:

Though one can understand that the Munshi was disliked, as favourites nearly always are, it is difficult to believe that he was 'so personally repulsive', for Queen Victoria was as sensitive as any woman to male attraction. One cannot help feeling that the repugnance with which he was regarded by the Household was based mostly on snobbery and colour prejudice. There were few English people in those days who would sit down at table with an Indian were he not a Prince.[4]

The Munshi was certainly no Prince. He aspired to be a nawab, was proud of the decorations that the Queen bestowed on him and soon became incredibly wealthy, but his low birth and lack of formal education did not win him friends from the upper classes.

Looked down upon by Indian Princes like Sir Pertab, the Maharajah of Jodhpur, and alienated from the other Indian attendants, who were jealous of him, he too cut a lonely figure in the Court, with only the Queen by his side. Their last moments together on that January morning in Osborne, as the Munshi stood praying over the Queen's coffin, captured a tender story. While the King had summoned the Munshi at the very end to pay his respects to the Queen, purely because he disliked him so vehemently, his action only ensured that the Munshi became the last person to see the Queen alone before the coffin was closed. Inadvertently, Edward VII had scripted the perfect ending.

The Viceroy's office in Calcutta was flooded with mail. The Queen's death had led to a clamour for a memorial for her. Lord Curzon wrote to Hamilton that the scores of letters he was getting from the native societies or individuals all referred to the late Queen as 'mother'. He was beginning to realise just how much Queen Victoria meant to her Indian subjects.

'They truly loved her as a mother, even more than they revered her as a Queen,' he wrote.[5] 'All India is seething with a desire to raise some sort of memorial.' The Viceroy felt the memorial should be some sort of building or structure on a 'sufficiently noble scale' that would possess the requisite connections with the Queen's reign and personality. He felt a central gallery could house the relics of the momentous crises through which the Empire had passed, and capture the 'thrilling scenes and drastic incidents both of war and peace and the famous men by whom it has been served'. A statue – paid for by public subscription at the time of the Diamond Jubilee – could be placed in the front of the hall.

Curzon energetically set about raising funds for the memorial and addressed a large gathering in the Town Hall in Calcutta on 6 February 1901. He recalled the Queen's great love for India 'as no other monarch from a motherland had done', and said the fifteen Governor Generals who had served under her were witness to this love.

The role of Karim in the Queen's life also proved an effective fund-raiser for Curzon. The Viceroy told the gathered crowds: 'As we know, she learned the Indian language when already advanced in years. She was never unattended by Indian servants, and we have read that they were entrusted with the last sorrowful office of watching over her body after death.' Curzon did not name the man who had helped the Queen learn Hindustani and brought her closer to India. Karim was not invited to the function, though funds were being raised on the basis of what he had achieved.

The Viceroy held forth on the Queen's love for India. He pointed out that in her two Jubilee processions she had decreed that the Indian Princes, and the pick of her Indian soldiers, should ride in her train. He said:

> There are many of those Princes, who could testify to the interest she showed in them, to the gracious welcome which she always extended to them when in England, and to the messages of congratulations or sympathy which they often received from her own hand. But it was not to the rich or titled alone that she was gracious. She was equally a mother to the humble and the poor, Hindu and Mahomedan, man and woman, the orphan and the widow, the outcaste and the destitute. She spoke to them all in the simple language that came straight from her heart and went straight to theirs. And these are the reasons why all India is in mourning today.

The very qualities in the Queen that the Household and the Indian Office had despaired of during her reign were now being used to appeal to the Indians and get them to donate. Barely a few months ago, Curzon had expressed his annoyance at the fuss made over the Maharajah of Kapurthala by the Queen and the fact that she had invited him to Balmoral. 'It is hopeless for me to endeavour to take a strong line about the unworthy and dissolute members of the princely class, if they receive encouragement and compliance from the Queen at home,' he had written angrily to Hamilton in November 1900. 'I am afraid that every Indian prince, whatever his character or personality is invested with a sort of halo in HM's eyes, and so strong are her sentimental feelings about the matter that I have not of course ventured to say anything about it in writing to her.'[6]

He had also complained to Hamilton that: 'At home every man with a turban, a sufficient number of jewels, and black skin is mistaken for a miniature Akbar, and becomes the darling of drawing rooms, the honoured guests of municipalities and the hero of newspapers.'[7]

Neither had the Household approved of her retinue of Indian servants and her closeness to the Munshi and the trust she placed in him, but these were of no consequence now that the Queen was dead. The fund-raising appeal for her memorial had to rely principally on her love for India and the Indians. Despite a severe famine in India, the cash flowed in. The Maharajah of Gwalior pledged Rs 10 lakhs (Rs 1 million), the Maharajah of Kashmir pledged Rs 15 lakhs (Rs 1.5 million), and the Maharajah of Jaipur pledged Rs 4 lakhs (Rs 400,000) to famine relief and Rs 5 lakhs (Rs 500,000) to the memorial fund.

So quickly were the funds flowing in that a cut-off premium was set at Rs 1 lakh (Rs 100,000) for further donations, though the large amounts already accepted were retained. India was welling with emotion at the Queen's death and the native Princes and the principalities were all prepared to stretch themselves for a memorial in her name.

Meanwhile, in London, the fund-raising efforts for a memorial were not
going half as well and the King appealed to Indian Princes to bankroll the
English memorial. This led to a clash with the Viceroy and Curzon decided
to put his foot down, saying the Indian funds should be kept for the Indian
memorial. By the end of February the Viceroy had collected Rs 1.6 million
from the native Princes, and by March this figure had reached Rs 2.3 million or
nearly £170,000.

'The Indian Empire is held by the British crown, partly by the justice and
sanity of our administration, partly by personal loyalty to the Sovereign,' Curzon
wrote to Hamilton. 'No Sovereign will be well advised who does not extend
to the uttermost the influence of the latter factor.'[8] Ever since the death of the
Queen, the Viceroy had found himself locked in argument with the King and the
India Office over what he thought was the excessive exploitation of the native
Princes. He vehemently objected to the proposal by the India Office that the
Indian Princes be asked to pay their way to attend the King's Coronation. He had
begun to realise how important the goodwill that the Queen had enjoyed was to
the Empire and he did not want the new King rocking it. He also objected to the
fact that Indians were being asked to pay for the visit of the Duke and Duchess of
Connaught to India, and asked Hamilton whether he thought it was 'possible or
practicable to make us pay for our Royal guests whom we did not invite, but who
offered themselves here, at the very moment that you are declining to pay for the
Indian guests whom you specially invited to England.'[9]

Instead of the Princes travelling to England at considerable expense to themselves, Curzon felt it was better to hold a grand Coronation Durbar in India
which could be attended by the native chiefs. He received the permission to
do so, and the Durbar was held in Delhi between December 1902 and January
1903. Curzon took personal interest in everything, from the setting down of the
train track and the design of the plaster to the position of the flower beds. A local
newspaper reported: 'Fifty-six native Indian chiefs arrived in an elephant procession with the Duke and Duchess of Connaught acting as representatives for the
King. Curzon spoke for 29 minutes and had to speak slowly as there were 13,000
people in the arena.'

Curzon informed Hamilton that the Duke and Duchess were 'delighted by
everything'. The former accepted a sword of £20,000 from the Maharajah of
Jaipur, something that did not please the Viceroy. He noted that there was a 'general feeling of disgust: for the impression already exists that an Indian chief exists
only to be bled'. The present King, noted Curzon, gave presents in India of £20–
25,000 and 'took away presents worth over 1 million sterling'.[10]

Curzon warned Hamilton that the Royals were prone to freeloading. 'When
the Prince and Princess of Wales come next year, it will be necessary to lay down
the strictest of rules. They really must not loot the Chiefs. The Associations,
Municipal and Communities will give them excellent gifts.' Curzon also felt

strongly that the Duke of Connaught should not have imposed for three weeks after the Durbar.

Meanwhile, the statue of Queen Victoria arrived in Calcutta by March 1902 and was placed temporarily in the Maidan where it was 'surrounded by thousands of admiring Natives'. The Viceroy also visited Agra in April 1902 and noted that the monuments being erected there would be the most beautiful. It is not recorded whether the Viceroy met the Munshi while in Agra or whether the Munshi was invited to any of the Viceroy's Durbars in the city.

The Munshi had built a new house, Karim Lodge, in the heart of Agra, on the land that the Queen had given him. He lived comfortably on his sizeable income and was seen riding through the city in his carriage. Often he could be heard regaling people with his tales about life in Queen Victoria's Court.

In December 1905 George, Prince of Wales, went on a tour of India and visited Agra, where he was captivated by the beauty of the Taj, and gave an account of it that his grandmother would have so loved to hear: 'After dinner we paid a short visit to the Taj Mahal which looked quite lovely in the moonlight. It is, I should think, the most beautiful building in the world, the white marble looks so dignified and peaceful and yet so grand, it impressed us immensely.'

The next day he visited it again and spent a good hour and a half examining it 'most carefully, both inside and out from every point, both near & far & I must say it is the most graceful and impressive building I have ever seen'.

The Prince of Wales also made time to see his grandmother's favourite Indian, the Munshi. He wrote to his father:

In the evening we saw 'the Munshi'. He has not grown more beautiful and is getting fat. I must say he was most civil and humble and really pleased to see us, he wore his CVO which I had no idea he had got. I am told he lives quite quietly here and gives no trouble at all. We also saw dear Grandmama's last four Indian servants who were with her up to her death, they also live here.[11]

The next day, the Prince of Wales unveiled a statue of Queen Victoria by Sir Thomas Brock which was erected in the centre of MacDonald Park in Agra. 'With the Fort on one side and the Taj on the other, no more perfect site could have been found, and the statue can be seen a long way off. Dear Old Sir Pertab was quite affected when I unveiled it, as you know how devoted he was to Grandmama,' said the Prince, who wore full military uniform for the occasion. He did not notice the figure of the Munshi also quietly wiping a tear as the Queen took her place in his city with a thirty-one gun salute fired from Agra Fort and the troops in full attendance. The day-long event ended with a dinner attended by all the leading people of Agra followed by a reception. The Prince described the evening as a 'tedious affair'. It was one of the last formal engagements with the Royal family attended by the Munshi.

He was not invited to the laying of the foundation stone of the Victoria Memorial Hall by the Prince of Wales in an elaborate ceremony in January 1906, where the 'whole of Calcutta, both English and Indian' made an appearance. It was followed by a state ball at Government House, Calcutta, attended by 2,000 people, where the Prince danced till 1.30 a.m. Lord Curzon, the main motivator behind the project, was also not present as he had left for England.

In his letter to his father, George wrote that he had a 'very successful' month in Calcutta as it was successful politically as well, given the negative feelings about the British government following the partition of Bengal. 'Our visit too was most opportune, as the feeling was very strong against the government owing to the Partition of Bengal and it made them think of something else, and the Bengalis most certainly showed their loyalty to the throne in a most unmistakeable manner,' wrote the Prince of Wales. He also added that he had killed during his month's stay in India thirteen tigers and four panthers.

The Indian political landscape was changing rapidly. Within three years an Indian was appointed to the Viceroy's Council to keep revolutionary sentiments against the British in check. The appointment was vehemently opposed by King Edward VII, who wrote a strong protest to Lord Morley, the Secretary of State for India, after he was forced to approve of it. The Prince of Wales wrote to the King: 'I think it will be fraught with grave danger to our rule in India.'[12]

In Agra, the Munshi had fallen ill. He had aged quickly over the last few years and was often melancholy. All the material wealth that he had could not compensate for the precious moments he had spent with the Empress of India, the warmth of her presence as she visited his house and had tea with his wife, and the quiet lessons that they had enjoyed together. He spent his last days riding in his carriage to MacDonald Park, sitting by the statue of Queen Victoria and watching the sun set over the Taj Mahal. His mind drifted back to the wintry days in Balmoral, the fresh smell of Highland heather, the sound of the River Dee as it flowed behind Karim Cottage and the feel of the leather-bound volumes of the Hindustani Journals passing through his hands. As the harsh winter turned to spring in 1909, the Munshi died quietly in Karim Lodge with his wife and nephew by his side. The colourful spring festival of Holi, which he had so often described to the Queen, had just been celebrated in Agra.

15

ⷀⷀⷀ

ENDGAME

On 20 April 1909 King Edward VII was sailing on the *Victoria and Albert* enjoying the gentle lapping of the waves against the yacht when he received a piece of unexpected news. It was the announcement of the death of Munshi Hafiz Abdul Karim. Eight years after Queen Victoria's death, her beloved Munshi had died in his native town of Agra. He was only forty-six.

The Times had carried a small obituary, written by its Lucknow correspondent, briefly giving the Munshi's duties in the Court and the Queen's high regard for him.

> The Queen reposed the utmost confidence in her Indian secretary. He was made a companion of the Order of the Indian Empire in 1895 and a Companion of the Royal Victorian Order in May 1899 only three years after the institution of the Order. Her Majesty continued her lessons in Hindustani until stricken by her brief final illness … Owing to the pressure of the daily duties of state, she had not the leisure to make rapid progress in this study, but the fact that she understood it and became able both to write and speak the language with some facility gave profound gratification to her Indian subjects.[1]

Somewhat discreetly the correspondent added: 'Munshi Abdul Karim was liberally pensioned and returned to India. He lived a quiet estimable life at Agra, his closing years being clouded by indifferent health. He cherished the memory of his illustrious pupil with profound veneration.'

Arthur Bigge, the Prince of Wales's private secretary, had bluntly written to Lord Knollys, the King's private secretary, saying: 'You will have seen that "the Munshi" is dead – I can have no regret!'[2] Knollys immediately passed on this information.

Shocked by the news, the King cast his boxes aside and pencilled a note to the Viceroy of India, instructing him to immediately transmit a telegram from the yacht: 'The King hopes you will take discreet precautions to ensure that any existing correspondence of the Munshi Abdul Karim, whose death is announced, does not fall into improper hands.'[3]

The King's relationship with the Munshi had always been uneasy. Though he had raided Karim's house after the Queen's death and burnt all her letters to him, he was now consumed by a feeling of panic and suspicion. He wanted every letter retrieved from the family, every bit of correspondence seized. He had heard from one of Queen Victoria's servants – Ahmed Husain – that the Munshi had kept a few letters from the Queen hidden, fuelling the sixty-eight-year-old's unease that compromising letters from his mother to the Munshi could be made public by the Munshi's family. The image of the portly Munshi and his mother floated before him again. The King recalled his mother's unyielding faith in Karim and how she had often reprimanded him for his criticism of the Indian, insisting he treat him with respect. He recalled the Munshi's smug expression whenever he won a round against the Court, the hoard of medals he always wore with pride and the sword that he was allowed to carry by the Queen. His feelings of revulsion flooded back and the King was determined not to rest until he was certain every part of the correspondence had been destroyed.

At the Viceroy's camp in Dehradun in India, Lord Minto was enjoying the weather, a soothing respite from the heat of Calcutta. It had been a hectic year; terrorism and militancy had reared its head in the state following the partition of Bengal by Lord Curzon in 1905. Militant groups of Bengali youths were planning an escalation of assassinations and bombings. In Calcutta, Bengali papers like the *Jugantar* were fanning this nationalism by backing the militants, and the government was coming under considerable pressure to grant representation to the Indian people.

Along with the Secretary of State for India, Lord Morley, Minto had reluctantly put together an urgently necessary package of reforms – which became known as the Minto-Morley Reforms – designed to contain the rising forces of Indian nationalism. The Reform Act granted Indian representation in Provincial Councils. Muslims would be given special representation so they didn't feel excluded. The Act was making its way through Parliament, and Minto was hoping it would be cleared.

The pleasant surrounds of Dehradun were a relief compared to Calcutta. The liveried attendant brought in the telegram from the King. It demanded a further visit to the Munshi's house. Minto sighed in disbelief and shot off a letter to Sir John Hewitt, Lieutenant Governor of the United Provinces.

Hewitt was staying at the Government House in Nainital, a town nestling in the Uttar Pradesh hills, where he too was enjoying a break from the heat. He sent a letter to W.H. Cobb, the Commissioner of Agra, and informed him of the Royal request.

The Commissioner and the Collector left immediately for Karim Lodge, the Munshi's house in Agra. It was the house that he had received as a gift from the Queen. They were met by his grieving family, the Munshi's widow, his brother, Abdul Aziz, and his nephew, Abdul Rashid. The Munshi had no children. The family listened in disbelief as the King's officials came, not to offer sympathy at the death of the Munshi, but demanded that they hand over any remaining letters written by Queen Victoria to him. They protested that the letters had already been handed over but, on the insistence of the Commissioner, eventually gave up the Munshi's entire box of correspondence. As the Munshi's wife wept silently behind her veil, the young Abdul Rashid, who had attended school in St Andrews in Scotland and played with the Royal grandchildren, entered solemnly carrying the letters and documents in a bag.

Seizing the letters, the Commissioner returned to his office and despatched a letter to Hewitt, who reported back to the Viceroy:

I have heard from the Commissioner of Agra that he and the Collector went yesterday to Karim Lodge and were shown the entire correspondence of the late Munshi. It included only two letters of a date up to her late Majesty's death, one from the Queen herself, and one from Sir Thomas Dennehy. There was nothing in either of them which might not be published to the world at large. The only point worthy of note was that the Munshi's nephew had not produced the Queen's letter in the first instance: it was only when he was asked whether no letter at all had been kept as a special memento of the late Majesty that he showed it. The letter had however been brought into the room in the same bag which held the other papers, so that there was apparently no intention of suppressing it.[4]

Cobb gave only sketchy details of what had actually been an emotionally charged scene. They had entered a house of mourning and made harsh demands. The Munshi's distraught nephew, Abdul Rashid, had told them that there were no letters left. He told them he had been present with the Munshi eight years ago in Frogmore Cottage in Windsor when the first raid had taken place on their house after Queen Victoria's death. He described how Queen Alexandra and Princess Beatrice had come to their house and demanded all the letters from the Queen to the Munshi. The letters had been burnt in the presence of Karim, his wife, his brother and Abdul Rashid.

The Collector went through the pile that young Rashid brought out. The letters included friendly correspondence from members of the Court, Christmas cards and other trivia. In one letter, the Munshi was found fault with for asking favours from His Majesty. The Munshi had kept all his letters carefully, even those that were critical of him.

The Collector noted: 'Only one letter contained a political allusion.' It was from Sir Dighton Probyn, who mentioned that the 'war between Russia and Japan was the general subject of conversation and that England hoped that Japan would gain the victory which her bravery and honesty entitled her to.'[5]

The Commissioner said he drew Abdul Rashid's attention to this letter and pointed out how the changed relations existing between Russia and England rendered it 'undesirable that such a letter should become public and impressed on him that he should seek out any other such correspondence that might have been overlooked and bring it to his notice'.

It was significant that a senior courtier like Sir Dighton Probyn, secretary to the Prince of Wales and a recipient of the Victoria Cross for his bravery during the Indian Mutiny, was discussing matters of political importance with the Munshi. Clearly, he considered him astute enough to discuss subjects like the war between Russia and Japan, even though he knew the nationalists in India had backed Japan as they had seen it as a small country taking on a mighty Imperial power with obvious parallels. The Commissioner and the Collector left Karim Lodge with the letters, convinced that the family had shown them all the correspondence they possessed.

They informed Hewitt that the Munshi had left two widows. He had taken a second wife, as Muslims were allowed to do, and she lived in Delhi. The family thought the second widow may give them some trouble. The first wife, who had travelled to England and had known the Queen, continued to live in the family home in Agra.

Hewitt himself clearly felt that there was nothing more to be done. Privately he felt that the seizure of the letters was hardly justified. He told the Viceroy: 'It does not appear to be possible to take any further action as regards the papers and unless your Excellency directs me to I do not propose to do anything more.'[6]

The letters were duly sent to King Edward VII with all the covering correspondence. However, he was not completely satisfied. On 21 May another memo arrived from Buckingham Palace: 'No doubt but that it will be necessary to watch the relatives of the late Abdul Karim for a certain time. Edward.'[7]

The scent of pine leaves was strong in the air. In the Viceregal Lodge in Simla, the summer capital of the British in India, the Viceroy, Lord Minto, was enjoying the fresh air after the monsoon. The deodar trees framed the grounds of the Lodge, which had been completed in 1888 under Lord Dufferin to provide the Viceroy and his office a refuge from the scorching sun of the plains in the summer. Every year the entire administration of the British Raj moved desks to the hills, the coolies carrying an army of cabinets, files and boxes up the steep slopes so that the business of the Empire could continue uninterrupted, 7,200 feet up in the tranquil surrounds of the Himalayas. Minto looked forward to this break and the opportunity it provided for a little relaxation: watching the latest plays from London staged by the Simla Amateur Dramatic Club in the neo-Gothic surrounds of the Gaiety Theatre on the Mall, scones and tea in the afternoon, the whirl of the summer parties, pink gins and the occasional round of golf on the nearby slopes.

He had reason to feel particularly pleased this summer. The Minto-Morley reforms had been passed in May and the Indians had been satisfied by it. The Indian leader, Gopal Krishna Gokhale, had praised it, saying that Minto and Morley had saved India from drifting 'towards what cannot be described by any other name than chaos'.

Minto was watching the changing colours of the snow-capped Himalayas in the late afternoon sun when he received another message from the King; more on the Munshi and the troublesome letters. The King wrote tersely: 'I am not satisfied in my mind that there may not be still letters in Queen Victoria's handwriting in their possession.' He recommended 'discreet investigations' and suggested that 'they [the Munshi's family] should be told to return them at once, or risk being "the sufferers thereby"'.[8] The fact that Ahmed Husain, the Queen's former servant and the Munshi's arch-rival, had hinted that the Munshi still possessed a few letters from the Queen was playing on the King's mind.

Not too pleased, the Viceroy wrote once again to John Hewitt. A few days later Hewitt visited the Viceroy at Simla. As the two men walked along the Observatory Hill and looked out over the valley below, they discussed what they should do about the King's further instructions to revisit the Munshi's house.

Hewitt decided there was nothing to do but obey. Once again, the Commissioner and the Collector of Agra were despatched to Karim Lodge. One morning in September, four months after their first visit, the King's representatives rapped on the door of the late Munshi's house again. This time the language was stronger, there were angry threats and talk of heavy repercussions on the family. The three family members pleaded and begged but the officials were intimidating. At last, the Munshi's widow pulled out eight letters from the Queen that she had kept as mementoes. Weeping, the lady who had once been visited regularly by Queen Victoria begged that the letters were of no value to anyone but her. They were personal letters and she would like to keep them as long as she lived. The production of the letters led to more harsh words and accusations that the family were probably hiding more.

The distraught nephew, Abdul Rashid, pleaded that there were no more. In desperation he brought out a copy of the Koran and swore on it that there were no more letters in the Queen's handwriting. The Commissioner and his team marched out of the house with the letters. Feeling like criminals, the family watched as the uniformed officers of the Raj rode away. The Munshi's wife wept uncontrollably, more for the humiliation she had suffered and the insulting manner in which the family had been treated.

She remembered her days in England when Queen Victoria would visit her house and stay for a cup of tea. Then she would lift her veil and sit with her. The Queen would try to speak in Hindustani, while she replied in broken English. Often a member of the Royal family or visiting European Royalty would come with the Queen. She remembered the last Christmas present the Queen had given her and how she had driven to their house personally to give it. Nothing remained with her now, not even a memento of the Munshi and Victoria. The photographs were handed over, the letters burnt. Her husband had died, still grieving for the Queen and never forgetting his days spent by her side. She felt a dull ache in her heart as she remembered the past years.

The seized letters were sealed and sent by the Commissioner to Hewitt who forwarded them to Minto with the note: 'I enclose the original letters in possession of the late Munshi's representatives ... the widow is particularly anxious to be permitted to keep letters dated 12 October 1893, 15 February and 15 September 1894 and 6 November 1898 as long as she is alive. Her wish seems a reasonable one.'[9] Minto in turn sent them to Knollys.

Hewitt, clearly quite unhappy at the whole affair, said he did not believe the family were concealing any letters from the late Majesty. He pointed out that in addition to the Munshi's widow, both the descendants – the brother and the nephew – were in government service and were unlikely to conceal anything. The bureaucrats at the India Office, and the Viceroy himself, clearly disapproved of the hounding of the Munshi's family by the King. At a time of political discontent and the government trying to balance the relations between the Hindus and Muslims, this persecution of a Muslim family did not seem an ideal situation to Minto. He felt he did not need any aggravation of an already delicate situation, least over what he perceived as some irrelevant personal letters and postcards.

Though he had pressing administrative matters to attend to, Minto sent off the letters to Lord Knollys, private secretary to the King, along with copies of the letters to Arthur Bigge. The clutch of letters included some Christmas cards sent by the Queen with 'Good Wishes' and 'xxx' marked on them.

In the pile of letters sent to Knollys, there were three letters written by the Queen to the Munshi. One, in the Queen's own handwriting, was addressed from Balmoral. It was headed: 'Extracts from the Prince of Wales's letters to the Queen in answer to hers.' These showed the humbling of the Prince of Wales by his mother. In the first letter, dated 28 September 1899, the Prince of Wales wrote: 'I shall always be ready to notice and speak to the Munshi when I meet him.' The second, dated 2 October 1899, authorised the Queen to assure Abdul Karim 'that I [Edward] have no ill will against him and only trust that matters should go smoothly and quietly.'[10] The Queen had copied her son's correspondence and given it to the Munshi.

Two other letters in the pack were marked as 'True copies'. They were of a slightly earlier date. One was written in February 1894 by the Queen and declared: 'I have given to the Munshi Abdul Karim (for whom I have specially written this) a gun as a present and have allowed him to wear a sword here and in India since the year 1890. Victoria R.I.' The other was written in 1896 and defined the Munshi's duties. None of them, apart maybe from the one in reply to the King's original letter on the Munshi, could have caused the King any embarrassment, but he was determined to mop up even the smallest scrap of paper that could have passed between his mother and her Indian confidant.

While sending the letters to Knollys, Minto added a note: 'I hope the King will allow the letters the widow wishes to keep to be returned to her. It seems natural that she should like to have them and their return to her would be much appreciated and would do good. I sent you all these details to avoid a long explanation to the King but will write to His Majesty to say I have sent the letters to you.'[11]

It was clear that the persecution of the Munshi's family after his death had not gone down well with the representatives of the Crown in India. The Munshi was perceived as an important man in Agra and his closeness to the Queen was legendary. The Viceroy did not want to ruffle unnecessary feathers and escalate a situation where the King's actions would be seen as unfair and heavy handed. India was already becoming a political tinder-box and the Viceroy was anxious to send the right messages. He wrote a separate letter to King Edward VII saying he would be glad to know that 'the descendants of the late Munshi Abdul Karim have given up some further letters from Queen Victoria'.

The Viceroy informed the King that he believed these were all that existed and the King could now be assured that there were no more. Expressing his wish that the widow of the Munshi be allowed to keep a few souvenirs, he said: 'The widow of the late Munshi is very anxious that some of the latter, which are of little importance except to herself should be returned to her for her lifetime and the Viceroy is sure that if such a gracious act is possible, it would be very gratefully appreciated.'[12]

In a veiled warning to the King, the Viceroy updated him on the political situation in India, pressing home the point that it would be unwise to upset the community at this present junction. He told the King that though his political position in India had improved, the plots of agitators were certainly still smouldering. Minto expressed the hope that things would continue to improve.

The King realised the Viceroy's sensitive position and agreed to return the four letters mentioned by Lord Minto to the Munshi's widow. However, he wanted the government in India to take steps 'to ensure their being returned to the King in the event of her death'.[13] Edward VII retained the remaining four letters, in all probability tossing them into the crackling fire at Buckingham Palace.

After much deliberation, the four letters that the King conceded to return were sent back from London to Agra and restored to the Munshi's wife. Nor was this a simple procedure. They were handed over only after the Munshi's brother, Abdul Aziz Tehsildar, travelled personally to Agra on leave and handed an agreement in writing to the Commissioner of Agra, agreeing to 'return them to His Majesty the King on her death through the Collector of Agra'. The letter was signed in triplicate by him, the Munshi's widow and his nephew, Abdul Rashid Tahsildar, and handed to the Collector of Agra.

The details of the agreement were sent to Hewitt on 23 November by the Commissioner. Hewitt conveyed them to Lord Minto, who responded wearily from the Viceroy's Camp in Bangalore: 'Many thanks for copy of the Commissioner of Agra's letter ... I suppose the agreement will be filed in the Commissioner's office or in your own – otherwise its existence might be lost sight of as years go on. Believe me, yours very truly, Minto.'[14] Nearly seven months had passed since the death of the Munshi.

With the last batch of Queen Victoria's letters divided between Agra and Windsor, the story of the Queen and her Munshi was finally confined to bureaucratic files. It is not known whether the letters held by the Munshi's widow were ever returned to Windsor after her death. King Edward was to die a few months later, on 6 May 1910. Few after him were interested in pursuing the letters. George V would rule a world torn apart by revolution and war.

Bigger events were overtaking British rule in India. A tide of political unrest was sweeping the sub-continent and the first stirrings of the nationalist struggle were beginning to rattle the Imperial administration. Not since the Mutiny of 1857 had the powers-that-be in Westminster witnessed the wave of feelings against the British government and the growing demands for independence. The cries of '*Vande Mataram*' (Bow to the Mother) were beginning to fill the air again and Bengal was gripped by revolutionary zeal. Women handed in their jewellery to help fund the revolutionaries, bonfires of British goods were organised, and the air was heavy with plots, secret meetings and assassination attempts. From jute mill workers to farmhands, students to the landed aristocracy, all of Bengal was seething with nationalistic fervour following the partition of the state.

Far away in London, on 1 July 1909, a twenty-two-year-old Indian engineering student, Madan Lal Dhingra, while attending the annual function of the Indian National Association, pumped five bullets into Sir Curzon Wyllie, Political Aide-de-Camp to the Secretary of State for India, Lord Morley, as he entered the hall of the Imperial Institute. It was just over a decade ago that the foundation stone of the Institute had been laid by Queen Victoria in far happier circumstances. Dhingra was arrested immediately and refused to have a defence counsel, saying the courts in Britain had no right to try him. It took the judge at the Old Bailey only twenty minutes to sentence him. On 17 August 1909 he was hanged in Pentonville Prison.

Dhingra was defiant in death. 'I believe that a nation held down by foreign bayonets is in a perpetual state of war ... the only lesson required in India at present is to learn how to die,' he declared before he was hanged. He showed no remorse or fear and said he believed that the English would have done the same had the Germans been occupying their land. Dhingra became the first Indian nationalist to become a martyr on British soil, inspiring later revolutionaries like Chandrashekhar Azad, Bhagat Singh and Udham Singh, all of whom went to their deaths fighting for freedom.

Later that year, Minto and his wife were themselves to survive an assassination attempt while on a visit to Ahmedabad in western India. Two bombs were thrown at the carriage in which they were driving. The explosives did not go off, but they succeeded in injuring a water-carrier who picked them up.

By 1911 all of Delhi was transformed for the Durbar of George V, which saw the British government make an important announcement. The capital of the government would be moved from Calcutta to Delhi. It was clear that the political climate in Bengal had become much too hot. The new Viceroy, Lord Hardinge, successor to Lord Minto, entered Delhi on an elephant in 1912 to inaugurate the construction of the new city, but was met with a daring bomb attack. He survived, but only just. Hardinge was carried away on a stretcher as the elephant and mahout collapsed in a sea of white dust.

It was the time of assassination attempts around the world. Two years later the assassination of Archduke Franz Ferdinand in Sarajevo would see the outbreak of the First World War. Queen Victoria's grandchildren, who had knelt together at her deathbed, were now at war, drawing the whole world into a conflict which was to leave millions dead. One million Indian soldiers were recruited and sent to fight on the front line, dying in trenches in far-off lands. The smell of gunfire, the sight of the injured and the dead were to become the signs of the day.

Barely a year later, in January 1915, an astute young lawyer stepped off a boat from South Africa at the Bombay docks. His name was Mohandas Karamchand Gandhi. A new chapter in Indian history was about to be written. It was a time far removed from the sunny days spent in marquees in the gardens at Frogmore and Osborne, when an elderly English Queen sat learning Hindustani from a young Indian, who told her tales of his homeland and won her heart.

EPILOGUE

The Regional Archives of Agra – a small house located in a sleepy residential area – had a forgotten air about it. 'We only open it if someone needs a document,' apologised the junior official, who had driven up in a scooter from another building to let us in. It was clear that he did not need to do this too often.

The register indicated that the last person had visited over a month back. After handing me a handwritten catalogue, the official – clearly at a loose end – said he was going for some tea. Would I like some? I certainly would. Searching for the Munshi's records in this neglected place seemed like a hopeless task. The room smelt of open drains. A sleepy dog lay on the verandah, surveying me through a half-closed eye. The mosquitoes under the table had already started making a meal of my legs. I thought longingly of the cosy surrounds of the Round Tower in Windsor where the other half of the Munshi's records lay. At the Queen's Royal residence, they rang a bell at eleven and served us tea and biscuits. The contrast could not have been more obvious.

Miraculously, the cataloguing actually worked. In the languid surrounds of the room, in steel almirahs with rusty handles were filed records of the Munshi's life in Agra: letters, land documents and detailed arrangements for the Viceroy's Durbar. Before long, I had forgotten about the mosquito bites and was staring at a crumbling parchment map spread across the table. It was a map drawn by an official in the Collector's Office in Agra in 1896, showing the area of land occupied by the Munshi. A black border had been marked around the plots numbered 11–125. These were already owned by the Munshi and gifted to him by the Queen. Marked in red was the huge chunk of government land adjacent to it, which the Munshi wanted to buy. It numbered up to plot 314 and covered an area of 141 acres. There was a road running through it, with several trees including *jamun*, mango and *neem*. There was farmland and fallow land. The Munshi had clearly acquired a giant stretch of land, shaped amazingly like the map of the United States, in the heart of Agra. On plots numbered 177–187 he had built his dream house, Karim Lodge.

We seemed to have been in the car for nearly an hour, driving through what was once the Munshi's estate, passing large gated houses covered with bougainvilleas, jasmine and fragrant flowering plants. Palm trees and brightly painted flower pots lined the streets. Occasionally, one got a glimpse of manicured lawns. The rich and prosperous of Agra had built their houses here now. 'All this belonged to Abdul Karim,' said my guide from the local Agra estate agents. 'It is now a whole area in Agra.' Finally, he pulled up outside what looked like the remnants of an old stone wall and a gate with a carved medieval arch. On it was stuck an announcement by the Rashtriya Lok Dal, a political party. Next to the gate were rows of chemists' shops, the makeshift shacks running for nearly a mile along the wall that had once cordoned off Karim's property.

All that remained of the original Karim Lodge was the brick wall, the arches and the living room with its high ceiling. The back of the house had been modernised and turned into a nursing home and medical practice. The front of the house had been further divided into two residential houses. Prakash Hingorani, the present owner of the original house, knew only a few sketchy details about Abdul Karim. He showed me a letter from Karim written on Windsor notepaper. It gave the date and time of his arrival by the mail train to Agra. Hingorani had laminated the yellowing page and kept it as a souvenir. It was one of the things he had found lying among the papers in the house.

His grandfather, Hiranand Vaswani, had occupied Karim Lodge when the family had come from Pakistan after the partition in 1947. The biggest movement of people in history had seen nearly 15 million refugees crossing the border on both sides between India and Pakistan, leading to riots, looting and wanton killing. In the darkest days after independence, Hindus crossed over from Pakistan to India, and Muslims from India moved to Pakistan for fear of becoming minorities in their homeland. The descendants of Karim's extended family, the grandchildren of his brother and sisters, left the acres of land that they owned and went to Pakistan. The land was seized by the Ministry of Rehabilitation in Agra and distributed to Hindu refugees from Pakistan.

'We lost our land in Pakistan and we were housed here. Those were troubled times,' said eighty-seven-year-old Himesh Chand Chaturvedi, who lives in one of the smaller original houses of the estate, a few hundred yards from Karim Lodge. The sprightly man with a flowing beard gave me a mischievous smile. 'I found a pile of letters in this house written by Karim. My wife made me throw them away, as they were of no use to anyone. How did I know you would come looking for him after all these years?' Chaturvedi remembered some of Karim's descendants who had not left immediately for Pakistan. 'Some of the family were still left here,' he said, trying to recall the names and faces of the people all those years back. 'The children used to play in the garden. Karim had no children of his own, so they were his brother's grandchildren.' I figured they would have been the children of Karim's favourite nephew, Abdul Rashid.

Chaturvedi recalled how people would still talk about Abdul Karim, the *ustad*, and his relations with Queen Victoria. There were many stories about how he was trained for the job, how he became the Queen's teacher and acquired a special place in the Court. There were stories about how Karim Lodge was built with bricks and labour from Agra Jail, so it could be ready for him on his return. He recalled how he had read some of the letters which were lying in the house. They were from Karim to his wife, asking her to send him certain spices, or his favourite *pan* and *supari* (betel nut). 'He would give her instructions about which mail company to send the parcels with. There were many, many letters …'

Suddenly the old man sprang up and walked to the main entrance of Karim Lodge.

'This is the gate that Abdul Karim's carriage would drive up to. Here he would alight in his smart clothes and turban and walk indoors,' said Chaturvedi, his mind racing back to the stories he had heard. 'People spoke about him for years …'

The Munshi had lived quietly with his memories after his return from England. Though he knew the strength of the feelings against him in the Palace, he had never spoken any ill of the Royal family or the Household. The Queen's family never understood that he had provided her with the companionship over the last decade of her life, which they themselves had not been able to offer.

An ambulance rattled past us to the nursing home at the back of the house. A nurse in starched whites was briskly attending the line of patients sitting in the neon-lit room, the silence broken only by the occasional cough and the sound of her white shoes clicking on the marble floor. Karim's carriage had stopped coming here a hundred years ago. A forgotten grave, a laminated telegram and the memories of an old man were all that was left of him in his native city. Agra had moved on.

NOTES AND SOURCES

RA – Royal Archives
QVJ – Queen Victoria's Journals
QVJ/HIND – Queen Victoria's Hindustani Journals
ADDL/MSS – Additional Manuscripts
IOR – India Office Records

1. AGRA

1. RA VIC/MAIN/QVJ/HIND/3: Article on Karim in *Black* magazine, 15 June 1895
2. IOR MSS/Eur/F130/8b, Viceroy to Secretary of State, 8 September 1887, Simla
3. IOR MSS/Eur/D558/1, Queen to Viceroy, 18 December 1890, Windsor

2. A JUBILEE PRESENT

1. IOR MSS/Eur/F130/6, Dufferin to Cross, 20 March 1887, Calcutta
2. IOR MSS/Eur/F130/9, Cross to Dufferin, 22 April 1887, London
3. Ibid., 28 April, London
4. Sunity Devi, *The Autobiography of an Indian Princess*, quoted in Lucy Moore, *Maharanis* (London: Viking, 2004), p. 104
5. RA VIC/MAIN/QVJ/1887: 21 June
6. Ibid.
7. Ibid.
8. IOR MSS/Eur/F130/9, Cross to Dufferin, 24 June 1887
9. RA VIC/MAIN/QVJ/1887: 22 June
10. Ibid., 23 June

3. AN INDIAN DURBAR

1. RA MRH/MRH/HH/1/214a: 3 July 1887
2. RA MRH/MRH/HH/1/214b
3. Arthur Ponsonby, *Henry Ponsonby, His Life From his Letters* (London: Macmillan & Co., 1943), p. 383

4. RA VIC/MAIN/QVJ/1887: 28 June
5. Ibid., 30 June
6. Ibid.
7. Ibid.
8. RA VIC/MAIN/QVJ/1887: 28 July
9. Ibid., 3 August
10. Ponsonby, *Henry Ponsonby*, p. 130
11. RA VIC/MAIN/QVJ/1887: 6 August
12. Ibid., 11 August
13. Ibid., 20 August

4. Curries and Highlanders

1. Reid Archives, Scrap Book, 1887, Vol. 1
2. Ibid.
3. Queen Victoria, *Our Life in the Highlands* (London: William Kimber, 1968, revised edition), p. 14
4. Reid Archives, Scrap Book, 1887, Vol. 2
5. RA VIC/MAIN/QVJ/HIND/7: 24 May 1899
6. RA VIC/ADDU/104/1
7. RA VIC/ADDA12/154
8. RA VIC/MAIN/QVJ/1887: 18 September
9. IOR MSS/Eur/F130/9, Cross to Dufferin
10. RA VIC/MAIN/QVJ/1887: 29 September
11. IOR MSS/Eur/F130/9, Cross to Dufferin
12. IOR MSS/Eur/F130/6, Randolph Churchill, Secretary of State, to Dufferin
13. RA VIC/MAIN/QVJ/1887: 9 October
14. Ibid., 2 December
15. RA VIC/MAIN/QVJ/HIND/7: 24 May 1899
16. RA VIC/MAIN/QVJ/1887: 31 December

5. Becoming the Munshi

1. Reid Archives, Scrap Book, Vol. 2
2. RA VIC/MAIN/QVJ/HIND/9
3. Michael Nelson, *Queen Victoria and the Discovery of the Riviera* (London: Tauris Parke, 2007), pp. 21–22
4. RA VIC/MAIN/L/24/30, Ponsonby to Queen, 31 July 1888, St James's Palace
5. RA VIC/MAIN/QVJ/1888: 11 August
6. RA VIC/ADDA/15/5188, Queen Victoria to the Duchess of Connaught, 3 November 1888, Balmoral
7. RA VIC/MAIN/Y/172/85, Queen Victoria to Sir Theodore Martin, 20 November 1888, Windsor
8. RA VIC/ADDU/104/2: 25 September 1888, Balmoral
9. RA VIC/ADDU/104/3: 25 September 1888, Balmoral
10. RA VIC/MAIN/QVJ/1888: 2 November
11. Christopher Hibbert (ed.), *Queen Victoria in Her Letters and Journals*, (London: Penguin, 1985), p. 314
12. IOR MSS/Eur/D558/1, Queen to Viceroy, 22 February 1889, Windsor

13. Ibid., Viceroy to Queen, 21 April 1889, Viceregal Lodge, Simla
14. Ibid., Queen to Viceroy, 22 March 1889
15. Ibid., Queen to Viceroy, 8 April 1889
16. Ibid., Queen to Viceroy, 17 May 1889
17. Reid Archives, Scrap Book, Vol. 2, Queen to Reid, 13 May 1889
18. Reid Archives, Scrap Book, Vol. 2
19. Ibid.
20. Ibid.
21. IOR MSS/Eur/D558/1, Queen to Viceroy, 18 July 1889, Osborne
22. Ibid.
23. Ibid., Viceroy to Queen, 15 June 1889, Viceregal Lodge, Simla
24. Reid Archives, Scrap Book, Vol. 2

6. A GRANT OF LAND

1. Reid Archives, Scrap Book, Vol. 2
2. RAVIC/ADDU/32/1890: 17 May
3. IOR MSS/Eur/D558/1, Telegram No. 28, Queen to Lansdowne, 11 July 1890, Windsor
4. Ibid., Telegram No. 32, Lansdowne to Queen, 6 July 1890, Viceregal Lodge, Simla
5. Ibid., Telegram No. 29, Queen to Lansdowne, 1 August 1890, Osborne
6. Ibid., Telegram No. 32, Queen to Lansdowne, 27 August 1890, Balmoral
7. Ibid., Telegram No. 33, Queen to Lansdowne, 28 August 1890, Balmoral
8. Ibid., Telegram No. 36, Lansdowne to Queen, 2 August 1890, Simla
9. Ibid., Telegram No. 39, Lansdowne to Queen, 23 September 1890, Simla
10. Ibid., Letter No. 41, Lansdowne to Queen, 21 October 1890, Simla
11. IOR MSS/Eur/D558/3, Cross to Lansdowne, 30 October 1890, India Office, Whitehall
12. RAVIC/MAIN/QVJ/1890: 7 October
13. IOR MSS/Eur/D558/3, Lansdowne to Cross, 19 November 1890
14. Ibid.
15. IOR MSS/Eur/D558/1, Telegram No. 39, Queen to Lansdowne, 29 October 1890, Balmoral
16. Ibid., Telegram No. 42, Lansdowne to Queen, 30 October 1890, Viceroy's camp
17. Ibid., Telegram No. 40, Queen to Lansdowne, 30 October 1890, Balmoral
18. IOR MSS/Eur/D558/7
19. RAVIC/ADDU/32/1890: 2 November
20. IOR MSS/Eur/D558/3, Lansdowne to Cross, 12 November 1890, Jeypore
21. IOR MSS/Eur/D558/1, Telegram No. 41, Queen to Lansdowne, 21 November 1890, Windsor
22. Ibid., Telegram Nos 43–44, Queen to Lansdowne, 23 November 1890, Windsor
23. IOR MSS/Eur/558/1, Telegram Nos 44–45, Queen to Lansdowne, 24 November 1890, Windsor
24. IOR MSS/Eur/D558/1, Telegram No. 45, Lansdowne to Queen, 26 November 1890, Agra
25. Ibid., Lansdowne to Cross, 27 November 1890
26. IOR MSS/Eur/D558/3, Lansdowne to Cross, 2 December 1890
27. Ibid., Cross to Lansdowne, 18 December 1890, India Office, Whitehall
28. IOR MSS/Eur/558/1, Telegram No. 49, Queen to Lansdowne, 18 December 1890, Windsor
29. IOR MSS/Eur/D558/1, Telegram No. 55, Queen to Lansdowne, 26 January 1891, Osborne
30. Ibid., Telegram No. 57, Queen to Lansdowne, 30 January 1891, Osborne

31. Ibid., Telegram No. 65, Lansdowne to Queen, 15 February 1891, Calcutta
32. Ibid., Telegram No. 60, Queen to Lansdowne, 15 February 1891, Osborne
33. IOR MSS/Eur/D558/3, Cross to Lansdowne, 24 December 1890, India Office, Whitehall

7. Indian Affairs

1. IOR MSS/Eur/D558/4
2. Reid Archives, Scrap Book, 1891, cutting from *The Standard*, 26 March 1891
3. Michael Nelson, *Queen Victoria and the Discovery of the Riviera* (London: Tauris Parke, 2007), p. 52
4. IOR MSS/Eur/F130/6, Letter to Lala Jhinda Ram, 1 May 1891, Moscow
5. IOR MSS/Eur/D558/7, Cross to Lansdowne, 25 July 1890
6. IOR MSS/Eur/D558/3, Cross to Duleep Singh, 1 August 1890, Whitehall
7. RA VIC/MAIN/QVJ/1891: 31 March
8. Reid Archives, Scrap Book, 1891, cutting from *Dundee Evening Telegraph*, 10 September 1891
9. Gabriel Tschumi, *Royal Chef*, 4th edn (London: William Kimber, 1974), p. 69
10. RA VIC/QVJ/MAIN/1893: 26 August
11. IOR MSS/Eur/D558/4, Cross to Lansdowne, 15 October 1891, Balmoral
12. Ibid., Cross to Lansdowne, 1 October 1891, Balmoral
13. Ibid., Cross to Lansdowne, 19 August 1891, Broughton-in-Furness
14. Reid Archives, Scrap Book, 1891, Vol. 2
15. Reid Archives, Scrap Book, Vol. 2, 'Abstract of conversation with John Tyler'
16. Quoted from *Life*, Vol. 1, Marie of Romania, in *Heart of a Queen* by Theo Aronson, p. 240
17. RA VIC/ADDQ/5/116, Alex Profeit to Queen, 8 May 1892
18. Reid Archives, Scrap Book, Vol. 2
19. RA GV/PRIV/AA10/41, Queen to Duke of York
20. IOR MSS/Eur/D558/12, Queen to Lansdowne, June 1892, Balmoral
21. IOR MSS/Eur/D558/10, Secretary of State to Viceroy, 15 March 1893
22. *The Times*, 24 March 1893
23. RA VIC/MAIN/QVJ/HIND/1: 11 May 1893
24. RA VIC/MAIN/QVJ/1893: 18 November
25. *The Times*, 19 November 1893
26. Letter from Queen Victoria to Empress Frederick of Germany, 9 December 1893, quoted in Sushila Anand, *Indian Sahib*, p. 45
27. The first five of the Hindustani Journals have not survived and hence the 6th book is numbered 1 in the references
28. RA VIC/MAIN/QVJ/HIND/1: 14 November 1892
29. Ibid., 31 December 1892
30. RA VIC/MAIN/QVJ/ADDU/104/12, Queen to Karim, 28 December 1893, Osborne
31. RA VIC/MAIN/QVJ/ADDU/104/13, 15 February 1894, Osborne
32. RA VIC/MAIN/ADDU/104/10, 12 December 1893, Windsor
33. Reid Archives, Diary, 16 December 1893
34. RA VIC/ADDU/104/11
35. RA VIC/ADDU/104/14: 15 September 1894, Balmoral
36. RA VIC/ADDU/104/15: 9 October 1894, Balmoral
37. RA VIC/ADDU/104/16: 11 October 1894, Balmoral
38. IOR MSS/Eur/D558/1, Telegram No. 123, Queen to Viceroy, 15 August 1893, Osborne
39. Ibid., Telegram No. 124, Queen to Viceroy, 25 August 1893, Osborne
40. IOR MSS/Eur/D558/1, Telegram No. 151, Viceroy to Queen, November 1893
41. Ibid., Telegram No. 126, Queen to Viceroy, 21 September 1893, Balmoral

42. Ibid., Telegram No. 134, Queen to Viceroy, 8 December 1893

43. Ibid., Viceroy to Queen, November 1893

44. Ibid., Telegram No.134, Queen to Viceroy, 8 December 1893

45. IOR MSS/Eur/D558/1, Telegram No. 167, Viceroy to Queen, December 1893, Government House, Calcutta

8. The Viceroy Receives a Christmas Card

1. Reid Archives, Scrap Book, Vol. 12

2. Ibid.

3. Ibid.

4. Ibid.

5. Ibid.

6. Arthur Ponsonby, *Henry Ponsonby, Queen Victoria's Private Secretary, His Life From His Letters* (London: Macmillan & Co., 1943), p. 131

7. Ibid.

8. Reid Archives, Scrap Book, 1891

9. RA LC/LCO/AR/1894

10. Reid Archives, Diary, October 1894

11. RA VIC/MAIN/Z/477/6

12. IOR/MSS/Eur/F84

13. Frederick Ponsonby, *Recollections of Three Reigns* (London: Odhams Press), p. 12

14. IOR MSS/Eur/F84/126 ff/47/v, Fritz Ponsonby to Lord Elgin, 25 January 1895

15. IOR MSS/Eur/F84/126b, Durand to Fritz Ponsonby, 13 February 1895

16. Ibid., Elgin to Fowler, 15 February 1895

17. RA VIC/MAIN/QVJ/HIND/3: 1 January 1895

9. The Household Conspires

1. *Strand Magazine*, December 1892

2. RA VIC/MAIN/H/37/46, Queen to Prime Minister, 16 October 1895

3. IOR MSS/Eur/F84/126a

4. IOR MSS/Eur/L/PS/8/61

5. IOR MSS/Eur/F84/126

6. IOR MSS/Eur/F84/126b, Gadley to Elgin, 8 March 1895, Whitehall

7. IOR MSS/Eur/ F84/126a, Gadley to Elgin

8. RA VIC/MAIN/Z/477/207, Queen to Duchess of York, 11 March 1895, Windsor

9. Reid Archives, Scrap Book, Vol. 15, newspaper cutting

10. Ibid., cutting from *The Galignani Messenger*, 22 March 1895

11. Ibid., newspaper cutting

12. IOR MSS/Eur/F84/126b, Fritz Ponsonby to Elgin

13. RA VIC/ADDU/32/27, April 1895, Darmstadt

14. RA VIC/ADDU/104/17, Queen to Karim, 15 May 1895, Windsor

15. Reid Archives, Diary, 24 June 1895, Windsor

16. IOR MSS/Eur/F84/126b, Fritz Ponsonby to Elgin, 6 June 1895, Guard's Club, London

17. Reid Archives, Scrap Book, Vol. 16

18. *The Aberdeen Journal*, 6 September 1895

19. Mary Lutyens (ed.), *Lady Lytton's Court Diary 1895–1899* (London: Rupert Hart Davis, 1961), p. 44

20. *The Times* Court Circular, 11 November 1895
21. Giles St Aubyn, *Edward VII, Prince and King* (London: William Collins, 1979), p. 142
22. IOR MSS/Eur/F84/126 a/b, Hamilton to Elgin, 15 November 1895, Whitehall
23. Michaela Reid, *Ask Sir James* (London: Hodder and Stoughton, 1987), p. 142
24. *The Times*, 19 December 1895
25. *Black*, 15 June 1895
26. RA VIC/MAIN/QVJ/HIND/3: 2 December 1895

10. REBELLION IN THE RANKS

1. IOR MSS/Eur/F84/126b, Elgin to Sandhurst, 14 March 1896, Calcutta
2. IOR MSS/Eur/F84/126/f3, Hamilton to Elgin, 21 February 1896, Whitehall
3. Ibid.
4. IOR MSS/Eur/F84/126a
5. Ibid.
6. Ibid.
7. IOR MSS/Eur/F84/126/f16
8. Victor Mallet (ed.), *Life With Queen Victoria: Marie Mallet's Letters From Court 1887–1901* (London: John Murray), p. 96
9. Ibid., p. 2
10. *The Times*, 12 March 1897
11. Reid Archives, Diary, 13 March 1897
12. Ibid., 27 March 1897
13. Ibid., 28 March 1897
14. Ibid., 30 March 1897
15. Ibid.
16. IOR MSS/Eur/F84/126, Elgin to Hamilton, 3 April 1897
17. Reid Archives, Diary, 4 April 1897
18. Reid Archives, Scrap Book, Queen's memo, 23 April 1897
19. IOR MSS/Eur/F84/126/f22, Fritz Ponsonby to Babington Smith, 27 April 1897, Hotel Regina, Cimiez
20. Ibid., Hamilton to Elgin, 30 April 1897, Whitehall
21. Reid Archives, Scrap Book, May 1897
22. IOR MSS/Eur/D509/4, Elgin to Hamilton, 21 April 1897, Simla
23. IOR MSS/Eur/D509/5, Elgin to Hamilton, 18 May 1897, Simla

11. 'MUNSHIMANIA'

1. Reid Archives, Scrap Book, Queen to Reid, 6 June 1897, Balmoral
2. Ibid., Queen to Reid, 28 June 1897, Balmoral
3. RA VIC/MAIN/QVJ/HIND/5: 20 June 1897
4. Reid Archives, Diary, 28 June 1897
5. Reid Archives, Scrap Book, Queen to Reid, 5 July 1897
6. Reid Archives, Diary, 21 July 1897, Osborne
7. Reid Archives, Diary, Queen to Reid, 28 July 1897, Osborne
8. Reid Archives, Scrap Book, Ahmed Husain to Reid, 4 August 1897
9. Reid Archives, Scrap Book, Fritz Ponsonby to Reid, 2 September 1897
10. Reid Archives, Scrap Book, cutting from *The World*, 15 September 1897
11. Michaela Reid, *Ask Sir James*, letter from Queen to Reid, quoted

12. Reid Archives, Scrap Book, Queen to Reid, 22 September 1897
13. Ibid., Reid to Queen, 23 September 1897
14. Reid Archives, Diary, 16 October 1897
15. Reid Archives, Diary, 21 October 1897
16. Reid Archives, Scrap Book, Queen to Reid, 21 October 1897
17. Reid Archives, Scrap Book, Queen to Reid, 22 October 1897
18. Reid Archives, Scrap Book, Reid to Queen, 26 October 1897
19. RA VIC/MAIN/QVJ/HIND/5: 26 October 1897, Balmoral
20. Reid Archives, Scrap book, 1897–98. Newspaper report on the Queen's departure, 12 November 1897

12. REDEMPTION

1. RA VIC/ADDU/104/20, Queen to Karim, 12 February 1898, Osborne
2. Reid Archives, Diary, Reid to Salisbury, 29 January 1898, Osborne
3. Reid Archives, Diary, 18 February 1898
4. Ibid.
5. Reid Archives, Scrap Book, Queen to Reid, April 1898, Cimiez
6. Reid Archives, Scrap Book, Davidson to Reid, May 1898
7. RA VIC/MAIN/C/20/20, Queen to Rowton, 27 June 1899
8. RA VIC/MAIN/QVJ/HIND/6: 13 August 1898
9. Agra Archives, Serial No. 3/File No. 14/Box 50
10. Ibid.
11. Ibid.
12. RA VIC/MAIN/QVJ/HIND/7: 24 May 1899
13. RA VIC/MAIN/QVJ/HIND/8: 31 October 1899
14. RA VIC/MAIN/O/7/22

13. DEATH OF A QUEEN

1. Victor Mallet (ed.), *Life with Queen Victoria: Marie Mallet's Letters From Court, 1887–1901* (London: John Murray), p. 216
2. RA VIC/MAIN/QVJ/HIND/13: 7 November 1900
3. Reid Archives, 'Report on Queen's health/death' by John Reid, 23 January 1901
4. Reid Archives, Diary, 25 January 1901
5. IOR MSS/Eur/D510/7, Curzon to Hamilton, 24 January 1901, Calcutta

14. LAST DAYS IN AGRA

1. Reid Archives, Diary, 22 February 1901
2. Victor Mallet (ed.), *Life with Queen Victoria: Marie Mallet's Letters from Court, 1887–1901* (London: John Murray), p. 172
3. Letter from Lady Curzon quoted in Sushila Anand, *Indian Sahib*, p. 102
4. Mary Lutyens (ed.), *Lady Lytton's Court Diary 1895–1899* (London: Rupert Hart Davis, 1961), p. 42
5. IOR MSS/Eur/D510/7, Curzon to Hamilton, 31 January 1901
6. Ibid., Curzon to Hamilton, 28 November 1900
7. Ibid., 27 August 1902

8. Ibid., 14 March 1901

9. IOR MSS/Eur/D510/11, Curzon to Hamilton, 30 July 1902

10. IOR MSS/Eur/D510/12, Curzon to Hamilton, 5 November 1902

11. RA GV/PRIV/AA27/12, George to King Edward VII, 8 January 1906, Agra

12. RA GV/PRIV/AA27/51, George to King Edward VII, 20 March 1909, Marlborough House, London

15. ENDGAME

1. *The Times*, 24 April 1909

2. Giles St Aubyn, *Edward VII: Prince and King* (London: William Collins, 1979), p. 144

3. RA VIC/MAIN/X/14/20, Edward VII to Viceroy, 20 April 1909

4. RA VIC/MAIN/W/5/74, John Hewitt to Lord Minto, 27 April 1909, Nainital

5. Ibid.

6. Ibid.

7. RA VIC/MAIN/W/5/75, Edward VII to Minto, 21 May 1909, Buckingham Palace

8. St Aubyn, *Edward VII*, p. 145

9. RA VIC/MAIN/X/14/29, Minto to Knollys, 27 September 1909, Viceregal Lodge, Simla

10. St Aubyn, *Edward VII*, p. 145

11. RA VIC/MAIN/X/14/29, Minto to Knollys, 27 September 1909

12. RA VIC/MAIN/X/14/30, Minto to Edward VII, 28 September 1909, Simla

13. Ibid., Edward VII note to Minto, 20 October 1909

14. RA VIC/MAIN/W/5/100, Minto to Hewitt, 7 December 1909, Viceroy's Camp, Bangalore

BIBLIOGRAPHY

Primary Sources
Royal Archives, Windsor (RA)
Queen Victoria's Journals (QVJ)
Queen Victoria's Hindustani Journals (QVJ/HIND)
Additional Manuscripts (ADDL/MSS)

Reid Archives, Jedburgh

India Office Records, British Library, London (IOR)
Dufferin Papers
Lansdowne Papers
Elgin Papers
Curzon Papers
Minto Papers

Regional Archives, Agra
Abdul Karim files

Newspapers and Magazines
The Times
The Telegraph
Illustrated London News
The Daily Graphic
Black
The World
The Standard
Lloyds Weekly
Aberdeen Weekly
Birmingham Daily Post
Pall Mall Gazette
The Era
Glasgow Herald

Secondary Sources and Select Bibliography

Anand, Sushila, *Indian Sahib, Queen Victoria's Dear Abdul* (London: Duckworth, 1996)

Aronson, Theo, *Heart of a Queen, Queen Victoria's Romantic Attachments* (London: John Murray, 1991)

Devi, Sunity, *The Autobiography of an Indian Princess* (India: 1921, reprint Tarang Paperbacks, 1995)

Erickson, Carolly, *Her Little Majesty: The Life of Queen Victoria* (London: Robson Books, 1999)

Harris, Russell, *The Lafayette Studio and Princely India* (Delhi: Roli Books)

Hibbert, Christopher, *Queen Victoria, A Personal History* (London: Harper Collins, 2001)

—— *Lives and Letters, Queen Victoria in Her Letters and Journals* (Penguin reprint 1985)

—— *Edward VII: A Portrait* (London: Allen Lane, 1976)

King, Greg, *Twilight of Splendour, The Court of Queen Victoria During Her Diamond Jubilee Year* (Canada: John Wiley and Sons, 2007)

Latif, Syad Muhammad, *Agra, Historical and Descriptive* (Calcutta: Calcutta Central Press Company, 1896)

Longford, Elizabeth, *Victoria R.I.* (London: Weidenfeld and Nicholson, 1964)

Lutyens, Mary (ed.), *Lady Lytton's Court Diary 1895–1899* (London: Rupert Hart-Davis, 1961)

Mallet, Victor (ed.), *Life with Queen Victoria, Marie Mallet's letters from Court 1887–1901* (London: John Murray)

Moore, Lucy, *Maharanis: The Lives and Times of Three Generations of Indian Princesses* (London: Viking, 2004)

Nelson, Michael, *Queen Victoria and the Discovery of the Riviera* (London: Tauris Parke reprint, 2007)

Nevill, Barry St John, *Life at the Court of Queen Victoria* (Stroud: Sutton Publishing, 1997)

Ponsonby, Arthur, *Henry Ponsonby, Queen Victoria's Private Secretary, His Life From his Letters* (London: Macmillan & Co., 1943)

Ponsonby, Frederick, *Recollections of Three Reigns* (London: Odhams Press)

Queen Victoria, *Our Life in the Highlands* (London: William Kimber, 1968)

Ramm, Agatha (ed.), *Beloved and Darling Child: Last letters between Queen Victoria and her Eldest Daughter 1886–1901* (Stroud: Sutton Publishing, 1990)

Reid, Michaela, *Ask Sir James* (London: Hodder and Stoughton, 1987)

Rennell, Tony, *Last Days of Glory: The Death of Queen Victoria* (London: Penguin, 2001)

St Aubyn, Giles, *Edward VII, Prince and King* (London: William Collins, 1979)

Tschumi, Gabriel, *Royal Chef, Forty Years with Royal Households* (London: William Kimber, 1954)

Vadgama, Kusoom, *India in Britain* (London: Robert Royce, 1984)

Van Der Kiste, John, *Sons, Servants & Statesmen, The Men in Queen Victoria's Life* (Stroud: Sutton Publishing, 2006)

INDEX